THE
BUGATTI
QUEEN

*In Search of a
Motor-racing Legend*

MIRANDA SEYMOUR

SIMON &
SCHUSTER

London · New York · Sydney · Tokyo · Toronto · Dublin

A VIACOM COMPANY

First published in Great Britain by Simon & Schuster UK Ltd in 2004
A Viacom company

1 3 5 7 9 10 8 6 4 2

Simon & Schuster UK Ltd
Africa House
64–78 Kingsway
London WC2B 6AH

Simon & Schuster Australia
Sydney

www.simonsays.co.uk

A CIP catalogue for this book is available
from the British Library.

ISBN: 0-7432-3146-5

Typeset by M Rules
Printed and bound in Great Britain by
Mackays of Chatham plc

To my mother,
with love and admiration

'The thing I like best in the world is adventure'

– Hellé Nice

CONTENTS

DISGRACE

INTRODUCTION

A collection of photographs spreads across my desk this morning. Three are of places. Three show an attractive woman with a film star's sense of how to make her face speak to a camera. One is of a car crash.

Places first. 1900. A sepia-tinted postcard shows what is plainly intended to be a typical everyday scene of the time in Aunay-sous-Auneau, a tiny village forty miles west of Paris. Three women stand in the road, hands on hips, thickly stockinged legs set well apart. Aunay's local historian, Raymond Barenton, wants me to look, not at the gossiping ladies, but at the building behind them. Small, low and shabby, this is the house in which Hellé Nice (Hélène Delangle) was born in 1900, although 1905 was her preferred year of birth. Peering closer at the card and using a magnifying glass, I can make out the words 'Postes et Télégraphes' on the wall of the drab little rectangle. Not a cheerful home in which to start a glorious career.

Place Two is the Villa des Agaves, Hélène's home on the Côte d'Azur in 1937. A white house, up-to-the-minute in its curvaceous design, it juts out from the side of a cliff above Beaulieu-sur-mer, looking down on the elegant spit of Cap Ferrat. The Villa des Agaves stands near the summit of the climbing, serpentine route of boulevard Edward VII, where neighbours in Hélène's heyday included a handful of European royals and a gang of sports stars. Below, almost overlooked from the terrace of the main bedroom, lies the magnificent Villa Tunis, bought by Hélène's patron Ettore Bugatti from Jean-Pierre Wimille, one of his most successful drivers. Bugatti's thirty-year-old marriage to a Milanese opera singer was in bad shape by the mid-thirties; the Villa Tunis was bought as a bolthole, a seaside palace just made for a man who collected houses as easily as carriages and racehorses.

Place Three jumps forward almost fifty years. This house lies at the back of the port in old Nice, an area where the tobacco-workers used to rent rooms in the thirties. The handful of streets separating rue Edouard Scoffier from the mountains behind the town are shady and mean. Opposite the tatty façade behind which Hélène's life leaked away in obscurity, a garage keeps itself in business by respraying trucks. This was the house where she lived on charity, although not the landlord's, for almost twenty years. In 1984, she died in a public ward at the local hospital. Among her few possessions were two large, stained boxes full of old newspaper cuttings, letters and photographs. The landlord, impatient to clean the place up and relet, sent them off as rubbish. Her trophy cups and her treasured book of stamps, collected over seventy years, were either sold or given away.

So much for places: now for personalities. The first of the second clutch of photographs shows a gorgeous young woman with no clothes on, laughing, and raising her arms to capture a fluttering white dove. It isn't indicated exactly where she is performing, but it clearly isn't the town hall of Aunay. She is probably in her early twenties; she has a glow on her skin that makes you want to reach out and touch her.

The next photograph shows the same young woman, but in a startlingly different pose. Here, she is sitting at the wheel of what, as I have learned to appreciate, is the supercharged version of the world's most beautiful sports car, Ettore Bugatti's model 35. She is wearing white overalls and a cloth helmet hides her blonde curls.

Her smile has a nervousness which is rare in her photographs. You can't tell the time of day (other evidence shows that it is early on a December morning in 1929). The weather forecast is bad: the men lined up like a row of Chicago heavies behind the car are shrouded in waterproofs. The smallest of them, looking anxiously at the car, must be her mechanic, Joseph Cecci, to whom she has inscribed the photograph in her bold looping writing.

We need to spend a little more time with this photograph. It is a record of the celebrated day when, driving at an average of 198 kph over ten laps on the uneven surface and high banked walls of France's first speed track, Hélène Delangle, now calling herself Hellé Nice, became the fastest woman in the world, skidding around the top of Montlhéry's goldfish bowl at a rate of 48 seconds a lap with the knowledge that a blown tyre, a loose screw, a faulty brake could send her flying over the concrete rim. Steering a Bugatti at that speed was, they said, like trying to slice a knife through hot butter.

And how did it feel? It's a shame and a puzzle that so few of the novelists who could have done justice to the subject chose to do so. Racing was, after all, one of the biggest entertainments the 1920s had to offer. Artists from Lautrec and Matisse to Tamara de Lempicka, painter of the iconic *Woman in a Green Bugatti*, relished the challenge of how to express speed in a linear form. Writers, if we set aside some poems that Paul Eluard and Apollinaire might have preferred to be forgotten, and a few set-piece scenes, kept away from it.*

The best-known account of a woman driving at speed comes in

* We could add some passages from Dornford Yates, a gripping scene climax to Michael Arlen's *The Green Hat*, the chillingly indifferent driving-scene in *The Great Gatsby*, some stray passages from Anthony Powell, W. E. Henley's 1903 poem, 'A Song of Speed'; and *Christopher Strong*, a powerful novel about a girl racing driver by Gilbert Frankau. The film version of Frankau's novel, starring Katharine Hepburn, omitted the car-racing altogether.

Vile Bodies, which Waugh wrote in 1929, the year of Hélène Delangle's record-breaking run when she was just short of thirty. Chapter 12 describes young Adam Syme and Myles Malpractice setting off for a long, grubby day at the track with their friends Agatha Runcible and Archie Schwertz. Sporting Miss Runcible – Waugh modelled her on his racing friend Elizabeth Plunket Greene – enters the race as a co-driver and beats the champion before leaving the road at speed. Carried off to hospital, she continues to relive the experience for as long as the nurses will permit:

> There was rarely more than a quarter of a mile of the black road to be seen at one time. It unrolled like a length of cinema film. At the edges was confusion; a fog spinning past: '*Faster, faster,*' they shouted above the roar of the engine. The road rose suddenly and the white car soared up the sharp ascent without slackening speed. At the summit of the hill there was a corner. Two cars had crept up, one on each side, and were closing in. 'Faster,' cried Miss Runcible, 'faster'.
> . . . Another frightful corner. The car leant over on two wheels, tugging outwards; it was drawn across the road until it was within a few inches of the bank. One ought to brake down at the corners, but one couldn't see them coming lying flat on one's back like this. The back wheel wouldn't hold the road at this speed. Skidding all over the place.
> 'Faster. Faster.'
> The stab of a hypodermic needle.
> 'There's nothing to worry about, dear . . . *nothing at all . . . nothing.*'

Hellé Nice – her professional name – was the most audacious woman driver of her time and she first proved it on that chilly morning at Montlhéry in front of a group of cynical sports writers and select members of the Bugatti works team. Ettore's signature brown bowler hat isn't visible in the photograph, but he was taking a close interest in her achievement. Her courage and skill were remarkable; what interested him still more were the seductively half-closed eyes and joyful smile which were already her trademark on stage. Put the saucy, radiant face together with the speed at which she was prepared to risk her life for a record or a win and Hélène Delangle became an irresistible commodity for a car company which relied on personality as much as victories for its sales.

The third of the photographs is a romantic mystery and not by any means the only one in Hélène's promiscuous life. It has been taken on a liner bound for South America in 1936, and we know that the man who has snapped her in close-up is her new lover. The photograph is an exact match to the one in her album of a man on a liner, sitting in an identical chair. 'Naldo', she has written helpfully at the side. Her lover, Arnaldo Binelli, is a young man of arresting beauty, dark-haired, soft-lipped, a mouth, you'd guess, that was used to laughing and kissing. Like her own. They must have had fun, those two. Always photogenic, Hélène looks young and vulnerable here, hair tucked back, head slightly tilted. Her large eyes are dreamy, liquid with love.

The last photograph on the desk is of a crash. This is a horrifying shot, taken at the moment of disaster, by Hélène's lover, who was standing by the finishing line. The place was São Paulo in Brazil and the year was 1936. She was racing an Alfa on that occasion, and racing well. But something has gone terribly wrong. The picture shows a figure like a doll, legs and arms stiff as star spokes as it whirls through the dusty air. The car is hidden in a blur of smoke. After the race, they laid her body out with the dead beside the track. Incredibly, she survived and went on to help set ten new world records the following year. 'Elle a du cran,' the papers said, as they had when she went to race on the speedbowls and dirt tracks of America in 1930. 'The girl's got guts.'

Acknowledged in her time as the fastest woman driver in the world, Hélène Delangle's career was destroyed, not by a crash but by the moment when one of the most famous racers of the pre-war years chose to denounce her as a Gestapo agent. Disgraced, despite a fight to clear her name, she was banished from the racing community. Her reputation never recovered, her former lovers deserted her and she was reduced to selling tickets for a charity at seaside cinema matinée performances. She died in complete obscurity. Her name does not even appear on the family gravestone.

The search for her story is told here in the Afterword. It has, for a writer who knew little about cars, music halls or life under occupation in France, all of which are vital elements in her story, been a wonderful adventure. My aim has been to do some kind of justice to one of the boldest and most attractive women of the last century. Hélène deserves to be remembered and, more than that, celebrated. She liked reading: I think this is a book that she might have enjoyed.

I shall miss her.

London, June 2003

AUTHOR'S NOTE

Researching the life of Hellé Nice has led to the discovery of a treasure-trove of material about her life and career, most of which has never been gathered together or published until now. *The Bugatti Queen* therefore represents the most comprehensive account of her life we have ever had – or, I like to think, are likely to have. There are, inevitably, gaps in the archive, details of her early life which will remain forever unknowable; in the interests of creating a narrative that does justice to her remarkable story, there are occasions in the pages that follow where I have had to employ some creative reconstruction. I hope to have made it clear where fact dissolves into speculation. I feel that, having been immersed in Hélène's story for several years, I am probably better qualified than most to make such assumptions. And, since we are talking about someone who continued to reinvent herself throughout her fascinating life, I feel that she herself would not disapprove too much.

The French franc lost or changed its value during the years of Hellé Nice's career. Below are shown rough equivalents to today's sterling.

One franc of the year	Equivalent in present-day sterling
1901	£2.06
1914	1.79
1915	1.49
1916	1.34
1917	1.11
1918	0.86
1919	0.70
1920	0.50
1925	0.44
1930	0.30
1935	0.41
1939	0.25
1940	0.21
1941	0.18
1942	0.15
1943	0.12
1944	0.09
1945	0.06
1950	0.014
1955	0.011
1959	0.008
1960	0.84
1965	0.70
1970	0.56
1975	0.36
1980	0.21
1990	0.12
1995	0.108
2000	0.101

THE POSTMASTER'S DAUGHTER

1

BEGINNINGS

'In my end is my beginning.'

MARY, QUEEN OF SCOTS
(ALLEGEDLY)

Nice, winter 1975

She had kept the gloves because they reminded her of the way in which one of her most charming lovers, Philippe de Rothschild, had introduced himself to her. She had been sitting at a café table in Paris, chatting to a friend, when she first noticed that a man, strongly built, well-dressed, bronze-faced, had stopped as he walked past. He hadn't moved for about a minute. He was looking directly at her. She wondered if he was after an autograph; he didn't look like a journalist. Good eyes; nice mouth. She gave a wide bold smile and watched him come towards the table. He spoke her name, asked how long she had been back from her American tour, indicating familiarity with her career. She said she seemed to know his face too, and burst out laughing when he identified himself. A racer himself, and of Bugattis: no wonder that he had such a familiar look. She introduced her friend, a girl she had met when they were

3

both dancers at the Casino, and gave her a quick significant glance. Diana took the hint, remembered an appointment, smiled at them both and moved out of the yellow shade of the awning into the hard afternoon light of the Champs-Elysées. That was when Philippe de Rothschild lifted her left hand from the table and, correctly, identified the name of her glovemaker. Turning her hand over, he undid the four tiny pearl buttons which held the moulded kid tight against her wrist, smooth on her flesh as a second skin. Her bare arms were sunburnt; here, at the pulse point, the skin was white as a baby's. Smiling, he lifted her hand to his mouth and, looking into her eyes, touched the tiny area of revealed skin with his mouth and, very lightly, the tip of his tongue. It was the most delicate of gestures. She knew at once that the experience of being made love to by this man would give her pleasure.

Sitting on the edge of her bed at four in the morning, she lifted the gloves to her face, as if to bring back some scent of the past. Nothing remained but the softness of the kid. As for Philippe de Rothschild, she didn't even know whether he was alive or dead. Sighing, she stretched out her toes, feeling for her slippers before she knelt to pull the precious trunk from its hiding-place – she trusted nobody – beneath the iron bed-frame. Wincing at the effort, she levered back the heavy lid.

There they were, her hoard of treasures, the tarnished racing cups, the silver commemorative plate from Brazil, the book of stamps collected from her travels: all were safe. She lifted the plate aside to reach the sheaves of yellow cuttings. Two envelopes of photographs and a handful of letters were taken out, ready for the day's work.

Sitting at the table under the window, she laid them carefully out. A cat mewed in the darkness and her head jerked up eagerly before she remembered that Minette, her companion over ten years, had been banished from this, the most desolate of her homes, by a landlord who refused to have pets on the premises. True, he had offered a bottle of champagne in consolation when he saw her distress, but you couldn't stroke a bottle or talk to it, or please it with a scrap of fish. Beggars couldn't lay down the law; given the choice between the cat and the room, she let Minette find a new home with the tobacconist at the end of the street. Now, the little minx didn't so much as open her eyes when she hobbled in to buy the week's supply of cigarettes. Faithless, in the end, as all the rest had proved to be.

Brushing a skin of glue over the back of the tiny black and white photographs, with their images of better times, she began the daily task of sticking them to the pages of the scrapbooks, building up a record of the past, drumming her heels on the floorboards as she tried to remember a date for each one. It was a young interviewer from Monte Carlo Radio who had given her the idea when he came – five years ago? six? – to ask about the great day in 1929 when she drove a Bugatti at the Montlhéry circuit near Paris and beat the world record. He was a nice boy, and a good listener. She had enjoyed talking to him, but she couldn't make him understand the joy of driving that car. He ought to drive one himself, she told him; that was the only way to do it. She showed him her trophy cups, watched his eyes widen in respect. He hadn't, he said, realized how much she had achieved. Before he left, he urged her to try to put together a record of her career.

It was something to do, to fill the long night hours when sleep refused to come. (The years when she slept as soundly as a child had ended for good in 1936, when a crash had nearly robbed her of more than the comfort of peaceful nights.) Now, the scrapbooks had become her solace, taking her back to another life. Another person, she sometimes thought, looking down at a news item about her American tour of 1930 which proclaimed the first-ever appearance of a woman racing-driver on the most dangerous board track in New Jersey, where she was expected to set a new speed record.

The landlord was too mean to provide her with more than a single-bar heater for the two rooms she occupied at the top of the house. Shivering, she dragged a blanket off the bed and wrapped it tightly around her as she sat down again at the table. The photograph before her now was yellow, the images faint with age. A lace-smothered baby perched on the lap of a countrywoman wearing a long, heavy skirt and wooden sabots. 'Mother and I, 1902, at Sainte-Mesme,' she wrote on the back; no, that couldn't be right. In 1902, they had been living at Aunay-sous-Auneau, outside Chartres. Was this a photograph of herself, or of Solange, her sister? That was the trouble with babies: swathed in bonnets and shawls, they all looked alike. It could very well be Solange, in which case the photograph was going back in the trunk. Where it would stay. Her family were going to have no place in her record of triumph.

Boissy-le-Sec, 1898

Boissy-le-Sec was a dead end of a village between Paris and Chartres, buried in the cornfields that stretched from one horizon to another. The women and their daughters wound the water up with an iron wheel that took four hands to turn it, from a well so deep that you could drop stones all day and never hear a sound come back. Léon Delangle and his wife blamed the icy water of Boissy for the deaths of their oldest boy, Maurice, who died there in 1897, aged only three, and the youngest, Gabriel, whom they buried in the same summer. Lucien, the middle child, cursed with long pale cheeks and a croupy cough, survived. Alexandrine Delangle was expecting again when a welcome offer came to leave the village.

Léon Aristide Delangle was a postmaster, a government appointment which gave him a thousand francs a year (see conversion table on page xviii) and a roof over his head, and which licensed him to look down on his blacksmith cousin at Boissy. They had both married Alexandrines; it was all they or their wives had in common.

Alexandrine Estelle Bouillie was a gaunt girl of nineteen when she married the thirty-year-old postmaster. Her own family were of simple origins and Alexandrine was intensely aware of her new and superior standing; it pleased her that Léon and she shared a big fourposter bed while his cousin the blacksmith's wife lay in a humble tester. It was also gratifying to know that her husband and she had the only telephone in the village.* As the *facteur-receveur*, Léon Delangle was the local banker; sacks of coins were placed in his care. He was an educated man, able to read and write without difficulty; Alexandrine drew further satisfaction from the knowledge that the Boissy schoolmaster, who had never shared a table with the blacksmith's family, had been to dinner with her husband and herself twice during their first year in the village.

The postmaster Delangles made annual voyages to the coast, alternating between Deauville and Dieppe. They had been to Paris, twice, and had stayed in hotels. The blacksmith Delangles took pride in the fact that they never travelled beyond Rambouillet, once the forest of kings, lying on the northern edge of the great Beauce plain. Here, the green woods rustled with the wings of chaffinches, nightingales, turtle doves and larks. With a smithy full of guns to use on Rambouillet's wildlife, there seemed no point in travelling twice as far to catch cold on an Atlantic beach. The postmaster was, in the opinion of his cousins, altogether too ambitious in his ways. Boissy had always been good enough for them. A man came to no harm by knowing the landmarks of his own horizon.

Never comfortable together, the two branches of the family

---

*One of only 20,000 in all France at that time.

separated easily as oil from water when the postmaster received offer of a transfer to nearby Aunay-sous-Auneau in June 1898. Alexandrine, while pleased by the opportunity to escape from her husband's cousins, and a village she now associated with death, was anxious about moving at a time when their new baby girl was shedding weight at alarming speed. But word came down from the great Gothic headquarters of the postal service in Chartres that the process must not be delayed; they could take their chance now, or stay. So the house at Boissy was stripped of its modest furnishings. Kitchenware, chairs, bed, linen, a wooden chest and three down-stuffed quilts were roped on to the carrier's cart and trundled away on the long white ribbon of track to Plessis, Garancières and Aunay. The family did not look back and their cousins did not come out of the smithy to wave them off.

Aunay-sous-Auneau, named for the alder trees which are no longer in evidence on its river banks, was larger than Boissy and, having at least two big fêtes every summer, a little livelier. It was, nevertheless, another one-street village locked in by the golden carpets of the cornfields around which its existence revolved. Here, too, the landscape was enormous and featureless: size is the only claim the Beauce has ever made to a character. Clambering down from the cart as it halted on the road above the village, Alexandrine Delangle ignored the old church of Saint-Eloi and trained her eyes on the distance, searching the broad yellow ring of the horizon. Beyond it, out of view, loomed the grey spires of Chartres. Overhead, the sky stretched in cloudless calm, blank as the fields beneath.

Their new home, squat and tiled in slate, stood opposite the smart new town hall and school which, ranged together, dwarfed it. Beyond, standing on the road to Chartres, defended by a high and rose-spattered wall and looking down an avenue of chestnuts, a recently embellished chateau lent an air of grandeur to the village. The owner, Dr Poupon, was more admired for his ownership of a touring car which lived in the chateau stables between a dogcart and a secretive closed sedan, home, in Aunay legends, to every star-crossed relationship the village had ever been sufficiently aware of to prattle about. The car was the village's equivalent to a royal carriage. Every spring, the machine was ceremoniously unshrouded from dustsheets and towed into the light by two burly cart-horses belonging to Charles Foiret, principal landholder in the village. Dr Poupon, taking his role seriously, wore goggles, cap, gauntlets and a yellow coat which served to keep off both rain and the clouds of dust which rose from the Beauce's unsurfaced roads. His groom, relishing the elevation to mechanic and chauffeur, wore a smart cap which hinted at a military background.

Dr Poupon had recently been elected as the mayor of Aunay, giving him responsibility for the welfare of almost a thousand residents, most of whom were of farming stock. Conscious of ceremony, he was waiting outside the single-storey block of the little Maison des Postes et Télégraphes – the sign had just been repainted – when the Delangles arrived on the carrier's cart. It was Dr Poupon who unlocked the door and led them hastily through a damp little office into what was, if he might express a view, an unusually comfortable and pleasant bedroom. (Enthusiasm was required: the initial candidate had rejected the job on the grounds that the house was unsatisfactory.) The view from the back of the house was, the mayor indicated with a flourish at a window which looked straight into the side of a thornbush, admirably private. The floors – he thumped his heel – were sound. A new Thierry stove had been installed for their benefit.

The mayor paused, allowing this generous gesture to be appreciated before he delivered the one indisputable disappointment. No authority had been obtained for the provision of a bicycle to the new official and attempts to secure the services of a deputy postman had not proved successful. Deliveries must, nevertheless, be carried out to homes over a five-mile radius. And there, discomforted by the silence of the Delangles, Dr Poupon decided to bring his welcome to an end. They would, he said as he turned to the door, enjoy living at Aunay. The schoolmaster, Chopiteau, was a delightful man; Foiret, the principal farmer, was a good chap, always ready to help out with one of his carts if they were planning a trip to Chartres. He left before Madame Delangle, registering from his title that this small and strutting man was a doctor, could seek advice about the sickly baby girl who lay in her arms.

Lucienne Delangle, aged four months, was buried two months later. At the end of August, with a mixture of gratitude and dread, Alexandrine Delangle found herself pregnant once more.

Her luck had turned; no more Delangles would join the row of doll-sized graves at the back of the cemetery. Solange Andrée was born late in the spring of 1899, almost a year after their arrival at Aunay. On 15 December 1900 Alexandrine went into labour once again in the family bed.

They named her Mariette Hélène. M. Julien the baker and Charles Foiret, the elderly farmer who had been commended by the mayor, were witnesses to the entry of her birth in the town hall register. Dr Poupon, who had been distressed by the Delangles' loss of a baby girl so soon after their arrival at Aunay, volunteered himself as a godfather. He even produced a tiny ivory crucifix which had belonged to his mother, offering it as a baptism gift. The christening itself was modest, not followed by the usual supper and dance; misfortunes had made the parents superstitious. Drawing attention to their remaining children seemed imprudent; the less fuss, the better.

Fretting over their growing family, the Delangles paid little attention to themselves. Several people in the village commented on the fact that the postmaster always looked in need of a proper meal. He was a good-looking man with lustrous eyes and a bold white smile. At Boissy, his cousins had made jokes about the postmaster's appetite which played on the affectionate glances he always drew from women. It angered Alexandrine to see him coming back from his rounds at Aunay with pockets full of fresh bread, pieces of cheese and even, on occasion, with a brace of birds or a hare weighing down the mailbag. Didn't the farmers' wives know that he got fed at home?

Weight continued to fall off the postmaster until his handsomeness became that of a starved Christ. His approach could be heard half a street away by a deep rattling cough; his stride became a painful hobble; neither Poupon nor the doctor who reluctantly came out from Chartres on two occasions could think of anything more useful to prescribe than warm poultices and dandelion tea, brewed with mallow root. Neither poultices nor tisanes produced an improvement: Léon Delangle was only thirty-nine in 1901, but he stooped and trembled like a man of twice his age. When discreet queries were made about his ability to continue work, his wife, fearing that a replacement might be suggested, offered to act as his deputy.

As an old woman, shivering in her attic on rue Edouard Scoffier in Nice, Mariette Hélène Delangle thought back to her first memory of her mother. She saw her by the dim glow of an oil lamp, bending to fold sheets of paper into her clogs and another under a close-fitting wool bonnet before she picked up the heavy mailbag, lit the wick in her lantern and went out into the freezing damp of a winter morning before dawn. The slap of wooden shoes trod away, echoing, down the silent street. A clock ticked. Above the high side of the rocker where she and Solange had lain, mummified in their separate quilts, she remembered the rattle of breath which came steadily down, hollow as pebbles in a glass jar, from their parents' bed. She could not remember a time without that noise, familiar and lacking in sinister content as the crowing of roosters. It was, quite simply, the sound of morning.

2

1903: THE RACE TO DEATH

What about racing?
Oh, that will go. Already it has gone. It was necessary in
the past for the testing of cars whose capabilities were
quite unknown.

THE HON C.S. ROLLS, INTERVIEWED BY THE
MANCHESTER GUARDIAN, 26 FEBRUARY 1907

She was three years old. In Paris, over two thousand people now owned cars; in Aunay, it is unlikely that anybody had heard of the 30 kph restriction which had been imposed on country lanes to protect the safety of cattle and their keepers. Life here proceeded at the tranquil pace of the carriage in which Madame Foiret the farmer's wife travelled to Chartres once a year, to honour the shrine of the Black Virgin.

Bicycles had become a part of daily life. Girls a few years older than Hélène raced their Petites Reines up and down the village street; Madame Delangle had a tall La Grande Star on which to take round the morning post, while her husband, racked by the coughs from which no relief came, watched over Henri Louis, the baby who had most recently taken possession of the battered wooden rocker. Lucien, grown into a tall, stringy boy of eight, attended the new village school beside the town hall, where his two sisters, when old enough to wear button-up boots, would be introduced to dressmaking, drawing, and the rivers, flowers and departments of France. The world beyond was only glimpsed in the foreign stamps which sometimes proclaimed the continuing existence of a runaway from Aunay's smothering tranquillity.

In 1903, Hélène was taken across the road by her mother, to join her older sister for the afternoon 'movement' class, her first experience of dancing. Drab as mailsacks in their serge smocks and black aprons, the little girls raised their arms in obedience to the teacher's call, fingers fluttering as they tried to imitate trees in springtime. Heads back and shoulders braced, they skipped around the yard. Hélène, jumping and waving as she grinned at the teacher, was praised for her enthusiasm. 'My sister Solange was jealous of me, even then,' Hélène wrote proudly seventy years later. 'She was eighteen months older, but I did everything – everything! – better, from the first day I went to school.'[1]

The great car race from Paris to Madrid was to commence on the last Sunday in May 1903; the papers of the Beauce region had been building up to it for weeks. People at Aunay, excited by their proximity to the first lap of the route, moving westwards to Chartres and down to Bordeaux, talked of little else. Some planned to join the fifty thousand who were expected to arrive at Versailles on the Saturday night in order not to miss the excitement of the dawn start of over 300 machines. Others, eager to experience the thrill of watching the machines travel at full speed, studied maps and decided to spend the day on the roadside, familiar to them from the bicycle races which had been crossing this part of the country for over a decade.*

The list of participants had already been announced in the press,

---

* The bicycle races from Paris to Bordeaux had drawn huge crowds from the local villages and towns since their inauguration in the early 1890s. When Chartres came under German occupation in 1940, the citizens instinctively fled south to Bordeaux, following the familiar road.

their vehicles divided into four classes according to weight. The heaviest and fastest machines would be stripped down to bare essentials in order to qualify, with the drivers seated on a plank of wood lacking even the luxury of a feather-stuffed cushion to spare them from jolts and bruises. Cars would depart on the minute, at the firing of a pistol shot, pursuing each other along roads above which dust, however carefully watered-down in advance, would arise in impenetrable clouds. Roadside spectators were urged to keep their distance and to remember that they might not be visible to the drivers until it was too late for escape.

Towns were another acknowledged source of concern. A few would be bypassed with wooden tracks, but this was too great an extravagance to be employed in more than a handful of cases. Elsewhere, it was predicted that the streets would be crammed with innocent spectators, unaware of the danger they presented to themselves and the drivers as they pressed close to the machines or ran in front of them. (Gloomily, and with a certain relish, the newspapers reminded their readers that pedestrians and dogs had, to date, been the major causes of fatal automobile accidents.)

A banker, a count, a jeweller, a lady who had already shown her courage in the 1901 race from Paris to Berlin: the entry-list of drivers ranged from the celebrated to cranks who entered for fun, never expecting that their cars would take them further than a six-hour run to Tours or, at best, Poitiers. Among them were two young car-designers from Alsace, Emile Mathis and his Milanese associate, Ettore Bugatti. More serious candidates were the Americans Tod Sloan (it seems likely that he was the celebrated jockey in the United States and Great Britain during the 1890s) and William K. Vanderbilt Jr in his formidable mile-a-minute Mercedes; British car salesman Charles Rolls and his compatriots, Lorraine Barrow and Charles Jarrott; René De Knyff, always driving a Panhard; Marcel, Fernand and Louis Renault – and a mysterious 'Dr Pascal', the pseudonym masking the identity of the millionaire playwright and motoring enthusiast, Baron Henri de Rothschild.

Camille du Gast was the only woman brave enough to volunteer for a race of 872 miles over largely unfamiliar roads; to the disappointment of the Versailles spectators familiar with poster-portraits of ladies who went driving in their finest Paris dresses, Madame du Gast arrived dressed for battle. Goggled, masked and wearing heavy gauntlets to protect her hands from the burning heat of a metal wheel and gearshift, she was a sexless lump. There were unchivalrous comments until her mechanic hit on the ingenious idea of feminizing the bonnet of their powerful De Dietrich car. (Camille du Gast's expensive taste in machines was subsidized by a doting husband.) Ropes of pink roses and cornflowers restored the driver to iconic status in a moment; an enthusiastic crowd rallied to wish her well.

Hélène's chance to witness one of the greatest events in the early history of automobile races almost didn't happen. The baby, Henri, was too sick for Alexandrine Delangle to leave him and the postmaster was also unwell. His friend Chopiteau, the schoolmaster, offered to take the children along, but Solange, perhaps from nervousness, had a bad stomach. The expedition eventually comprised only Chopiteau, Lucien and Hélène, barely visible under her lace sun-bonnet. Lucien, to whom the sturdy little girl still seemed like a charmingly animated toy, clasped his thin arms tightly round her stomach as they sat on the jolting cart bound for Bourdinière, some twenty miles to the west. Even through a layer of white lace, Lucien could smell the warm, sweet scent of her skin, like hay.

At eight in the morning, the fields below the long slant of Bourdinière hill were already crowded; Aunay was not the only village to have calculated where the race could best be viewed. Nobody was sure when the first cars would be coming through, but every sound, every gust of wind, was greeted by a flurry of expectant shouts, a surge of bodies towards the road. There was the sense of a fair about the occasion; dogs ran in and out of the wheels of farm-wagons and carts on a hunt for dropped crumbs; babies with surprised eyes lay on quilts which scattered colour across the patches of shadow under the plane trees. Heavy-bellied horses of the Percheron region cropped at the grass verges of the dusty track, while a couple of pedlars in the bright clothes of circus-people hawked trays of ribbons and strips of lace through the crowds, calling attention to the elegance of their wares.

Did a three-year-old girl absorb all this and store it away for future recollection? Probably not. But photographs of her suggest that she was already pretty enough, with her big blue eyes, for several of the mothers to have stooped to stroke her round cheeks and tickle her, wheedling for a smile. Years later, friends would tell Hélène Delangle that whatever she gave away, she must never lose that glorious, unforgettable smile of hers. You could see a hint of it already in the baby face shaded by the bonnet, a grin of beaming confidence that spread and stayed, cheerful as the sun. The ladies smiled back; the schoolmaster, enjoying his paternal role more than he had anticipated, knelt to retie the satin ribbons of his charge's white bonnet.

Ten o'clock. A gust of wind brushed the planes, spattering the white road with the shadows of their broad five-fingered leaves. The men were smoking furiously, scribbling calculations on folded sheets of newspaper; the women, faintly excited by the thought of the proximity of the approaching drivers, hitched up their skirts, enjoying the coolness of the grass under their thighs as they lay prone, black shawls spread over their faces. The schoolmaster felt in his pocket for a pipe. He was on the point of lighting up when one of the men gave a shout.

The women threw off their shawls and rose, staring intently up the hill to where a silhouette against the sky had signalled an approach with a raised flag. Far away, soft as a whisper, the sound wavered towards them. It rose to a hum, a whine and then, with sudden fury, to the rattle of nails being hurled around a tin barrel as the machine burst on them from above, burying the flag-holder on the hilltop in a dense cloud of white dust before it plunged forward.

The sound of the car was, briefly, drowned by screams. For many in the crowded fields, this was their introduction to the automobile in motion. A few stood still, hypnotized, unconscious of others behind them who were running away, shrieking as they fled to safety from the demon motor.

Schoolmaster Chopiteau's pipe dropped from nerveless fingers. He was close enough to the road to glimpse the eyes of a hawk behind the white mask before a dust-cloud rose and forced him to cover his face. 'Take me!' he heard little Lucien Delangle screaming. 'Take me!'

And then the car, with young Louis Renault grasping the vibrating wheel in flayed hands, was past them, rattling into the distance on a long ribbon of track that carried him from their sight. A low sound went up from the crowd, a sigh empty of emotion, an extension of the engine's roar. There was pride in it, somewhere. This was the future, and they had been a part of it. The feeling of weightless absorption might have encompassed even a small girl in a lace bonnet, to whom the rite of speed had been experienced only as a rush of noise and dust, the flinty glitter of falling stones, the sudden whiteness of the grass, the smell of sweat on the frightened horses, a sharp tang in the air, the smell of sand and oil. So this, thought the schoolmaster, as they slowly began to brush the dust from their clothes and faces, this was what the Greeks had meant by the words: sacred terror. And it had taken him fifty years to discover it. Looking down, he saw Lucien, still standing by the road, his arms stretched out. The car, Chopiteau realized, must have missed him by centimetres.

Even the grim reports which began to filter in by the end of the day failed to extinguish the wonder of the country folk who witnessed Louis Renault's record run of 140 kilometres an hour down the hill of La Bourdinière. They had shared in his triumph too closely to relinquish it at once for grief. On Sunday night, back at Aunay, Lucien tried to explain what he had seen. Finding that no words could make his parents understand the wonder of the great rushing machine, the noise, the dust, the smell, he wept.

The Monday papers brought nothing but horror stories. The Race to Death! screamed the headlines, over violent illustrations of burning bodies, scattered limbs. Hundreds killed! Hundreds had not died, but the truth was bad enough. Marcel Renault was dead (a camera snapped his brother Louis in the moment of pushing back his ear-flaps to learn the news).* An amateur English driver had burnt to death when his car overturned on a corner and caught fire. Lesna, the great champion cyclist, had been injured so badly that he would never be able to race again; Lorraine Barrow, swerving to avoid a dog, hit a tree and killed his mechanic while he himself lingered for a painful few hours. Another driver managed to avoid a child on the road before he lost control and rumbled into the crowd, killing three and scattering injured bodies, too many for the local hospital to cope with. Camille du Gast, gallantly renouncing her own chance of victory, briefly withdrew to nurse another De Dietrich driver before racing on to take 45th place.

From Châtellerault to Bordeaux, the journalists reported, the road was littered with wrecked machines. Six of the 224 cyclists and drivers who set out from Versailles had been killed outright; ten more had been injured beyond hope of recovery. News that the

---

* Louis Renault left racing to develop cars after the death of his brother. In 1944, he was arrested and imprisoned as a collaborator, having offered his factory to the German occupiers for their own use.

winner, France's champion Fernand Gabriel, had maintained a remarkable average speed of 105 kph, was diminished by the sense of a national tragedy. The level of catastrophe was too great for there to be any question of continuing with the race beyond Bordeaux; in Madrid, the garlanded pillars which should have welcomed the victor down a triumphal avenue of flowers were silently dismantled. There would be no more town to town races. The cost had proved too high.

Two months later, the first Tour de France took place and was greeted as an unprecedented success. Nothing now would halt the advance of the car, but the spectacle of roads that hummed with spinning wheels and pumping thighs was welcomed by spectators as a less dangerous celebration of speed.

3

LOSS AND LEARNING

Quand tu reverras ton village
Quand tu reverras ton cloche
Ta maison, tes parents, tes amis de ton age . . .

CHARLES TRENET

'Ton village' was noted down by the old lady in Nice as one of her favourite songs, but she seems never to have returned to the house at Aunay, or to the church where, as a small girl, she knelt beneath a pink vaulted roof and joined in prayers for the restoration of her father's health.

Léon Delangle died in the autumn of 1904. The funeral took place in his father's village, Lèvesville-le-Chenard, out in the heart of the Beauce. We can imagine how, kneeling on stone slabs from which a damp chill brought a smell of the underworld, they prayed for his soul. Tasting her first glass of cider at the lunch which followed the burial, the child looked up and noticed an old man glowering down the table. This was her grandfather, angry today because the occasion had forced him to come into the house of his son-in-law, the ploughman; they hadn't spoken to each other for quarter of a century. Saying his goodbyes to the widow and her children outside the house – he had kept his honour by saying nothing at the table – Frédéric Delangle glanced at Hélène and remarked that Léon had produced at least one child who didn't look half-witted; just as well Alexandrine had a government pension to help her bring them up. It was his way of making it clear that his daughter-in-law could expect no generous gesture from him.[1]

The Delangle children have a desolate air in the only photograph to have been preserved from this early period of their lives. Lucien stands tall, large hands hanging loose at his sides. He is not a handsome boy. Studying his build and square stance, you might suppose that he had learnt to defend himself with his fists. Henri, a small curly-headed child in crumpled shorts, peers anxiously at the camera, seeming on the verge of tears. Solange and Hélène are dressed like twins, neat clips pinning back their heavy brown curls. Solange is perched on a stool, ankles crossed, feet swinging clear of the floor. Hélène is holding on to her. There's no sign in this formal pose of the radiant smile which made Hélène the centre of attention in later photographs; even so, you can appreciate the strength of character in her face.

This is the only family photograph which the old lady kept from her early years. It may have commemorated some special event, such as the annual visit to nearby Auneau, for the three-day fair held there every summer in honour of Saint Jean. Did it bring back memories of the few sous she was given by her mother to spend on riding a flared-nostrilled wooden horse on the carousel, or on a miniature box filled with sweet jam which a child's careful tongue could lick out, clean as a cat's? Perhaps she carried home a trophy from one of the stallholders, a gift for a pretty child, a butterfly flapping bright paper wings on the crest of a stick. Jolting home to Aunay on the cart past a moon-bleached expanse of cornfields, a determined little girl might hold her prize fast, clasped so tightly that not even in sleep could her fingers be prised apart.

Or it might have been a school picture. The Aunay records of school attendance during this period have not survived, but this

The Delangle children in 1906 – left to right, Lucien, Henri, Solange, Hélène.

was where Hélène began her education in a school system which was, after thirty years of bitter dispute, under the direction of the state rather than the church. The school at Aunay was proudly modern; here, if she chose, an enterprising girl had the chance to move beyond the limited aspirations of a barely literate family. Her father had done it before her, pushing to raise himself from the Delangle ranks of shepherds and *journaliers*, day-labourers who competed annually against an invasion of Bretons for employment on the farms of the Beauce. She had an example to follow.

As an old lady, Hélène Delangle took pleasure in emphasizing the fact that she had excelled in everything she did, easily surpassing the modest achievements of her sister. This, if true, could explain the sense of bitter rivalry which became an unbreachable rift between the two women in later life. Certainly, the evidence – Solange never rose beyond holding down a job as a telegraph clerk – would seem to bear out Hélène's claims. She spelt and wrote well all her life, in a strong and slanting hand. A glance at one of the carefully prepared route-maps she made before embarking on a race shows an impressive attention to detail and an ability to compress information. A passion for stamp collecting which must have derived from her father's occupation led her to take an interest in geography and history.* In later years, she found it easy to learn both English and Italian. She sang well and loved reading. Drawing up a list of her favourite authors in 1936, she included Stendhal, Maupassant, Cocteau, Anatole France, the journals of Marie Bashkirtseff and the novels and stories of Colette. She enjoyed poetry; her gift for drawing was above the ordinary. One of her lovers, a professional artist whose subjects included Colette,† teased her by saying that she had entered the wrong profession.

---

*The collection of stamps which she described as her greatest treasure vanished after her death. It has probably been broken up.

† René Carrère's portrait of Colette appears on the cover of Yvonne Mitchell's *Colette: A Taste for Life* (Weidenfeld & Nicolson, 1975).

Exercise played a large role in the new secular school system. Hélène had begun her schooling by frisking around the yard in the afternoon movement class; at ten, she was expected to concentrate on strengthening her muscles and learning how to conserve her energy. The extraordinary, androgynous bodies of the 1920s girls were the product both of the undernourished war years and the devotion to physical culture which began at their schools. Look forward to the legendary achievements of Suzanne Lenglen in women's tennis during the 1920s, long limbs moving at full stretch to seize each point of every game from her opponents; to the formidable boxer, weight-lifter and javelin thrower Violette Morris who, after finding that heavy breasts impeded her control of the steering wheel of her Donnet racing car, chose to have them lopped off in February 1929. Think, even, of Colette, fighting the soft flesh of encroaching years with a home gym: the passion with which these women strove to transcend their bodies was formed during their schooldays.

The role models for girls of the pre-war generation were achievers, breakers of moulds. In 1904, *La Vie Heureuse*, a well-behaved magazine for ladies, of a kind which could easily have been read by Hélène's teachers, celebrated the triumphs of a mountaineer, Madame Vallot, and a painter, Mademoiselle Dufau. The daily press, recording a disastrous speedboat race in 1905, paid enthusiastic tribute to the courage of intrepid Madame du Gast, dragged by the crew of a warship from the wreck of her own *Camille*.* From abroad, came accounts of a transcontinental all-female car race in America in 1909, and of Alice Ramsay driving coast to coast alone, on roads which were little better than cart-tracks. In England, Dorothy Levitt had won a coveted trophy in

---

* Prudently, perhaps, du Gast decided to relinquish her sporting ambitions after this disaster and devoted herself instead to giving recitals – she was a fine concert pianist – and to presiding over a society devoted to the care of stray and injured dogs.

1905 when she took a formidably large and heavy Napier car up to almost 80 mph (128 kph) in a speed trial held on Brighton's seafront. Condescension continued among the reporters: readers of the sports pages heard about Alice Ramsay's interest in her appearance and Levitt's skills as a hostess. Fearless, independent and shrewdly aware of the value of all publicity, these were the kind of women who were admired by schoolgirls of Hélène's generation.

Another side could be shown to life at Aunay in the years before the war. Marie-Josèphe Guers, in a book based largely on oral records of the village, describes picnics in the hayfields, the pleasure of threading a wreath of cornflowers and poppies around the rim of straw hats, the weekly task of helping mothers to carry baskets of linen down to be scrubbed at the washing stands on the river. Hélène might have been among the little girls who stared with fascination as the local butcher rammed a pump up the backside of a dead calf, swelling the body until its pelt could be stripped off as easily as a peach-skin and sent to the tanners. She, too, would have been taught to sing the Angelus, looked forward to fête days when she could put on a fancy dress and parade in the street, joined her friends to gather chestnuts among the fallen leaves in the long avenue leading up to the Château Grand-Mont.

In the summer of 1914 a solitary drum called the harvesters of Aunay to drop their scythes and return to the town hall, to be told their military duties. Lucien, not, perhaps, sorry to be given a reason to escape from a dutiful life as the oldest male in the family, kissed his mother goodbye and told her not to worry. Everybody said that it would be a short war. He expected to be home by Christmas. A year later he had not returned.

In 1915 Alexandrine Delangle decided to leave Aunay and its sad memories behind her. Perhaps she wanted to be nearer to Jean Bernard, the man she lived with 'en concubinage', as the French saying goes, in later life. (They never married, although she called herself by his name. Neighbours discovered the truth only from her gravestone.) She may have grown weary herself of those endless cornfields, the screech of rooks, the heavy odour of the smothering autumn carpet of manure. Independently, she rented and then bought a small house in a secluded part of Jean Bernard's village, Sainte-Mesme, just to the southwest of Paris; later, she acquired a larger second home on the village's main street. Behind this second house, formerly a café, Alexandrine thriftily converted a fertile half-acre of ground into a vegetable plot, producing beans and marrows for the city markets.

The landscape of Sainte-Mesme has not changed much. Its principal features are the luxuriant woods which separate it, to the east, from the plain of the Beauce, and the pale blockade of a disused cotton factory which had once brought prosperity to the village but which, by the time the Delangle family settled there, had become a summer school for young missionaries. Standing guard in miniature effigy over a well at the edge of a small path in the centre of the village, Sainte-Mesme's medieval persecutor still wields his wooden axe above a pious sister's head (her sacrifice allegedly brought water to the village, and thus, in due course, the mills for its cotton industry). It has, like many French villages, an air of languor bordering on torpidity in the afternoons when shutters mask the housefronts and shadows shrink back from the vacant street.

This, in the year 1916, was still the home of Hélène Delangle, a slight, strongly built girl with a mop of brown curls, big blue eyes and an enormous, heart-stopping grin.

In January 1916 Ettore Bugatti's younger brother Rembrandt returned from church to his modest white studio room on rue Joseph-Bara, not far from the Jardin du Luxembourg. At thirty-one, he had already made his reputation. He was only twenty-five when he received the Légion d'Honneur for his arrestingly graceful studies of animals in bronze. Friends who had seen

Rembrandt sitting in the cages of panthers at the Jardin des Plantes or modelling the elephants at Antwerp zoo joked that he preferred such wild company to their own. Few of them, however, understood the anguish Rembrandt felt when, in the year that war broke out, the elephants of Antwerp and the panthers and tigers of the Jardin des Plantes were all destroyed to save the cost of feeding them. To a young man of fragile psyche, this was a more painful loss than the abrupt closure of the Hebrard gallery which had always represented him. Loss of commissions meant nothing to Rembrandt; he had lived for years on the verge of destitution.

Returning to Paris from Antwerp in 1915, Rembrandt had found his brother Ettore established in style at the Grand Hotel on

Rembrandt Bugatti – seen here with one of the statuettes he modelled from life at the Antwerp menagerie.

the rue Scribe, having decided that he could not bear to spend the war in a German province, with his workshops in Alsace on France's eastern border being used to assist a German victory.* An old friend, Count Zeppelin, had enabled Ettore to make his escape; now, hankering for the country he thought of as home, Ettore had returned to France. Offered a commission by the military to design aero engines, he was full of optimism; all he needed was the space in which to work. Rembrandt, when asked to use his influence with one of his closest friends and chief patron, the Duc de Guiche, was able to help. A generous scientifically minded aristocrat who inspired Proust's portrait of Robert de Saint-Loup, Armand de Guiche kept a fully equipped laboratory and workshop in the industrial Levallois district to the northwest of Paris and this was immediately placed at Ettore's disposal.

Ettore, absorbed in designing a powerful new engine, had little time to spare for his quiet, elusive brother. Guilt may have played some part; Barbara Bolzoni, a beautiful young Milanese opera-singer to whom Rembrandt was once engaged, had chosen to marry Ettore instead. By 1915, the couple had two daughters and a six-year-old son, Gianoberto (Jean). Rembrandt had never ceased to love her, although he was too gentle to bear ill-will towards his brother.

His unhappiness had been apparent for some time to the artists Modigliani, Delaunay, Utrillo and Picasso, who thought of themselves as being Rembrandt's closest friends. They were aware that he had ceased to make any effort to see them by the end of 1915. There was talk of a broken love affair. Working on a crucifixion for de Guiche in these final months, the sculptor had attempted to nail the young Neapolitan model to the cross, an action entirely out of character in such a kind-hearted man.

---

* Alsace was annexed by Germany in 1870, following victory in the Franco-Prussian war.

On 8 January Rembrandt Bugatti closed the door of his studio, filled the cracks, shut the windows and placed two letters neatly on the table. One of the two was addressed to 'Ettorino' and signed 'Pempa', the nickname by which Ettore had known his younger brother since their youth. Its contents are not known. After turning on the gas he lay down on the bed, the medal of the Légion d'Honneur in his buttonhole, a bunch of Sunday violets clasped in his hands. The neighbours who called for an ambulance were too late: he died of asphyxiation before reaching the hospital.

Rembrandt Bugatti was known to have been deeply religious and, despite his suicide, arrangements were made for a church service to be held at the Madeleine and for his body to be given provisional burial at Père Lachaise until it could be taken to the Bugatti family tomb in Milan. Ettore, who had just signed a contract with the Italian firm of Diatto and who was on the verge of accepting a larger, more important commission to develop his aero-engine for American use, must surely have felt some responsibility for the tragedy. Their father Carlo had become immersed in his work as the wartime mayor of Pierrefonds, but Ettore, having gratefully used Rembrandt's introduction to Armand de Guiche, had found no time to worry over his brother's evident despair. To a close friend, Gabriel Espanet, Ettore wrote now of his sense of devastating loss. On the base of Rembrandt's final work in bronze, *The Lion and the Snake*, he inscribed the words: 'The last work of my brother', and added, with his own signature, the date of death. The newspapers, muted in their tributes, quickly forgot the brilliant young Italian's death in their rush to honour a fallen automobile hero, Georges Boillot, shot down in an air-battle that April. Ettore decided to make compensation for their deficiency. He may have been making peace with himself when, in the years after the war, he set about creating a museum for Rembrandt's work on the Alsace estate at Molsheim to which he had returned. The Bugatti Royale, Ettore's

Ettore Bugatti

favourite of his own designs, would carry on its gleaming seven-foot long bonnet the mascot of a silver elephant. It had been modelled by Rembrandt as his homage to the slaughtered inmates of the Antwerp zoo where he spent his calmest hours.[2]

In Paris, in 1916, the government decided to end the presentation of death announcements by post; the effects had proved too traumatic, the agony of suspense too great, when every visit by the postman became an occasion for dread, with families clinging to each other for support in the doorways as they saw a black-bordered envelope being withdrawn and slowly carried towards a still unknown destination. Instead, in 1916, the authorities decided to communicate bad news in a more discreet fashion; pairs of soberly dressed ladies were recruited to deliver the message in person and, if required, stay to offer advice and comfort.

Such thoughtfulness could not, for practical reasons, be extended to families living in the smaller towns of France, less still, to its thousands of villages and hamlets.

In 1916, 550,000 French conscripts died in the struggle to prevent German troops from taking the city of Verdun and marching south towards Paris. Lucien Delangle was in one of the last batches, sent out on the orders of Pétain, 'the hero of Verdun', to hold the grimly named Dead Man's Hill. The defence was successful. Twenty-one-year-old Lucien Delangle, however, was killed, shot or blown to pieces – the body was not identified – on 28 May.

This was the news which the postman brought to the Delangle household at Sainte-Mesme, sometime that summer.

THE DANCER

4

PARIS

'I've cut my dress, my slip, my hair: what next?'

CAPTION TO A CARTOON IN
LE JOURNAL, 1919

Hélène was sixteen when her brother Lucien died. She spoke of him rarely after this, and only to the closest of her friends.

At some point now, well before the age of twenty, Hélène Delangle left home to make a new life for herself in Paris. Asked by interviewers in later life to tell them how it was that she survived, she always laughed and promised an answer. 'It's a secret,' she repeated, 'but I might have time to tell you, soon!'

She never did.

From 1918 until 1928, Hélène occupied a series of rented rooms just off the Avenue des Ternes, of the sort in which the young Jean Rhys was living at much the same time, and in equally straitened circumstances.

The bed was large and comfortable, covered with an imitation satin quilt of faded pink. There was a wardrobe without a looking-glass, a red plush sofa and – opposite the bed and reflecting it – a very spotted mirror in a gilt frame.

The ledge under the mirror was strewn with [Julia's] toilet things – an untidy assortment of boxes of rouge, powder, and make-up for the eyes. At the farther end of it stood an unframed oil-painting of a half-empty bottle of red wine, a knife, and a piece of Gruyère cheese, signed 'J. Grykho, 1923'. It had probably been left in payment of a debt.[1]

A lodging of this sort was easily found. War widows were not, on the whole, fussy about the private lives of their tenants, so long as the modest rent came in. An attic room, unheated and without a water supply, cost little, and a midday meal was often included. Hélène's landladies were even prepared to overlook the two snappy little shih-tzus she acquired shortly after leaving Sainte-Mesme, and which always slept on her bed. During the first years of independence in a city where she knew nobody, they made welcome companions.

An early photograph from the trunk of memorabilia shows Hélène leaning back in a large armchair, smiling at the photographer and making the most of her beautiful, lively eyes. Her hands are neatly folded. She couldn't look more demure; all that is missing are a pair of the cat-fur mittens sold by pharmacists to an army of pretty, underfed young girls who shivered away the bitter months of winter in damp garrets, while the Seine performed its annual metamorphosis, reaching icy fingers into the city as it spilled over its banks.

She might be only nineteen or twenty in this photograph. She isn't at all well-off. Look closer, at the antimacassar draped on the back of the chair, the tattered wallpaper, the row of unframed prints, the shabby curtain. You can almost smell the cabbage soup being boiled up in the kitchen below street-level, five storeys down.

Hélène in her first flat.

These were the years when Hélène kept herself by working as a model, striking attitudes for the naughty French photographs which were sold in batches of six or ten to eager tourists, slipped under the counter in an unmarked envelope. One has survived, showing her draped in a length of gauze, an arm locked behind her head to accentuate the lifted roundness of an exposed breast. Look at the hand on her stomach and you can see that her fingers are saucily twitching the gauze aside to reveal a hint of what is supposed to be hidden from view. This isn't, we can be certain, the first time she has performed such work.

The man who may have been Hélène's first lover and whom she photographed, for a joke, while he was taking a bath, was René Carrère, an artist whose serious work was subsidized by sexy drawings which were published as postcards and used to advertise music-hall revues. One card which has survived shows a mildly sinister Don Juan sheltering a pretty naked girl under his cape. Don Juan bears a striking resemblance to René Carrère. The girl has a body very like that of Hélène Delangle.

Carrère, with his connections in the theatre world, was a man who might well have advised his young model-mistress to get herself some training as a dancer. This, for an athletic girl with plenty of stamina, a pretty face and a good sense of balance, was

René Carrère's signed theatre postcard of Don Juan and a victim.

one of the easiest semi-respectable ways to make a living in the post-war years. Paris had always been in love with dancing, long before the days when La Goulue first kicked up her legs in split knickers at the Moulin Rouge and Loie Fuller swirled her radiant chiffon veils. La Goulue was out of fashion and working for a circus by 1920, but Loie was giving a new performance at the Gaumont Palace, *Lys de la Vie*, while Isadora Duncan took time off from interpreting the music of Chopin, Brahms and Beethoven in barefoot performances of unforgettable intensity, to strut the tango with her latest lover in a Montmartre nightclub. Dancing had kept up the spirits of Parisians throughout the war; in 1920, new music halls competed against hastily renovated old friends in the struggle to meet an ever-growing demand for huge, spectacular shows. Each promised more gorgeous girls, more nudity and more lavish expense, than the last.

Hélène may have earned her rent and the money which bought her first car, a Citroën she nicknamed Maisie, by working, dark curls hidden under a helmet of bleached horsehair, in one of the chorus lines at Concert Mayol or the Ba-Ta-Clan. Somehow, she had also acquired some formal ballet training. The poses which she struck for publicity shots a few years later are easily analysed; ballet critics who have examined them are able to see, as I cannot, the way she presents a dance position, the way she angles her hips, the way she manages her pointework and tilts her head. They can study the pointe shoes – no box in the toe for protection and a shank as unrelenting as an iron caliper. Here, they are ready to confirm, is clear evidence of formal training. Poses of this kind cannot simply be struck for the camera by an inexperienced dancer.[2]

The likelihood is that she listened to René Carrère's suggestion and went to take lessons in one of the shabby first-floor drawing-rooms which, stripped of their rugs and rococo mirrors, were rented out as dance studios after the war, their social atmosphere, faint as the scent of dried rose-petals, banished by a cloying combination of sweat, rice-powder and Guerlain's L'Heure Bleu. It has proved impossible to discover who taught her. A member of the newly formed Ballets Suèdois is one possibility: we know that she made friends in these early years with the chubby jazz-loving young Swiss composer Arthur Honegger, who took several commissions from the company. It's conceivable that she joined the strenuous classes held by the illustrious Madame Egorova in a room above the Olympia. Madame's terrible candour to another pupil, Zelda Fitzgerald, suggests that the rest of her flock turned into swans; it wasn't so. The room above the Olympia was where some of the best vaudeville dancers took a few lessons before they were spotted by the talent scouts who came visiting every week; classical and popular entertainment were enmeshed, during the post-war years in Paris, in a way that is now almost impossible to imagine. This arabesque might take you into the corps de ballet at the Opéra; that one, into performing a nude adagio number at the Casino de Paris. And the latter was no disgrace.

Let's imagine. It's a summer morning in 1923.[3] Lesson time over, Hélène joins some of the dance pupils for cigarettes and a slug of coffee, then wanders off to kill an hour before her next modelling appointment. She strolls with a long sideways glance past one of the big new brasseries, thronged with beefy American men and smart, skinny girls. She carries her money – no bank accounts for a girl on her own in those days – in a cotton purse stitched into her underclothes. When, brushing through a crowd, she feels a hand nudge her waist, she lifts her leg and brings a spiked heel smartly down, nailing the thief until he swears and falls away, a black shadow glimpsed through a sea of bright dresses. Passing the matt black doors of Harry Pilcer's new club, the Florida, she remembers the shrill whistles and shrieks of a South American band, the husky voice of a red-lipped girl singing Mistinguett's latest hit, 'The Java':

'Tout contre moi/serre toi/ bien fort dans mes bras/ Je te suivrais/Je ferais ce que tu voudras./ Quand je te prends / dans mon coeur je sens / Comme un vertigo . . .' Humming, she turns to flash a smile and widen her eyes at a window-show of the latest line in striped silk jockey caps and pilot-style hats with side-flaps trailing like spaniel's ears. Staring at her own dim reflection in the glass, she's startled to see another face beyond it, gazing out at her. For a brief, shocked moment, she sees her mother before realizing that this second darker image is also of herself. Unnerved, she crosses herself, even though she hasn't stepped inside a church for five years.

Passing the entrance to a vast new hotel, still unfinished, she glances down rue Marboeuf, where an illuminated arrow above the palatial garage of Alfa Romeo flashes on and off over a row of rakishly elegant sports cars which include a stylish Bugatti touring car. (Ettore was represented in Paris by the Marboeuf garage at this time.) Clicking one red heel on the cobbles, Hélène stands and yearns. Modern in her tastes, she admires the cool curves of Mallet-Stevens's architecture – 'The garage is one of the purest expressions of design', another fan will gush to readers of *L'Art Vivant* in February 1927. But what she wants is one of the cars. Who wouldn't hanker for an Alfa or a Bugatti, when all they possessed was a Citroën, one of the 20,000 being turned out every year on Quai Javel and sold for a little over 7,000 francs to people who had never dreamed, before the war, that they might one day be able to afford a fuel-driven vehicle?

Soon after passing her driving test in 1920, Hélène Delangle decided to spend her earnings from modelling on taking her little Citroën out of Paris and off on a thousand-mile tour of France. It was the beginning of a love-affair which lasted for the rest of her life.

At approximately the same time, she discovered a new and

fashionable car accessory shop on rue Saint-Ferdinand, up at the west end of the Champs-Elysées. Carrère is likely to have mentioned it to her, for the shop was owned by one of his closest friends, a former fighter-pilot called Henri de Courcelles.

No heroes, in French eyes, matched up to the men who had engaged in aerial combat during the war; something of the awe with which they were regarded is communicated in Jean Renoir's film *La Règle du Jeu*, where the airman is both the popular hero and sacrificial victim, too noble for the corrupt world in which, after the isolation of the skies, he is as bewildered as a child. Their exceptionally swift reactions enabled them to become some of the finest racing drivers of the postwar era. These were the men who frequented the Saint-Ferdinand store. Young Philippe de Rothschild came here as a car-mad boy of fifteen, swaggering in the shadow of his aviator brother, James; so did André Dubonnet, the heir to a vermouth fortune, and Frédéric Coty, of the cosmetics empire. Robert Benoist was a former pilot whose father had been one of the Rothschild gamekeepers at their estate near Sainte-Mesme. Albert Guyot, older at forty than any of this group, was a hero to them all, a man who had raced for Sunbeam, Delage and the American Duesenberg on the brick circuit of Indianopolis and performed exhibition rolls and spins in a Blériot biplane, high above Russia, back in the innocent, pre-war years of flight. His new passion, however, was for manufacturing cars.

The store owner, Henri de Courcelles, was a gangling, squashy-nosed man in his late thirties. His smile was shy but unexpectedly wide; his charming eyes often wore an expression of secret amusement. A stranger might have been surprised to discover that 'Couc' had won a Croix de Guerre with five palms as a Sopwith fighter pilot; nothing in his appearance suggested this kind of heroism. His taste in clothes was awful – his preferred style of off-duty dress was a check shirt, baggy shorts and Scottish-style knitted socks, turned over just short of sturdy knees. His ancestry was elegant, reaching back to the Norman Conquest (there are still members of his family spread around England), but the money had disappeared long ago. The shop was the means by which he helped to finance an expensive taste in sports cars, about which, as he was the first to admit with a cheerful smile, he knew absolutely nothing except that he enjoyed driving them. For the mechanical side of things, he relied on his business partner, a burly man with broad, slightly Asiatic features and an imperturbable manner. This was Marcel Mongin, considered by many to be one of the best sports-car drivers around.* He had an agreeably playful side: a sketch by René Carrère shows Mongin laughing as he strums a banjo.

These three men, Carrère, Mongin and Courcelles, became Hélène's closest friends and allies in her twenties. Mongin's curious, almost gloating photographs of her naked body stretched on a bed, and hers of René Carrère peeping over the edge of his bath, leave no doubt about the intimacy of their relationship. The photographs of Courcelles outnumber all others; she kept sheaves of them stowed away in her trunk. He, it seems reasonable to assume, was her first great love. There is no clear indication that it was requited.

It is simpler to perform the physical act of leaving home than to escape the invisible, sticky web of family obligations. Hélène did not find it painful to walk away from the house at Sainte-Mesme. Her mother, grieving for Lucien, could take comfort from her new companion, Jean Bernard. (The daughters, whose relations with him were not warm, always alluded to Bernard as Monsieur Père.) It is possible that she missed Henri, the young brother she always called 'Didi', but he had none of her ambition and drive. The job which he took in Paris as an upholsterer's assistant never prevented Henri from returning, week after week, to the reassurance of his

---

* A second source of revenue was the Neuilly garage from which Mongin sold second-hand sports cars.

familiar surroundings in the village. He was, by all accounts, a gentle young man.

Solange had nobody. Questioned about her ambitions, she curled up like a winter leaf and said she had none, other than a steady job in the postal service which had been offered to her because of her family connections. Hélène, fuelled by dreams of glory, found this tragic; Solange responded that it was secure. But how, her sister wondered, could anybody want to settle for safety when they had never taken a risk? Returning home on a rare visit, she watched Solange grimly hauling on the water-wheel at the back of the house, dark hair pinned up in an untidy knot, skinny legs scratched from clambering up and down the river bank with the week's washing. It seemed a miserable existence. Impetuously, she decided to improve it.

The photographs kept and erratically annotated by Hélène in her old age do not suggest that Solange was especially grateful for her sister's efforts; on the contrary, they hint that her invitations were accepted in the spirit of a martyred guardian. One picture shows Hélène, curly-haired and laughing, on the beach at Le Touquet; Solange appears as a streak of darkness in the corner of the shot. Another is of a group, lounging on a vine-shaded terrace, chairs and hats tilted as the models offer sleepy smiles to the camera. Solange stands in the shadows, towards the back of the terrace. She looks isolated, sullen and bored.

It can't have felt agreeable to be beholden to a brighter, cleverer younger sister; Solange may not have wanted to be pulled into Hélène's giddy orbit. But there was no escaping her kindness, or her need. Leading an increasingly peripatetic and unstable life, Hélène wanted somebody she could depend on and in whom she could confide: one of the most surprising facts to emerge from 'Totote's' infrequent communications with Hélène is her remarkable familiarity with the gang of lovers between whom her younger sister casually shared her favours. Solange knew everything about them, their gossip, their business lives, the details of their finances. She dined with them in Paris when Hélène was away; she sympathized when they complained about her sister's refusal to commit, her frightening rages, her voracious childlike need for praise and reassurance. The sisters spoke to each other on the telephone more often than they exchanged letters, but one thing is apparent from the correspondence which has survived. Hélène never took a final decision until she had consulted Solange.[4]

Mongin and Couc took Hélène on her first journey out of France in the autumn of 1921; the occasion, for which both men had entered themselves in Grégoire cars to be supplied by an agent on their arrival, was the 200-mile race at Brooklands.[5] They started off with a visit to Brighton, where Courcelles dutifully photographed his companions standing side by side outside the new garage of the Old Ship Hotel. We don't know whether it was he or Marcel Mongin who took the pictures of Hélène naked and fast asleep in what is clearly a double room. We don't know which of the two men occupied the brass bed which is visible behind that taut and muscular body. Some of the photographs seem to hint that this may even have been an easygoing threesome.

The two Frenchmen were scratched from the race when their cars – Grégoires were notoriously problematic and the firm closed in 1923 – failed to show up. But Courcelles had a friend in the race, and Mongin was curious to see what the circuit looked like since being reopened after the war; taking Hélène with them, they drove across the Downs in Mongin's Voisin.

Created in 1906 because of the English interdiction on road-racing, Brooklands in 1921 was still the most exciting and advanced circuit in Europe, a two-and-a-half mile track of pebbled concrete with banking that rose to a dizzy 1 in 2 gradient. Hélène's only experience of a race at this time was a faint memory, preserved from childhood, of a monstrous machine, enveloped in dust as it roared downhill and away across the plain of the Beauce. Now, she found herself in a jostling, beery crowd of tweedy men in flat caps, rosy-cheeked yapping girls in sturdy knickerbockers and unflattering rubber boots, all gathered in a vast paddock at the centre of what looked like a modern amphitheatre.

Distantly, outside the clubroom, a brass band crashed into a cheerful medley of marches; above the paddock, a Sopwith plane wheeled, swooped and flipped over on to its back before soaring away over the banking. The marshal's yellow flag, apparent in the

Left to right: Marcel Mongin, Hélène, still with her natural hair colour, and Henri de Courcelles ('Couc') in leisure clothes, at an unidentified location.

*Top to bottom: Hélène, Henri de Courcelles and Marcel Mongin,
holidaying in North Italy and the Lakes in 1925.*

distance, rose, waited for the rev of engines to rise to a hungry
scream, and dropped, to be instantly hidden in a cloud of acrid
black smoke as the cars, spitting fire as they raised their engine revs,
spread out across the track. Two, crossing the black painted line,
climbed rapidly towards the concrete rim where only a line of
straggling bushes separated the circuit from a grey sky. Hélène
stared as a third climber, identified by Mongin as a Salmson and
one of the lightest cars in the race, spun round, rocked, and came
skidding down the bowl to hit the inner kerb with a crack like a

pistol-shot. Courcelles, taking his pipe out of his mouth for a moment, wondered whether she ought to be taken back to the clubhouse. A quick glance at her face reassured him; her lips were slightly parted, her eyes narrowed as she watched two blue cars screaming around the circuit at the top of the banking. Bugattis, he told her; good taste, just what he would have picked for himself to drive in this field.

'And for me?' She was still watching them intently. He jabbed his finger down at the regulations printed on the back of her programme: no women. Not permitted at Brooklands, not in a man's race. He saw her scowl, and sighed. There'd be no rest on the journey back to Brighton that evening.

Their confidence astonished and enraged her. What made these drivers so sure that women were inferior? What about the hours most women worked, the weights they carried in domestic tasks, carrying gallons of water up flights of narrow stairs for a gentleman's bath, or a week's supply of sheets and clothes down a steep riverbank for the wash? Dancing had shown her that women were more flexible, quicker, lighter.

Smiling, her two friends changed the subject. Rules were rules; the discussion was pointless. If she really wanted to get involved, there were rallies, hill-climbs, gymkhanas. But grand prix driving? Had she ever considered the cost, the hiring of the mechanics, the transport arrangements?

Hélène's quick temper was seldom under control for long: listening to them, she lost it. They didn't believe a word of what they were saying, she shouted; they just didn't like the idea of being beaten by a woman, that was all. But now she had gone too far and her tone was growing shrill and they were bored of the conversation. Quietly, in the light voice which always sounded as though he was about to laugh, Couc put forward an idea for an expedition they might make down to Nice before the end of autumn. And, since there was plainly no way to win this argument and a visit to the Riviera was always good fun, she leaned forward and kissed the back of his neck.

A casual observer of Hélène's life during the six years which followed her first visit to England might have taken a bet that this charming, fearless girl specialized only in having fun and living dangerously. Photographs, presumably taken by René Carrère, show her always in the company of Mongin and Courcelles, always laughing. They spent their summers on the Riviera or the Côte Fleurie, at elegant resorts which never imposed a constraining influence on Hélène's high spirits. Sent to get herself photographed for passport purposes before joining her friends on a trip to inspect the new Italian circuit at Monza outside Milan, she decided to do outrageous impressions of Josephine Baker; skiing for the first time at Superbagnères in the winter of 1924, she threw up her arms and shouted in delight after beating her companions, both fine sportsmen, in a race. The fact that she had almost killed herself by taking a short cut through a clump of closely planted pines bothered her not at all.

Her fearlessness was admirable – and terrifying. Retrospectively, Mongin saw the fierce intentness of a competitor who was only ever interested in winning. So too was his friend Courcelles. In 1923, Couc entered the first Endurance race at Le Mans with a massive Lorraine-Dietrich and brought it in at 8th place; the following year, he came 3rd; in 1925, partnered by André Rossignol, he won; in 1926, Mongin and he took 2nd place. It was, for an amateur driver in his late thirties, a triumphant record. While Courcelles enjoyed this late blossoming and continued to break records on his runs between Paris and Deauville, Hélène charted out her own course of victories in the Alps. Bobsleighing and skiing in the winters, she spent each summer with Kléber Balmart, one of France's finest skiers, climbing L'Aiguille Verte, Le Greppon Blanc and Mont Blanc. In 1925, she noted with

Hélène on top of the world, with a climbing team, 1925.

satisfaction that she had climbed Mont Blanc again, and by the most dangerous route; photographed at the end of the climb, she beamed down at the camera, glowing with the pleasure of a goal achieved. When Mongin and Courcelles tested their car brakes by driving on an icebound lake at the end of the year, Hélène demanded a trial drive on her own. Mongin grudgingly acknowledged that her control was exceptional. He remained puzzled by her motivation. If asked, she laughed and said that she had always liked winning; it wasn't a sufficient answer. It occurred to both him and Couc that their friend might, in some way of which she was only half-conscious, have assumed the role of her older brother, the boy who had died at Verdun and of whom she always spoke in a different, gentler tone. But neither man was given to pondering the mysteries of the female psyche for longer than most of their sex; contemplation usually ended with a shrug and a laugh. She had a will of iron when she set her mind to meeting some new test of her athletic prowess; that was all they knew.

As an athlete, she had reached her peak; in 1926 she suddenly announced that she had decided to pursue her dancing career and give up the dream of racing. Her friends, surprised but relieved, drank to the new plan and took her out to dinner. They toasted her future. She would – anybody who spent time in her company felt it – become a real success on stage. She had the shining authority, the charisma, the presence. Her dancing, even to an untutored eye, was wonderfully graceful; she had, above all, a charming manner, a way of looking at you as she tilted her head and lifted her arms. Neither Mongin nor Couc was prepared to risk her wrath by saying so, but they felt, nevertheless, that dancing was a better, and safer, choice of career than the race-circuit for such a pretty, lively creature.

In 1927 Henri de Courcelles fulfilled a long-held promise to his friend Albert Guyot and agreed to race one of his cars in a free formula* contest being held on the new track at Montlhéry just outside Paris. Despite the month, July, the weather was grim. Rain sheeted down on the small crowd of spectators who included Mongin, Guyot and a svelte blonde Hélène, taking time off from a rehearsal in her new career. Mongin was in a bad mood. He had driven the car, worked through the night on improving it and ended with a feeling of nagging dissatisfaction. The last time a Guyot Spéciale had run, it finished three laps behind the nearest competitor; his own view, trenchantly expressed, was that the steering was still defective. Guyot received his verdict with a tight-lipped smile; Courcelles, graceful as always, embraced the car-maker before going down to the pits and waving away the crash-helmet which he had been offered.

* *Formule libre* (free formula) races imposed no restrictions on the entrants' cars.

His spirits had never been higher. The Guyot was not a highly regarded racing machine, but he seemed to see no possibility of being defeated by opposition which included Albert Divo, driving for Talbot, professional Louis Chiron in a supercharged 2.3 Bugatti – the car was owned by Freddy Hoffman's Nerka Spark Plug company and Chiron was having a flamboyant affair with Hoffman's wife, Alice – or by the big Sunbeams being driven that day by two outstandingly courageous drivers, Louis Wagner and Charles Grover, using his racing pseudonym of 'Williams'. But Guyot and Couc were confident of a victory; plans had already been made for a celebratory dinner at Maxim's that night, when Couc sauntered away from the pitstop and swung himself into the low driving-seat. He stretched his legs, shifted his weight, looked up once at the grandstand, and raised his hand in a salute. It was just past ten in the morning; rain hissed in the gutters and rattled on the racing bonnets like pistol shots. Shivering suddenly, Hélène pulled up her coat collar, dug her hands deep into the pockets where her clenched fists would not be seen.

Perhaps, after all, there was no cause for the feeling of sick apprehension which had gripped her as the cars moved away. The Sunbeams were forced to pull out of the race with mechanical problems before the end of the second lap; the Guyot appeared to be holding its own when it roared past the pitstop for the third time without stopping. Courcelles, his face masked by the Meyrovitz goggles, raised one hand briefly, as if he scented victory. Mongin was bending to say something to her when she saw the pointed tail-end of the Guyot swerve across the track, jittering, out of control. She gripped Mongin's arm as the car skidded from view, towards a distant row of trees. She heard a crack, like a cannon shot. Guyot, ashen-faced, was looking upwards, raising an arm to point. She followed the line, to where the rain had thickened like smoke, obscuring the heavy mass of the Château Sainte-Europe. A van with a cross painted on its back began to circle the track, moving fast; away in the distance, she saw two flags being raised and waved, white and yellow, signalling the drivers to be on guard. Mongin was pushing his way down; limping on her high heels, she followed him, tugging at the scarf around her neck and twisting it round her hands, ready to use it as a bandage.

He was lying face-down and crumpled into something smaller than himself. Pieces of twisted metal and rubber lay scattered across the track from where the Guyot had struck the tree; a smouldering wheel protruded, lolling sideways, from a bush; another was poised with odd delicacy on the corner of what looked like an iron bed-frame. It was impossible to believe that all these pieces had, until a few minutes ago, been bolted and welded into a single unit. She twisted the scarf around her hands, tightening it into a rope as she watched the ambulance men lift what was left of Henri de Courcelles on to the stretcher and carry it towards the back of the van. Distantly, she heard the whine of cars. Mongin held her arm, marching her towards the ambulance. Behind the acridity of spent fuel and burning leather, she identified the rusty smell of blood.[6]

Afterwards, somebody told her that the ambulance driver had been so bewildered that he set off in the wrong direction, straight into the face of the speeding cars. Louis Chiron, the young Monaco driver, had won screams of excitement from the crowd when he wrenched his Bugatti out of the danger-path and hurtled on past the wreckage, chasing Albert Divo, the winner of the day. She hadn't heard a thing. Sitting with Mongin in the back of the ambulance, she stared down at the hands which a pious doctor had folded on Henri de Courcelles' chest. They were the hands she had always known, long-fingered, narrow, making her think of one of those wooden saints in churches. She remembered how gently they had touched her. It was impossible to look at the face again, after the first shocked glance. Death had been quick for poor Couc: that ought to be a comfort.

Car designers seldom, if ever, take responsibility for the death of a driver in their fragile machines. In 1929, two years after the tragedy, Guyot abandoned car manufacture to become a consultant engineer to Citroën. In 1947, for reasons which were never apparent, he killed himself with cyanide, while sitting among a large group of friends in a restaurant. To Hélène, remembering the honourable and gentle Henri de Courcelles, Albert Guyot's closest friend and most loyal supporter, the only puzzle was that he should have taken so long about it.

5

THE DANCER

'J'adore des danseuses. Je demande des danseuses.'

FERNAND DIVORE,
LE JOURNAL DU PEUPLE, 1929

During the spring of 1926 Hélène had moved to a new apartment
on the small and elegant rue Saint-Senoch in the 17th
Arrondissement. On 10 May she gave this as her address when
signing a contract. Possibly, René Carrère, with his theatrical
connections, had put her in touch with the man to whom she now
agreed to pay a thousand francs a month, while he prepared a series
of dances for them to perform together. Celéstin Eugène
Vandevelde signed the contract with his stage name, Robert Lizet;
Hélène, for the first time, boldly added the name by which she
intended to make herself known as a star.

Hellé Nice; Belle et Nice, Elle est Nice or Hellish Nice to her
American fans; Hellé (with an accent emphasising that final 'é') to
her lovers and her family; Hell on Ice to those who crossed her.
Nice, to French ears, was a word full of promise: she's good, it
hinted. She's fun.

And she was. Lizet, who had been searching for a satisfactory

Hélène and her partner, Robert Lizet, in his adaptation of Ravel's
Daphnis and Chloë, *1926–7.*

partner for some time, was charmed by her liveliness, amused by her assurance and impressed by her determination. She had no modesty; when he suggested that her role as a Greek nymph might be more convincing if she took the sequinned bandeau off her breasts, she pulled her skirt off as well and went through the rest of the rehearsal in her knickers. Just as well, he must have thought, that he didn't feel the attraction of women's bodies; an affair would have complicated their partnership.

Lizet, whose name has now been forgotten, was a celebrity of sorts in the mid-twenties. He had featured in a few silent films, although the roles were small; his appearance in the romantic dance sequences which were then a regular part of music-hall entertainment seldom failed to draw admiring gasps for such a splendid physique. Muscular thighs and a misleadingly saturnine expression were his chief attractions; without a partner, however, they were useless. The last had returned to Hungary without warning, leaving him with three important contract dates and no leading lady. Hélène, with her brillilant smile, her training at a Paris ballet school and her offer of a thousand francs a month, had seemed to drop from heaven. He hadn't wasted a moment in signing the contract. By the time he had finished with her, he promised, she'd be making more in an evening than she was paying him for the entire twelve weeks.

The publicity shots were ready to be sent out by July. It's astonishing what had been achieved in such a short time, to transform the scruffy, cheerful tomboy who ran about the country with Couc and Mongin into a poised young lady whose manner conveys an exciting hint of wildness. Dark hair neatly bobbed in the style of Louise Brooks, she steps out in a foxtrot, takes up an arabesque position in a tutu, froths up a ballet skirt with a kick which conveys a hint of La Goulue's famous can-can, or leans confidently back from Lizet's muscular embrace, angling her head at a well-rehearsed angle to gaze at the viewer. He's handsome; she has something more, an ease, a radiance, the manner of a girl born to perform.[1]

Lizet had chosen his programme with care, blending art with titillation. The music, a Chopin nocturne, a Brahms waltz, a dark and moody composition by Massenet followed by a frothy operetta song, was just original enough to make the audience feel clever for recognizing it. The numbers, all with a classical theme, were based upon celebrated dance models. Costumes, although scant, were rich in texture, scraps of velvet and gauze which sparkled with bright beads of coloured glass. Nudity, as Lizet explained to his new dancing partner, was only vulgar if one went in for the fruit-and-feather-look, like the capering La Baker and her banana skirt; nakedness, at the upper end of the market which they aimed to please, was softly lit and always in the best of taste.[2]

He was right. Society audiences loved them. As the fame of the couple's act spread through the social network which has always governed Paris, they were even suggested as the perfect after-dinner show for a New Year's Eve charity ball at the Ritz, raising money for a monument to gas victims during the war. Interviewed for the commission by the Ball's president, the beautiful young Princess of Belgium, and sensing reservations about her suitability, Hélène drew a small muslin square from her crocodile bag and dabbed her eyes. To one who had herself lost a brother at Verdun, she might have murmured, the honour of performing would bring such happiness, such pride: she decided not to argue about the disappointingly modest fee. It was less than she usually received, but an appearance at the Ritz, and in such a respectable cause, would do her career nothing but good.[3]

Shortly before midnight then, in the presence of the Archbishop of Paris and enough aristocrats to fill a fourteenth volume by Proust, Hélène Delangle appeared on stage at the Ritz's Reveillon Ball, a radiant nymph in Lizet's adaptation of the Ravel ballet,

Daphnis and Chloë.* Her white body gleamed through a spider's web of gauze as, after being carried on to the stage over her partner's naked shoulder, she was gently released to enact her love. Her expression was enchanting, her movements were heartbreaking in their grace. The audience was under her spell; seldom, wrote an excited young reporter from *Le Journal,* had he been privileged to witness such perfection. Was he alone in remembering when Tamara Karsavina had first danced as Chloë in 1912? When would they be fortunate enough to see this ravishing new dancer again? Who could predict what her future might not be?[4]

Le Journal's reporter was not alone: the press fell in love with Hellé Nice wherever she appeared in that miraculous year. She was described – the comparison was a popular one with dance critics – as showing the grace of the delicate Tanagra dancing figurines prized by rich collectors of antiquities. There was a poignancy, a delicacy about her line, the way she inclined her head and raised her eyes, which made the fact of her near-nudity seem as appropriate as for the statue of a Greek girl athlete.

Little was ever said in reviews about the girl's male partner and choreographer, but she was not yet ready to leave him behind. In January 1927 the couple were offered a contract to appear onstage at the old-fashioned Olympia music hall, soon to become a giant cinema. The show, in which they were to provide a romantic interlude between a comic act and a circus turn, was being directed by the theatre's owner, Paul Franck. It was sheer luck that Hélène, scantily dressed as the nymph for their pas de deux, should have caught the bulging and appreciative eye of Colette's ex-husband, a man who was still one of the most influential theatre critics in Paris, and on her first appearance. Gauthiers-Willy, 'le bon Willy'

* The ballet was commissioned by Diaghilev for the Ballets Russes in 1909 and first performed in 1912.

to his colleagues, had fond memories of the days when his wife Colette had appeared in this same theatre, under the direction of the same Paul Franck. Even the role she had played, skipping on to the boards as a semi-naked faun, was evoked as he watched this pretty, smiling, large-eyed girl work the audience. Disinclined to waste space on descriptions of dancing performed in a light so subtle that his rheumy old eyes could hardly follow the steps, Willy confined his tributes to her looks. 'And with what a pretty little garden this charming Hellé Nice keeps herself from us,' he wrote, alluding to the silk flowers with which she covered two pubic inches. 'What a delight.'[5]

Willy's opinions were always noticed: another dance critic, Paul Varenne, repeated the sly compliment while adding a eulogy of his own to the gorgeous nymph, 'cette naïade, renversée, abandonnée, ballante [dangling], toute nue et toute fleurie'.[6]

It was pleasant to be admired for the full length of a column for her perfect technique and unspeakable grace by the local critic in Bordeaux ('la grâce acidulée, la technique parfaite'), but a casual phrase from a celebrated journalist in Paris was far more useful. The time had come to increase their demands. By the spring of 1927 Lizet and Hélène were in a position to command 4,000 francs a night; in May, she was approached by the dynamic little owner-manager of the Casino de Paris and offered solo billing in his up and coming revue. The wages were 250 francs a week, take it or leave it, Léon Volterra told her. She signed, and allowed Lizet to vanish into obscurity without, so it appears, a second thought.

Volterra, taking over the shabby old Casino de Paris in 1917, had spent a fortune on turning it into the most glamorous music hall in the city. His first show, *Laisse les Tomber* (Drop Them, Then), used squealing saxophones and revolver shots to mock the Big Bertha guns being trained on the landmarks of Paris. In 1919 he put the first naked dancer into action on a stage. The nudity craze caught on; by 1927, even respectable actresses such as Cécile

Sorel were willing to come and bare their breasts at the Casino.★
A spectacular ten-metre high staircase, a tank big enough for the
performance of aquatic ballets and an outsize cinema screen on
which, in 1922, amazed spectators watched frail Pearl White
circling the Eiffel Tower in a monoplane, were among his more
extravagant ways of drawing in the crowds. By 1927, the Casino
de Paris stood alone. Stravinsky, Raymond Radiguet and Cocteau
came here to watch an arrestingly beautiful transvestite, Barbette,
performing in queenly drag on a trapeze. The surrealist poet Paul
Eluard, under the spell of the dazzlingly efficient Hoffman girls
who could swarm up a backdrop of ladders as dashingly as they
could imitate a cageful of wild animals, paid tribute in verse to
their acrobatic skills: 'You glorious creatures, able to dance in the
ether like angels . . .'

Paris–New York was the revue in which Hellé Nice first appeared
at the Casino de Paris in 1927. (Volterra's titles were not
imaginative; the shows of 1927 and 1928 included *Bonjour Paris*,
Paris en Fleurs, *Paris qui Chante* and *Tout Paris*.) The attention she
attracted was slight; the audiences who came to the show were less
interested in a pretty soloist or a troupe of brand-new Russian
dwarfs than the city's favourite clown, woolly-bonneted Raimu,
and, topping the bill at an extortionate fee, the Dolly Sisters,
defying the passage of time with immaculate costumes and heavy
make-up as they went through their charming but slightly dated
song and dance routine. All was forgiven; the Dollys had recently
become the darlings of Paris when they sued Mistinguett and the
Moulin Rouge for 550,000 francs, won, and gave the entire
proceeds to charity.

★ Colette was one of the most enthusiastic supporters of the tradition of nudity
at the Casino de Paris, despite the fact that her friend Paul Poiret usually designed
the costumes for the shows. 'Go and look at the Casino,' she urged the first readers
of *Gringoire* in November 1928, 'go and see the gorgeous girls, their beautiful
breasts quivering as they step out to the rhythm of a march.'

It is not altogether surprising that Hellé Nice's name did not feature in the revues with which Volterra followed *Paris–New York* in 1927. Henri de Courcelles was killed in July and Hélène was devastated. But she had already begun to make friends in the easy-going raffish world of the music halls; instead of spending the rest of the summer with Mongin and Carrère, she went along with the Casino's regular performers to enjoy an extended holiday while spreading publicity. The cuttings books show her on the move from the northern beach resort of Le Touquet down to the Riviera, joining in bicycling competitions against her fellow-performers, or entering one of the increasingly popular gymkhana car shows which paired a celebrity or a socialite with a handsome new machine. For a high-spirited young woman of twenty-eight who enjoyed attention and loved driving, there was no hardship in spending an afternoon showing off her skills, even if they only consisted in demonstrating how elegantly she could swing her legs out of a car, or how swiftly she could drive it between a row of fixed posts. The pay was good; the publicity value was excellent. It passed the time.

She had already made a handsome sum of money, but the show which turned her into a star was *Les Ailes de Paris* (Wings over Paris), Léon Volterra's final spectacular before he sold out and took up racehorses. The show, written by the frighteningly productive team of Saint-Granier and Albert Willemetz, was a staggering 48-number showcase for the talents of Maurice Chevalier, one of the Casino's favourite stars. Chevalier, too, had been enjoying a summer on the coast and perhaps – his promiscuity was legendary – a brief affair with the pretty newly blonde dancer who was given star billing in his show. Hélène's name was far more prominent in posters advertising *Les Ailes de Paris* than it had been for previous Casino appearances.

Most people went to the show for two reasons. One was to see and hear Chevalier, whose number 'Quand On Revient' had become an instant hit. The second was to see a cruelly funny imitation of The Dolly Sisters, performed by two ravishingly handsome Norwegian boys who called themselves The Rocky Twins.

A dapper Maurice Chevalier, with an eye for the girls.

The Dollys were said to be furious; Hélène, who had not, perhaps, enjoyed being eclipsed by their celebrity, ganged up with their mimics and became The Rocky Twins' new best friend. For a time, at least, she, the Twins, and a pretty, sports-loving singer called Diana became a devoted foursome, spending all their time together and, since they were all startlingly attractive, receiving plenty of press attention.

In her old age, Hélène liked to pretend that she had been among the greatest dancers to perform on the music-hall stage.[7] When the names of other performers of the 1920s were mentioned, she described them as her friends while letting it be known that none, with the exception of Josephine Baker and Mistinguett, had been on her level. The truth was that she had never quite been on theirs. The dancer who attracted the most attention at the time in *Les Ailes de Paris* was dark-haired, fleet-footed Miss Florence, former leader of the remarkable Hoffmann Girls dancing troupe. Hellé Nice, appearing as Madame de Sévigné, as The Queen of the Night and, with her friends the Rockies, as a Greek March, was top of the second flight. It is, however, fair to note that at least one newspaper critic, for *Presse* magazine, noted that she had a ravishing body and danced with such skill and grace that a bigger role would have been justified.

The show was a phenomenon. It made the names and fortunes of many of its young stars and three million francs for Volterra, quite a triumph for a man who had started out selling programmes in the aisles of the Olympia. Most importantly, in an age when there was no support from the state for performers, the success of *Wings* brought invitations to appear outside Paris, at better rates of pay, and to audition for films. It would not have escaped the attention of Hélène, especially if she had been briefly involved with him, that Maurice Chevalier was off to Hollywood; everybody who worked in the theatre during the late twenties was plotting to expand into cinema work. The Rockys had already been in a film and so had Diana. The Gaumont Company, turning out as many as three films a day in their Paris studios, were always looking for new talent.

Later in life, during the years when her name had lost its magical resonance and the trappings of wealth – the furs, the yacht, the magnificently opulent Hispano-Suiza touring car which she bought on a whim – were gone, the old lady clung with pathetic tenacity to the programmes and photographs which kept the memory of her glorious youth.[8] The walls of the tiny lodging provided to her by the actors' charitable institution were hung with pictures taken in her dancing years. Anybody who showed an interest in them was invited to admire the pages of two heavy booklets, glossy with illustrious names. The Gala, she explained when her visitors looked blank. *The* Gala. You didn't get asked to take part in that event by being a nobody.

Indeed you did not; nothing, during the first years of her fall from grace, stood Hélène Delangle in better stead with a charity devoted to the care of dancers, singers and actors than the fact that she had given her services in this cause.

The Gala Union of Theatre Performers was put together shortly after the war. Its object, at a time when no help was available for performers too old or too frail to work, was to raise money for their care. In a city which was joyfully addicted to every form of theatrical entertainment, from the café-concert, at which singers entertained customers, to the ambitious works of the Ballets Suèdois, the Gala had a captive audience. By 1928, it was established as one of the great social events of the Parisian year. To be invited to participate in the Gala was an honour extended only to the cream of the performers. Hélène was among them.

Recalling such an event during the 1960s, by which time there was nothing comparable, she spoke wistfully of the fun, the excitement of the two weeks of preparation at the Cirque d'Hiver.

The evening was held in an amphitheatre, and it was presented as a circus. The joke and the fun of it lay in the fact that, for this one night of the year, even the most serious performers of Paris showed themselves in a completely different light, swinging through the air on ropes, dancing on trampolines, riding on elephants, sending dogs through paper hoops. And the audience, jewels blazing under the pink arc lights as they settled into their seats just after midnight, played along, clapping like children as Miss Dolly Davis wobbled her way up a free-standing ladder to perform a series of handstands, laughing with pleasure when the corps de ballet from the Opéra, last seen an hour earlier in *Swan Lake*, came shimmying and tapping across the ring to the backing of fourteen pianos playing Cole Porter and Gershwin in perfect unison.

Brightening as she recalled those distant days, the old lady was eager to show off the programme she had kept, and to point out her own name, teamed with the two biggest attractions of the evening as Les Harrys, two men and a girl, dazzling the crowds as they foxtrotted over a trampoline. Here she was again, at the Gala of 1930, up on a high wire and, she would like it to be noticed, performing without a safety net, after less than two weeks of training.[9]

In 1928, the two 'Harrys' who danced alongside Hélène on the trampoline had been celebrities. André Roanne, sometimes described as the most handsome man in French cinema, was already under contract to appear in G.W. Pabst's new vehicle for Louise Brooks, *Diary of a Lost Girl*, and to co-star with Constance Talmadge in a sports spoof, *Venus*. Harry Pilcer had established himself as one of the best-known dancers in France in a long partnership with Gaby Deslys, creator of the much-copied Gaby Glide; by 1928, he had acquired a Riviera home, a yacht, a magnificent touring car and a second nightclub, Les Acacias, which was said to be the best in Paris. José Noguero, with whom Hélène appeared as Les Stefano at the Cirque in 1930, was a smoothly handsome young Spaniard who was playing, with great credibility, the role of a charming gigolo in the theatrical hit of the spring season, *The Weaker Sex*, and who built up a successful film career over the next decade.* An unkind visitor might have been tempted to comment on the way Hellé Nice always managed to appear with the best-looking men.

Reviews of the two galas in which she participated suggest that Hélène did well in her new circus roles. Audiences – Colette and Anna de Noailles were among the enthusiastic regular attendants – were much freer with their opinions than they would have been in a theatre. They could, and did, show when they thought that a performance was feebly prepared or conceived. They booed pretty Miss Spinelli in 1930 when her troupe of performing baboons wilfully declined to dance on stilts. But Hellé Nice, boldly exposing herself on the high wire in a gold bandeau top and smaller shorts than had ever been seen in a real circus, drew warm applause, for her lack of fear – a professional trapezist had been killed in a fall only a few weeks earlier – and for a welcome return, after almost a year of absence from the stage.

Visiting her favourite resort, Megève, at the beginning of 1929, Hélène had suffered an accident which changed her life. She was skiing off piste when she heard the ominous rattle of stones behind her.[10] Speeding sideways as she tried to escape an avalanche, she attempted a leap which she would never, in normal circumstances, have risked. Saving her life, she damaged the cartilage of her knee, the worst fate that can overtake a dancer. Unable to participate in the annual Gala, she was forced, by the summer of 1929, to accept that she would never again be flexible enough to resume a

* The third of Les Stefano was Samson Fainsiber. Curiously, Hélène met him again as a fellow-recipient of La Roue Tourne's charity in 1962. No evidence of an earlier friendship between them was apparent.

professional dancing career. One reason for the warm applause which greeted her appearance at the Cirque d'Hiver in March 1930 was that the audience knew of her misfortune, and of the pain she must still have been in as, poised above the fixed bar, she slowly extended her legs to perform the splits.

Hélène herself would never have acknowledged the fact, but the accident was timely. She was nearing thirty, and if any reviewers were still comparing her to Karsavina when she danced, they kept the thought to themselves. The praises she received in 1929 were for her charm, her rapport with the audience and her beautiful body. One photograph which has survived from the late 1920s shows her in what appears to be a cabaret turn, dancing naked, with a white dove. Enchanting though she looks in the picture, it does not suggest that a glorious future of stage work stretched ahead.

There was another route. Hélène had already shown uncommon skill as a competitive driver. She had been excited by cars since the age of twenty. Fortunately for her, she was living in an age when the world of theatre was intimately connected to that of sport. The car-makers needed glamour to sell their machines; the stars saw the machines as a perfect accessory to their own good looks. With her wonderful smile, an unforgettable name and a genius for publicity, she was well-placed to attract a sponsor. First, however, she had to prove herself. She did so, quite spectacularly, through the remarkable occasions which were known as the Actors' Championships.

THE RACER

6

'LA PRINCESSE DES ALTITUDES, REINE DE VITESSE'*

'And now there was nothing – nothing on earth between her and victory save the hazard of the road.'

GILBERT FRANKAU,
CHRISTOPHER STRONG (1932), P.120†

On 10 June 1928 ten sporting balloonists agreed to be chased across country for a day, starting from Saint Cloud in a race against ten actresses mounted on Voisins, Peugeots and Ballots. (The balloonists won.) A month earlier, crowds had cheered on the waiters of some of the smart new brasseries of Montparnasse, running the length of a boulevard while they held heavily laden trays at shoulder height.

France has always loved competitive sports. In the spring of 1928, you could, when bored by steeplechasing, have taken bets on

* Title given to Hellé Nice by Rochat-Cenise, in *Le Journal*, 21 December 1929.
† Frankau's *Christopher Strong* was one of the few works of fiction of that time to provide a full and convincing account of the female experience of driving a Grand Prix car competitively against men, as Hellé Nice chose to do. Frankau's Lady Felicity Darrington, who drives a 'Straight Eight Courtland' at Montlhéry, is an intriguing cross between Hellé Nice and Gwenda Stewart, a formidable British record-breaker of the same period.

a newsboys' race, a newsgirls' race and a bakers' race. Between shows, the music halls hosted roller-skating competitions and issued endurance challenges to couples who were prepared to Charleston until they dropped. (The oddest of these events took place in complete silence as the smartly dressed competitors foxtrotted for twelve hours to the rhythm of 'Vitaphones' which transmitted radio music into their black plastic ear-muffs.)

Sylvia Beach, dragged away from her bookshop to the Vél d'Hiver by Ernest Hemingway for a true Parisian experience, was unable to decide which were the madder, the men who cycled around its banked wooden sides, day and night, for almost a week; or the spectators. 'Fans,' she wrote, 'went and lived there for the duration, watching more and more listlessly the little monkey-men, hunched over on their bikes, slowly circling the ring or suddenly sprinting, night and day, in an atmosphere of smoke and dust and theatrical stars, and amid the blare of loudspeakers.'[1] Similar events drew crowds to the Parc des Princes out at Auteuil and to the wooden-banked bowl of Stade Buffalo at Montrouge. This was where Ernest Hemingway, during a period when he became obsessed by the city's sporting events, saw a motorbike racer crash and die. His skull, Hemingway wrote with ghoulish precision, had crumpled under the crash helmet with the sound of a hard-boiled egg being cracked against a stone to peel it on a picnic.[2]

Hemingway, one of many young Americans who had been attracted to Paris by a truly magnificent exchange rate of almost 13 francs to the dollar (in 1921) saw the bicycle stadiums as battlefields. The velodromes had also, since 1923, been the setting for the city's most charmingly absurd competitive event, the Actors' Championship.

The Championships had evolved from the Bataille des Fleurs of the 1890s, an annual parade of flower-decked carriages, driven by beauties of the stage and high society. These parades had split in two directions after 1918, the car show and the competition. The first, the Concours d'Elégance, provided Hélène Delangle with plenty of attractive employment during her dancing years. The treasured collection of photographs and cuttings was thick with glamour-shots from those days. As an old lady, she loved to show them off, a finger moving slowly over the blurred prints as she pointed out the splendour of the machine beside or in which she was gracefully posed. The cars, the Rosengarts, Ballots and Voisins, were returned to the showrooms after the show; the jewels and furs and dresses, on the other hand . . . it all depended on which designer you were dealing with. Paul Poiret was a sweetheart, too generous for his own good, especially if you'd been dressed by him for one of the revues. Madame Schiaparelli, on the other hand, checked that everything came back, down to the last button. Still, one or two little bonuses had come her way, a spotted silk dress which she was still wearing ten years later, a glorious fur collar, a couple of expensive hats. But the main benefit of the Concours

Actress Maria Dalbaicin at the Actors' Championship 1928.

d'Elégance, as she was happy to explain, was the publicity.[3] The more appearances you made, the better the Casino de Paris liked it, and the better your name was known, the more money you could begin to demand. It made sense. And it was fun, a lovely day out. How many car shows had she been in? Too many to count, when you took account of the summer shows for holidaymakers held at Le Touquet, Trouville, Lyon, Limoges, Deauville, Cannes, Nice: thirty? forty? She couldn't begin to remember.[4]

The Actors' Championships, always scheduled to take place over the same June weekend as the car show at the Parc des Princes, was even more fun, a wonderful way for audiences to meet their favourite stars and give them support. Any actor or dancer or singer who enjoyed driving, and most of them did, wanted to enter the championship. A few of the performers took it seriously; others, like the comedian and film star Georges Biscot, who helped start a craze among the rich fathers when he tore around the course in a miniature Bugatti which Ettore had designed for his younger son Roland, treated the occasion as the high comedy which, in part, it was.

Hélène had always herself treated these occasions lightly until the disaster of her accident. Now, plotting a career change, she took note of the fact that the Actors' Championship of 1929 was due to take place in the same month as the only serious sporting event for female drivers, the Journée Féminine de L'Automobile. Marcel Mongin, from whom she took advice, thought she stood a chance of winning both, provided that she had a decent car and good coaching. Speaking to him in April, when she was first able to take a few steps without pain, she had neither. All she did have, other than a well-known name, was a ferocious competitive urge, the quality which had startled and impressed Mongin from the first time he had seen her on a ski-slope.

The conversations with Mongin and the mentor's role ascribed to him here are based on inference, not documentation. It is, however, striking that Hélène chose to drive an unusual car, the Omega Six, which Mongin himself had used successfully at Le Mans in 1924. It is likely to have been Mongin who approached the manufacturer, Jules Daubecq, and put it to him that his falling sales might receive a boost if a beautiful young woman drove one of the most ravishing sports cars of the time to victory. By 1929, Daubecq was worried enough to agree. A car was produced and prepared for her; possibly, Mongin supplied an experienced mechanic from his own garage.

Preparations were intensive and exhausting. She needed exercises to strengthen her torso, waist and shoulders for full control of the wheel, to harden her thighs and calves for braking, and to toughen her palms. Strenuous though the training was, she relished the sensation of a body growing daily more powerful. She knew Mongin was a superb driver; she had absolute confidence in him as a teacher. Memorize every corner, every uneven patch, he told her; know the course well enough to drive it blindfold. Keep your left foot down. Use it as a brace. Make sure you have spare goggles where you can reach them without looking down. Use two pairs of cotton gloves, thin enough to give you a feeling for the road, never mind the burnt palms. You won't notice the blisters until it's over.

Simple details, practically delivered, dutifully followed. Every day, twice a day, she drove ten laps of the circuit at Montlhéry, the first course in France to have been built specifically for cars. The most Mongin ever said was that she was picking up.

Publicly, her confidence was unassailable; alone, she was scared. What if she failed? Late at night, in the quiet hours, she sat on a kitchen chair, cold cream smeared on her cheeks and neck, a cigarette clenched between her teeth. She narrowed her eyes until she could see the circuit, brace her body against each jolt of broken surface under the tyres, tighten her fists and wrench the wheel until her shoulders ached, hold it there, hard, until she was safely round the bend, moving along the straight. Take a rest, her friends told her; it's not doing you good. And then she'd weaken and go drinking and come back with a handsome boy and she'd forget the irritation of his snuffles and snores as she lay wide-eyed in the darkness before dawn, listening for the rising whine of an engine, waiting for the wind to thump a fist against her face.

Once, circling the Montlhéry concrete bowl at a higher speed than Mongin or the manufacturer had licensed her to attempt – the bowl was excluded from the circuit for which she was rehearsing her skills – she nearly hit the barrier as a falling scrap of scarlet cloth flattened itself against the scrap of glass in her windshield. Blinded, she snatched it away. A pilot, flying low enough to have dropped a thoughtless souvenir, waved a jaunty hand before he pointed the little plane's nose skywards.

Couc had once told her that he always wore a red scarf around his neck when he went up in a plane. She wanted to believe that his ghost had come back to wish her luck. Mongin thought the idea ludicrous, but she kept the scarf tied around her neck. When she came home first in the preliminary elimination trial, the day before the main race, she was joyfully convinced that her amulet had played a part.

The Grand Prix of the third Journée Féminine was due to begin just after midday on Sunday, 2 June 1929. She reached the track with half an hour to go, wishing she hadn't spent the night before dancing at Les Acacias. A green-eyed boy, a friend of one of the costume-makers at the casino, had stayed the night. A mixture of morphine, champagne and sex had left her wanting to crawl into a coalhole when she woke up and now, with ten minutes to go, Mongin was worrying about the Omega's brakes. Dully, she watched the mechanic go to work again. She pulled her white beret down over her ears, lit a cigarette, stubbed it out. Her hands, she noticed, were shaking.

Given her state of nerves, she thought fifteenth place in the first race wasn't too much of a disgrace, from last starting position. Mongin, however, looked grim. Embracing her for the benefit of one of the camera teams sent by *Le Journal*, the sponsors of the day, he gave her a hard pinch. 'You'll have to do better than that if you're serious, ma grosse,' he murmured. 'And how many men was it, last night?'

She told him, which was true, that her knee was hurting. He gave her a thoughtful look and walked away without responding to speak to Charles, the mechanic.

Half an hour now until the big race. Acid bubbled in her stomach. Her eyes flickered from the busy row of mechanics to the fluttering banners and up to the clock, hanging like a full moon beside the start post. She watched the competition, Lucy Schell with one hand in a bandage; Dominique Ferrand, knowing she was the favourite, stroking the bonnet of her scarlet Amilcar as though she'd been given a new pony; Baronne d'Elern sulking at the news that her Rosengart wasn't up to the required safety levels; Violette Morris, marching around her vast Donnet like a policeman on duty, cigarette glued to the corner of her mouth as she barked out orders at a kneeling mechanic . . . Turning as if she could sense the watchful stare, Morris took the cigarette, dropped it and slowly ground it out, her eyes on the rosy-cheeked girl in the white beret. Even as an old woman, Hélène Delangle remembered that look.

A voice had called the warning for departure time. Mongin put a hand on her shoulder, smiled. She wondered if he, too, was thinking of Henri de Courcelles and wishing that their friend could be here to see her. She smiled back, grateful for all the time he'd given her. 'Charles?' She nodded at the young olive-skinned mechanic to accompany her as she strolled away from the pitstop and crossed to face the grandstand, giving the crowds just the hint of a shimmy. She heard a volley of hammering hands, laughter, a man's voice shouting her stage name. Let Morris or little Ferrand match that. She milked the moment, bit into a sandwich with strong white teeth, turned for the cameras to admire her as she tipped her head back to swallow from a water bottle before she thrust it into the front of her overalls with a straw jutting out high enough to be caught later by dust-parched lips. She flexed her feet in the narrow rubber-soled gymshoes, pulled a second pair of gloves over the thin cotton ones which would absorb some of the sweat. Bouncing on her toes as she walked towards the row of cars, she felt the familiar stab of pain shoot up from her knee. She bent quickly to hide the grimace.

The Omega was being given a last check by Charles and Mongin's nephew, Albert, named for their friend Albert Guyot. Head down so as not to meet the eyes of her competitors as the first machines began to rattle and belch smoke, she swung open the heavy blue door, settled herself into place, goggles on, right toes stretching out for the brake pedal, right heel ready for the centre-placed throttle, left foot just short of the clutch pedal. Far away, a band was thumping out the *Marseillaise*; nearer, the voice of the marshal came over the loud-hailer, giving the warnings. Blue flag, waved: give way to the driver behind you. Yellow flag, still: danger ahead. Yellow and red, the one to dread: oil on the track. Black flag with your number on it: back to the pit. And on. And on. She breathed deep and slow, stretched her fingers wide, reached for the gear stick as the mechanic spun the crank. Ahead of her, crouched on its appointed line, she heard the roar of a lion from Morris's Donnet.

The Amilcar was her biggest threat, according to Mongin. She looked for it and spotted the red and white bonnet jolt into a heavy shudder of anticipation.

The big clock on the dash showed two minutes to go. The flag was up. She pushed in the magneto switch, waited, laid a velvet foot on the throttle, opened, listened, watched the rev pointer shift, the needles flicker up, listened again. Oil pressure, oil temperature, blower pressure, engine temperature, noise rising, all in balance. Watch the flag, clear the mind, see, just before the flag fell, the emptiness of the road before a howl of sound took the cars forward, bunching too close as she pulled the lever back into third and saw the Donnet bonnet fall suddenly from sight.

The first corner came up at her. She squeezed the accelerator, aimed in on her familiar course line, out to see Ferrand's Amilcar ahead, dust rising to shroud the narrow projecting wheels as they straightened. She blinked as a shower of grit struck her goggles, waited for her breathing to regulate.

Her eyes narrowed as the next corner came at her. Sliding round it, she felt the car's wheels twitch and straighten in response to the small, deft movement of her hands. She liked this car. Pressing her right foot down, she tightened her grip, pulling the blue prow back into line, scanning the road ahead for the Amilcar.

Miss Hellé Nice, the charming Casino de Paris dancer, won the Grand Prix Féminin at Montlhéry yesterday.

The race . . . took place between the five fastest competitors in an elimination trial held the previous day. Two of the drivers broke down, leaving three to battle it out. The driving was magnificent: nobody who saw it would feel able to argue that women drive less well than men. Hellé Nice, the winner, maintained an average of over 100 kph: how many men could match that?

The victor was given a huge ovation. With a wreath of flowers garlanding the car bonnet, she performed a lap of honour before jumping out and pulling off her wind-protection cap. A slender figure in her white overalls and with a red scarf knotted around her neck, she ran across the track to the medical point, where I found her piercing the blisters on her fingers with a hot needle. (You could see how she must have gripped the wheel!)

I congratulated her. 'You raced with such passion! Up until the last moment, the public couldn't guess which was going to win, you, in the blue car, or Miss Ferrand in the red. And then, when we saw you come roaring past her, so near to the finishing line, the feeling of emotion in the crowd was fantastic!'

'I was chasing her for a long time,' Hellé Nice explained, 'but I couldn't spot her. I knew that I'd passed the others and I had to find the red one, and when I did see it, I'd lost count of how many laps I'd already done. And then I realized that we were on the last lap and there it was. I had to push the car really hard to get past – well, I'm happy.'

'I think you were doing 130 past the stands . . .'

'More, quite a lot more.'

The new champion told me a bit about her sporting tastes: 'Cars, of course, then skiing, although I had a bad accident this last season. I go climbing every year, Mont Blanc, the Grepon, the Aiguille Verte.'

I'm not surprised now by Miss Hellé Nice's coolness. The mountains are a tough school in which to learn the strengths she has shown here today.

Hastily, the new champion pulls off her overalls and changes into a beautiful dress for the results of the Concours d'Elégance. She's only just ready when we hear the announcement that the car she presented came first.

So, a double victory! Sport and elegance, the qualities that only the modern woman knows how to bring together.

Odette Marjorie, *L'Intransigeant*, 2 June 1929

Newspaper accounts are never to be trusted and Odette Marjorie was not given the scoop she suggested here. Instead, the poor interviewer from *L'Intransigeant* was obliged to wait for almost an hour while photographers from *Le Journal*, the day's sponsor, gathered around the Omega. Hélène's fingers may have been blistered, but she still managed to get most of the dust off her face,

*Hélène is snapped restoring her make-up after
winning the Grand Prix Féminin, 1929.*

freshen her lipstick and pull her beret on at a fetching angle before
taking up her victory pose, the winner of the first Grand Prix for
women in the history of racing.

Back in her apartment and surrounded by telegrams and flowers,
she gave interview after interview, flirting charmingly as she agreed
that, yes, speed was a great thrill and she'd never felt happier than
taking that last corner at 150 kph. Jean Pedron, a dazzled young
journalist on his first commission, dutifully noted Miss Hellé Nice's
words without picking up on the hint of a sexual invitation as she
told him of the greatest pleasure she knew, the feeling of a great
engine roaring and under your control ('entre les mains un bolide
qui ronfle et qui ne demande qu'à foncer').[5]

It was the beginning of a glorious summer. The day after the
race, she heard that the Bugatti showroom in Paris would be happy

to provide her with a car in which to perform at the Actors' Championship the following week. Bugatti: she didn't want to admit how many times she'd lingered outside the handsome showroom windows on Avenue Montaigne, her eyes drawn past the great poster of the racehorse, emblazoned 'The Thoroughbred Car', and on past the flowing lines of the great Bugatti Royale, a car like no other, to the pretty, witty shape of the 35, her favourite. The car they were asking – asking! – her to drive was off in a window of its own. The only person she knew who drove a T43A tourer was a duchess who used to come to the back of the casino, looking for a dancer to take home. A couple of the Woods' sisters, English girls, went along and talked for weeks of the thrill it had given them to sit up in front of the big car, roaring through the night towards Vincennes.

Fine to be a passenger, but to drive it! Sitting in the T43A in the showroom with her hands on the wheel, Hélène's face glowed with happiness. Jean Bugatti had designed the chassis, they told her, and it was Jean who had sent the message that they were to let the pretty dancer drive the car. She asked the sales manager to tell Mr Bugatti that she had never felt so honoured in her life.★

Albert Divo and Guy Bouriat, watching her wriggle her way out of the car and run her hand along the bonnet of Ettore's Royale before making some remark about how you could guess the level of a man's sex drive by the kind of car he chose, glanced at each other with raised eyebrows. Not the choice they would have made, but Jean, at twenty, was the firm's Crown Prince, able

---

★ Hélène's transfer to Bugatti, for whatever reason, was well-timed. The Omega Six's sales, already dwindling, were on the verge of being reduced to nothing by Daubecq's powerful rival, Hispano-Suiza. In 1930 the manufacturer who had risen from being a woodcutter to become a provider of sleepers for railway lines and then a car designer, committed suicide. He was already ruined; his strongbox, when opened, contained only a hunk of stale bread.

to do as he liked, so long as he didn't race himself. And he wanted, so it seemed, a showgirl to help sell his favourite car.

Their prejudices, weakened by the determination with which she set about mastering the car's ways with only a week to go before the competition, were forgotten in the joy of her triumph. *L'Auto,* the daily paper which helped sponsor the Actors' Championships, was dazzled by the ease with which she took the first prize in the gymkhana, handling the heavy car as easily as a pony while she paced it through the absurd requirements, opening a gate and closing it again without turning off the engine, leaning out to touch the ground, weaving at speed between a series of stakes. The crowd, reporters noted, adored this new champion with her delicious smile and her way of making a joke of everything she did, nonchalant in the display of superb driving skills. The real news of the day was that she had, for the first time in the six years of the championship's existence, taken the speed record of the day from the men. Blanche Montel, the foxy-faced veteran star of over sixteen films who usually scooped all the female prizes of the day and monopolized the camera shots, was photographed precisely once on this occasion and not as a champion, but as 'the charming actress who recently became a mother'. Hélène, carrying home her prizes while Guy Bouriat drove the car back to the showroom, had made herself another enemy.

By the end of the summer, as she rounded off her triumphs with a well-publicized appearance in a handsome 1928 Rosengart at Le Touquet, feelings about the new driving-star had polarized. Cameramen, car manufacturers and the crowds were captivated by her charm and courage; the singers and dancers who suddenly found themselves standing in her shade, heaped contempt on the shameless way she exhibited her body and used that grin to snatch all the attention. It was unbelievable, they said, how the little bitch got away with it: who had ever heard of driving a Rosengart in a bathing suit? It was pitifully apparent that Hélène Delangle wore one only to remind the world of her stripping-skills: as if anybody needed reminding.

The old lady had kept a favourite page of news items from this period. The top picture showed her in the Rosengart, one arm twined caressingly around the steering-wheel, long legs stretched out of the open driver's door, hair damp and curling, as if she had just come from a bedroom, or the sea. Lower down on the same page, the camera framed a group of solid young ladies displaying plump arms and sturdy legs in awkward poses around another of the entered cars. Their smiles are stiff; their eager, clumsy bodies do not please the eye. There seems to be a note of feline irony in a caption which describes the group as our 'charming competitors'. This provided the ageing Hélène with many pleasant moments. Was it any wonder, she asked, that photographers had preferred the look of the girl in the Rosengart, or that the women who took part in the car contests were so rude about her? Diana, her dancer friend from the casino, was the only exception, a perfect darling, sweet enough even to sign a photograph of herself, just after losing a bicycle race on the road above Deauville beach: 'To my best friend, the driving-ace!'

Diana was rewarded. An invitation arrived to join the champion and a few close friends on her new 22-metre-long boat, *La Vague*, for a sailing trip around the coast of Spain.

La Vague, like the newly acquired Hispano-Suiza, was an act of bold indulgence. Bills for the glorious, shining black car, with its stork mascot spreading silver wings above a radiator as big as a door, ran up to 40,000 francs a year; a single receipt for various repairs carried out on the boat, a beautiful second-hand ketch, added up to 250,000 francs. Hélène could afford such extravagance; success was turning her into a valuable advertising weapon. A seductive body and a cheeky, heart-stopping grin could sell products as well as cars. In 1929, shortly after her spectacular double victory in the

Lucky Strike poster.

Actors' Championship, Hélène became the new face of Lucky
Strike, 'cigarette of the championship winner'. Not, as she was
anxious to stress, that she ever lost her loyalty to untipped
Gauloises, but the money was good.

★

In the absence of any information from Hélène herself, conjectures have to be made about the development of her relationship with Bugatti. It seems reasonable to suppose that the connection began with her success in the T43A at the Actors' Championship in June. We can examine the radiant smiles with which Hélène and young Jean Bugatti were photographed gazing into each other's eyes the following year, as Jean presented her with the prize for coming 3rd in the Bugatti Grand Prix held at Le Mans. Later, he fell deeply in love with a dancing girl; perhaps Hélène set a precedent.

The initiative may have come from Jean; the idea of persuading her to set a new world speed record was his father's. Ettore, by 1929, was looking for a new woman racer to add glamour to the image and help him reach the female market. Elizabeth Junek, the most remarkable of female Bugatti drivers, had retired in July 1928, after the horror of witnessing her husband's death and that of a fellow Czech on the Nürburgring. Elizabeth Junek's most remarkable achievement was to hold the lead in the formidable Sicilian race, the Targa Florio, for nearly two laps of the five, in May 1928, two months before her husband's death. Two other women racers, Albertine Derancourt, and Jannine Jennky, the brilliant pupil of Albert Divo, stopped racing their Bugattis the following summer. Ernest Friderich's daughter Renée was still too young and inexperienced, although desperate to be given a chance to show her skills; a gap existed and this showgirl, Hellé Nice, seemed equipped to fill it.

The most probable place and time for Hélène's first encounter with Ettore and his oldest son is the great Paris car show which was held every year, towards the close of the season. She was in the news again, after her voyage around the coast of Spain. Ettore liked yachts and he shared his son's taste for attractive, adventurous women. Here, perhaps, he put forward his offer of a 35C, the most beautiful racing car she was ever likely to see, for a speed record, if she was confident that she could take it up to 200 kph.

86

Such an offer, to a woman who always told interviewers that the sensation of speed was the most exciting that she knew, was irresistible. Invited to come to the Bugatti estate at Molsheim and have the car prepared for her while she learnt how to handle it, she could hardly believe her good fortune. And all this in less than a year!

7

INTERLUDE AT MOLSHEIM

'Bugattis are élite cars created for the élite; the fact that they may be expensive to maintain, repair and tune, is therefore of no significance.'

ETTORE BUGATTI

Jean Bugatti's absence was the only disappointment, although it did not surprise her. She had noticed the sharp look which his father gave her at the Paris Show when, without thinking what she was doing, she touched Jean's arm with her hand. It was the kind of gesture she might have made twenty times a day and thought nothing about it, but the glance from Ettore told her that it wasn't a good idea. The Crown Prince was off limits, reserved for some semi-royal Miss, she supposed, picturing a film-star beauty running down a flight of steps from her chateau, and into his arms.

The flicker of regret was forgotten in the pleasure of being welcomed to Molsheim, not only by Ettore but also by his wife and eldest daughter. It was the latter, Lébé Bugatti, who escorted her to the estate's hotel – The Thoroughbred, of course – apologizing for the fact that they could not put her up in their own home. A meal could be brought to her room; or would she rather have something in the little bar downstairs? Looking at the young woman's dark, neatly tailored clothes, Hélène decided to leave her dashing Paris suits in the trunk. She was anxious to fit in.

Lébé hesitated in the doorway, murmuring something inaudible about her brother. Blushing, Hélène said that she hardly knew him. 'Well, please don't let him bother you,' Lébé said. 'Roland isn't supposed to come into the Hotel, but he does love meeting new visitors. Just send him off when you get bored.'

Not Jean, then; another, younger brother. She was glad she hadn't said more.

The hotel was unlike any she had ever encountered. When Lébé had left, she ran round the room like a child, inspecting the delights of this little palace of modernity. Running water in the bathroom, hot and cold, electric light, a well-aired bed, a clean set of overalls laid out on the chair for her first day of training, a dish of ripe plums, some new novels, Italian, German and French, on the shelf, bright-faced flowers in a yellow jug on the windowsill.

The bed was big enough for two people if they squeezed up close. Leaning out of the window and smelling the sharp tang of pines, hearing laughter from the bar below, she found herself thinking of Jean again and wondering where he took girls, when

Jean Bugatti, with a Bugatti Royale,
for which he designed the magnificent body.

he was here. Perhaps he didn't; the father looked as though he'd always be on the watch.

It was a shame Marcel hadn't come along to keep her company. They could have had a good time in here, just like the old days at Brighton. But Mongin was adamant. She'd do better on her own, he told her, so long as she remembered that she was there as a professional driver, not as a cabaret star. No drinking, dancing or silly stuff (by which he meant the morphine which she began using in 1929, to kill the pain of her injured knee; she continued to take it, as many of her friends did, for the sense of euphoric pleasure it delivered).

At five in the morning, she was dressed, desperate for activity and conscious that nobody else in the building was awake. Resting her elbows on the window ledge, she stared into the grey dawn, watching the lines of the distant hills take shape, wondering where her car might be locked away and whether she could get a glimpse of it, even sneak a practice drive.

It took her a while to find where the workshops had been hidden away from view, screened by what appeared to be a Roman temple. Behind it, walking on, she discovered the foundry, a carriage-work shop, a carpentry room, a garage especially built for the magnificent Royale, a car built to dwarf all competition. All were open and yet every door was fitted with a gigantic brass lock. Her curiosity had, it seemed, been anticipated. Still looking for the car, she walked past a stable where she counted fifteen horses, a further long room filled with antique carriages, all beautifully polished, and a gallery filled with animal sculptures. This was where she was standing, entranced by the grace and energy of the tiny figures, when Ettore, magnificent and absurd in a scarlet waistcoat and with his brown bowler hat planted at a rakish angle, made his entrance.

The sculptures were by his brother, he said; dead, unfortunately. Perhaps they might go around the estate later, if she didn't object to bicycling. He understood that she liked dogs; he had a splendid collection of terriers, prizewinners, the lot of them. And the yacht: she might appreciate that.

What she wanted most, she said, was to see the car; better still, drive it. A faint smile crossed Ettore's bland, clever face. Did she realize, he asked suddenly, that Léon Volterra was an old friend of his? He'd seen her, more times than she'd be able to guess, dancing at the casino. Very pretty. Very charming. Turning the handle of his whip over in his hand, he asked if she ever thought of going back to the stage. More money in that than racing, for a woman, after all. And more security.

She was, she realized, being interviewed. He asked what she liked about driving: an easy one. Solitude, she said, and a goal. As for a husband, his next question, she didn't plan on settling down. (No need, she thought, to mention the little ceremony she'd gone through with Mongin a year ago, to give herself some of the rights which a single woman was denied.) He seemed pleased by her answer and not, as she had first supposed, because he was worried about his precious son.

'Poor Madame Junek – our Eliska.' His bright blue eyes were studying her. 'You know her husband died while they were both at the Nürburgring last year. Very distressing. And she says – it's understandable, of course – that she'll never race again.'

'A great woman,' Hélène said cautiously, wondering what he wanted to hear.

He nodded. 'A good model for you,' he said. 'A fine driver who took no unnecessary risks. We never lost a car through Elizabeth.'

It chilled her a little to see that he was thinking not of the accident to Junek, or the distress to the widow, but of the cars. Smiling, she told him that she had never been involved in an accident yet and that this was one record she wasn't aiming to break. He liked that small joke. Not enough, however, to give in to her wish. 'No hurry,' he said. The car could wait.

*A poster bringing together Ettore Bugatti's passion for thoroughbred
horses with his superbly designed racing cars was the inspiration of his
daughter, Lébé. A private hotel called Le Pur Sang (The Thoroughbred)
on the Molsheim estate also played on Bugatti's twin interests.*

★

He was friendly, urbane and detached. A courteous and practised host who had already decided that she had no place in his inner circle. She wasn't grand enough. He made her conscious of the rough edges in her voice; he spoke in a way which kept her at a distance and a disadvantage. She didn't know what to say when he told her that her part of the little hotel had started out as a home for his pedigree chickens. Perhaps there was some sort of joke in the statement, a dig at the *poule de luxe*, the high class tart, she wasn't. It was impossible to tell. She took refuge in a policy of silence and, after the first two days, he seemed content to let her alone. She went for long walks beside the yellow autumn fields which reminded her of childhood landscapes. Above her, the purple hills of the Vosges sloped up to calm bright skies; below, the red-tiled roofs of small Alsatian villages clustered together. Sometimes, the only sounds she would hear in a whole afternoon were the chink of cowbells and the whistle of a gooseherd, broken by the insistent whine of an approaching Bugatti, racing back to Molsheim from a trial run.

And, at last, she was allowed to see her car, to sit in it, and, after the two mechanics had agreed that she needed a few alterations for it to suit her, the crank was turned, a pair of goggles were snapped down over her eyes and a warning was shouted in her ear to look out for animals on the road. Cecci, the smaller of the two mechanics, squeezed in beside her, just in case of a mishandling. Just like Ettore, she thought. The machines are all that matters.

Even today, a well-maintained 35C can reach 200 kph. The modern version is almost certain to have been restored. To know what it was like for Hélène, it's important to remember that the road, pitted with holes and clotted with cowdung, was visible through gaps in the metal floor; that the gear mesh would have crunched with every shift she made; that the wheels, standing well out from the body, were spindle thin and marvellously responsive, meeting each movement of the hand as if the car was a true thoroughbred, reined in by the turning wheel. The sensation was one of edgy, controlled poise.

Think of the sound, the sudden yelp of connection, turning to the high whine of an old-fashioned sewing machine being pulled at speed along an endless seam, a white track. Think of the intimacy, the mechanic's hand curving close over the tail, circling the driver to clasp the petrol tank's projecting cap; think of the whine rising as the long lever grinds into fourth gear, taking the car into its stride, up, pushing for the maximum, dancing down the road like a pony with wings, jumping and skittering, both sexy and sinewy, at ease in its own excellence.

To drive a car like this, she realized as she came racing back through the gates, fleet as a deer, was the nearest experience to pure joy that she'd ever known. Behind the mask of dust, her eyes were brilliant with pleasure.

'And again?' she said. 'Now?' And the drivers who had come out to watch her return nodded, amused and faintly touched by such guileless delight. She looked, laughing up at them and pulling her hands through her tangled hair, as though she and the car were one.

Remote though Molsheim was, all French Bugatti drivers looked on it as their Camelot, a kingdom to which they all belonged and which they represented in that romantic spirit of the chivalrous knights. They all, during their racing careers, came back to Molsheim, and Ettore, like any shrewd ruler, saw to it that they were welcome, their triumphs praised, their ideas heard, if not followed. On such a visit in 1929, Hélène would have met the men who helped to create the Bugatti legend. Tall, easy-going Meo Constantini, although homesick for Venice, had almost replaced

14

ETTORE BUGATTI
FABRIQUE D'AUTOMOBILES

SCH•MOLSHEIM (BAS-RHIN) le 29 Mars 19

Adr. Télégr. : BUGATTI-MOLSHEIM
Téléphone: MOLSHEIM 14 & 61

Reg. de Commerce : SAVERNE I/100

FACTURE pour

Com. No. 501
Fol. No.

Madame Hellé NICE

P A R I S .
-:-:-:-:-:-:-:-:-

La Marchandise est payable à Molsheim à la livraison net sans aucune déduction.

1 voiture Grand'Prix, type 35, d'Occasion

Moteur 8 cylindres 60x88 N°.4863

Carburateur Zénith

Magnéto Bosch

Pont AR.14x54

5 roues Bugatti avec pneus de la dimen-
-sion...28 x 4,95

Prix net:............ Frs 40.000.oo 40.000.oo

Hélène's receipt for the Bugatti 35 from Molsheim, 1930.

Ettore's lost brother. Constantini was his favourite driver, the only man to whom Ettore would listen when Constantini spoke out for Jean, and for his right to a share of the control. But Constantini was a quiet, reserved character; she would have been more intrigued by the awkward-mannered Englishman with a French mother who had just taken the winner's cup that year at the first Grand Prix ever to be held at Monte Carlo. Perched on one of the high bar stools at the Pur Sang hotel and drinking her favourite Gin Fizz or the hotel-keeper's speciality, a Paradise Cocktail of gin and apricot brandy, Hélène might have listened to Charles Grover's★ account of his great victory that year over Rudi Caracciola's intimidating Mercedes. Perhaps he spoke of his wife, Eve, the beautiful artist's model with whom he fell in love while he worked as a chauffeur for the portrait painter, Sir William Orpen. The artist, secretly relieved to disentangle himself from a relationship with no future, gave them his splendid Rolls for a wedding present, but both car and bride were conspicuously absent from Molsheim. Wives, as Grover might have had to explain, were not especially welcome here. They got in the way. And, in any event, his wife had no interest in the mechanics of racing; few did.

There is a possibility that Molsheim was where Hélène first encountered, face to face, the man who would one day destroy her, Louis Chiron. She knew him already as the man whose car had roared past as she cradled the dead body of Henri de Courcelles at Montlhéry, not a pleasant memory. Would she have liked him, meeting him again in 1929? It seems unlikely. Ambitious and flirtatious, Chiron was known as Louis the Debonair for his skills with women. They gave him another name for the viciousness with which he attacked those who rejected his advances. His relationship with Alice Hoffman, the beautiful and clever wife of his sponsor, the owner of the Nerka Spark Plugs

★ William Charles Grover is better known by his racing pseudonym, 'Williams'.

Agency, was common knowledge by 1929. But Chiron, in a mere two seasons, had won eight Grands Prix for Bugatti, using Nerka plugs; that for Bugatti and Alfred Hoffman was what mattered most.

There was bad blood between Chiron and Hélène Delangle from their first meeting; the reason has never been established. As a rival attention-seeker who visibly sulked when the cameras failed to focus on him, Chiron is unlikely to have shown his usual gallantry to a girl who was so adroit at capturing the interest of the press.

More to her taste were two rich and charming Bugatti owners who made regular visits to Molsheim during this period, and who she could already have met through de Courcelles. André Dubonnet, heir to the family's vermouth fortune and with his name emblazoned around every major circuit in France, was an ex-fighter pilot with the looks of a handsome pirate. His skills as a driver were matched by his engineering knowledge (the superb cars he designed in the late 1930s are now collector's items). Philippe de Rothschild, with whom Hélène became involved in later years, was only twenty-seven when she visited Molsheim in 1929. Bold enough to have already embarked on rescuing the family's great Médoc vineyards from dereliction, he had started racing a year earlier, hiding himself behind the name Georges Philippe just as his father had masked himself as 'André Pascal' when he took part in the ill-fated Paris–Madrid race of 1903. Starting his love affair with automobiles with a Hispano-Suiza, grandest of all the touring cars, Philippe bought his first Bugatti in 1929 and raced it on the demanding Nürburgring, in the Grand Prix de Bourgogne (which he won), at Monte Carlo and at Le Mans, after crashing badly in Antibes. The Bugatti family had a high opinion of Philippe; in the summer of 1929, he was invited to drive as one of the works team on the Sarthe Circuit at Le Mans.

The excitement of such encounters offered welcome relief from the relentless discipline of her coaching. Hélène prided herself on never showing a sad face in public. On several occasions at Molsheim, however, with her bedroom door locked shut and a pillow clutched to her face to muffle the noise, she might have allowed herself to weep. It tortured her to be so endlessly reminded of the responsibility she now carried. What if she failed in the speed test? Failure was not, Ettore told her, an option. The car would do what it could do; she had only to guide it. And besides, all the final preparations were now in hand. A film crew had been enlisted to record the occasion; the newspapers were all alerted. The car had been provided with a support for her back and a lengthened handbrake to increase her sense of control. Cecci would be driving the car to Montlhéry, Ettore told her; the Paris managers, Guy Bouriat and Albert Divo, would supervise her progress. A second car would be available at the track, in case of mechanical problems. There was no room left for turning back.

And what, she boldly asked as she said her farewells, would be the prize, the reward for her achievement? The honour, said Ettore with one of his suavest smiles. The honour of joining the élite who drove for the greatest marque in the history of the car. And that, to her incredulity, was where he chose to leave the conversation.

8

LAPPING THE GOLDFISH BOWL

'Few women, I think, have perfect control of a car at
anything over 80 mph . . . only half a dozen women may
be capable of driving an abnormally fast car.'

WINIFRED M. PINK, *WOMAN ENGINEER*, 1928[1]

Montlhéry, built in six months in 1923 as France's first purpose-
made circuit and speed bowl, lies 24 kilometres south of Paris. In
summer months, the track was in perpetual use (English drivers
were among the most regular users, preferring it to the battered
surface of Brooklands for their attempts at record breaking on
motorcycles and in cars). On an icy afternoon in December 1929,
however, the grandstand was empty, the sharp-angled circuit bare
as the branches of the trees which strained against the relentless
pressure of a bitter north wind. The fiercely banked concrete speed
bowl, thinly coated with ice, looked more menacing than usual
under a pewter sky. A hoarding which extolled the superior merit
of Dunlop tyres had been stripped by rain and wind of everything
bar the letter 'D' and 'du championnat!' Using it as a windbreak,
a group of heavily coated men huddled like plotting gangsters, iced
breath and cigarette smoke trailing wreaths around their black hat
brims. Two boys from the Pathé crew, sent down to record the

breaking of the women's world record for speed, began chasing
each other to keep warm, hands stuffed deep in their pockets as
they swerved and jumped.

The man from *L'Auto*[2] sauntered over to borrow a mike and
stayed to help them identify some of the group: Joseph Cecci the
mechanic was the little skinny one, Count Bouriat, the taller,
languid man, Albert Divo, the burly fellow with the cigar. The
three of them had been coming out from the Paris showroom to
supervise the girl's training for the past week. That was Carpe, the
timekeeper, leaving the group now to walk towards his glass booth.
All paid for by the Bugatti factory. The man from *L'Auto* winked.
Very special treatment.

The high scream of an engine turned their heads. A small, pale
blue car with a tail like an engorged dagger shot past them and
braked. The driver, rosy-cheeked and cheerful under her white
wind-cap, jumped out to embrace Bouriat and Divo while Cecci
folded back the side of the car bonnet to squint at the gleaming row
of pipes. One of the Bugatti team took a couple of photographs of
the girl standing beside the car, hands on hips, head cocked to one
side as Divo gave her some advice. The man from *L'Auto* had been
at the clubhouse lunch, paid for, like everything else today, by
Maison Bugatti. The girl was on good terms with everybody, he
said, a real little charmer, chatting, smiling, drinking gin and
lemonade, giving out gossip from the music-hall circuit. When one
of the journalists asked how she kept fit, she stood up and flipped
into a backwards somersault, landing light as a cat. Lovely smile. You
wouldn't have thought she had a care in the world.

The Pathé cameraman, worried about the best angle from
which to track the car, climbed his stepladder and propped the
heavy apparatus on his shoulder, tilting it skywards. Below him, the
engine yowled. Smoke burst upwards with a spit of flame; when
the Bugatti reached his circle of vision, it was racing around the top
of the bowl like a fly on a string.

Hélène's record certificate from Montlhéry in 1929.

Far below her, hurtling into her second lap, Hélène caught a glimpse of upturned faces, a ring of startled moons.[3] The rev counter showed 5500: good. Keep it steady. Her ankle throbbed as she clamped the rubber sole of her shoe to the throttle, gluing it down; the tyres swivelled on loose grit, bringing a shriek of rubber into the roar of the wind. Her small gloved hands held the wheel tight and high, twisting it hard as the bonnet reared at the barrier; she leaned forward a little, eyes wide and intent behind the goggles.

Third lap, fourth. A rat in a cage, that was what she felt like. Was the speed dropping? No warning flags showing from below. She didn't dare risk another glance at the rev counter; all she could do now was to keep it up, not let her concentration drop, even for a second. Think of nothing else, Divo had said. You're part of the machine. Feel everything it tells you. Listen to it and when you reach the limit, keep pushing. Up at the top of the bowl, when you're at top revs, your foot stays down on that throttle and you'll spin like a top. Just go with it.

And it was true. The thrust from behind her was being met by an invisible force in the bowl, pulling her round the rim, giving her, as she glanced swiftly down, the impression of a grey cliff falling away from the wheels. A pillar of wind was leaning out from the centre of the bowl, spinning the car around the bank of concrete at a speed so regular that she could catch the high note of its passage, echoed in the wail of perfectly replicated revolutions.

Six, seven. The heat of the wheel was scorching through her gloves. She caught a hot whiff of something unfamiliar in the cockpit. Her eyelids flickered with tension, her arm muscles tensed. With a grunt of relief, she registered the source, the singed cloth of her overalls where her thigh was pressing against the gearbox. Not pleasant, but nothing major.

Her eyes smarted in the dry vacuum behind the goggles; she swallowed, trying to force cooling saliva into the baked funnel of her throat. A bar, heavy as iron, was bending her shoulderblades forward as she struggled to hold the wheel at exactly the angle to keep the car below the barrier line. Beyond it, above her, darkness had begun to reshape the sky. Lights flickered, distracting; she kept her eyes fixed on the invisible ring laid down by the Bugatti, staying high on the edge, making the bowl work for her.

Ten. She heard something unfamiliar. Adrenalin crackled along the back of her scalp as the car started to vibrate. Fragments of black rubber, thin and mean, snapped across her vision line as she wrestled to keep control, slithered down the bank, braking and swerving, over the red line, and down to the flat. She reached for the handbrake, snapped off the power. Silence, while the wind whined. She dropped her head on the wheel for a moment, steadying her nerves for the disappointed stares, the rehearsal, useless now, of all the things she should have done.

So sure was she of failure that she shook her head when they told her the results, thinking she had misheard. But Carpe the timekeeper had written the figures down: there was no mistake. 197.708 kph for her fastest lap and an average over ten miles of

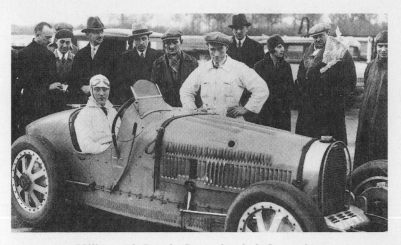

*Hélène with Joseph Cecci, shortly before making
her record-breaking drive in December 1929.*

194.266. Divo, whose praises were rarer than strawberries in
December, told her that he had never seen a woman drive better.
But she could get the speed average up, she whispered urgently;
give her a new wheel and she'd take it over 200. But they refused
to let her go: too late, too demanding and, anyway, irrelevant.
Hadn't she already made a new world record?

Everybody, even Cecci, wanted photographs. The man from
L'Auto shook her hand and said he'd be watching her career with
interest, no stopping her now. A couple of women, arriving late,
asked if she could explain the sensations to them. There weren't,
she realized, many words which would describe the feeling of joy
and excitement and terror, so intense, all confused. She could strike
a pose, cross her legs and throw her head back as well as
Mistinguett. Asked about driving, she could only tell them that
racing was what she wanted to do for the rest of her life. Nothing,
not dancing, or skiing or mountain-climbing, could touch the
exhilaration of the moment when the car and the driver fused.

★

For a whole week, she had been the most famous woman in France. Everybody wanted to meet her. Everything she said was noted down as of remarkable interest: her favourite food, her most enjoyable holiday, her most admired book, her ideal car. One woman writer had insisted on being driven around the Montlhéry circuit so that she too could experience the thrill which had been so winningly described. As an old lady, Hélène still grinned at the memory of the poor creature, holding on to her wind-cap with one hand and the safety-handle with the other, her face the colour of wet cement. She lasted half a lap before she passed out.

Fortunately, while several journalists had probed for her thoughts about young Jean Bugatti, none made the connection between herself and Bruno d'Harcourt. Which was lucky, considering Bruno's Bugatti had been parked outside the autodrome on the afternoon of the speed trial, as he waited to take her out to a celebration dinner. She warned him at the time that he shouldn't take such risks, not in his situation. It wasn't as though the relationship was serious. The serious thing about Comte Bruno d'Harcourt, father of four, was that he was married to one of the grandest women in France, Princesse Isabelle d'Orléans. Her mother was a Guise and Hélène knew her history books well enough to fear what a member of that ruthless family might do, if she were crossed.

So this had remained a discreet affair. Occasionally, when the princess was visiting her mother in the country, they managed a day together; for the most part, however, the relationship was an afternoon arrangement between friends. The date, like everything else in Bruno's life, was fixed: Hélène, while no snob, was fascinated by the elaborate rules of behaviour which still defined the life of a man who went, every Saturday, to visit his old nanny and eat a plate of almond biscuits. His mother and he had been having tea together at the Ritz every Wednesday since he was twenty.

Theirs was a relation of opposites. Buying a racing Bugatti was the boldest thing Bruno d'Harcourt had ever done; Hélène thrived in an atmosphere of audacity. She climbed mountains; Bruno preferred strolling over lawns. She could stay up all night; Bruno had been to every club in Paris once, and stayed in none for more than an hour. Tall, moustached and with a nose which would become eagle-like when the boyish roundness of his cheeks was gone, he resembled both a cavalry officer and a surprised choirboy. Hélène found his looks immensely attractive and could make him blush by saying so.

At thirty-one, Bruno d'Harcourt was still easy to shock; that, for her, was half the fun. It gave her a thrill to know that her elegant, bashful lover was watching when she performed in the Actors' Gala that March of 1930, stripped down to the smallest pair of gold shorts that she could slide over her hips. Lowering herself into the splits, she looked for Bruno's startled face in the crowd who, whether they liked it or not, were seeing more than they had paid for. They clapped her for being brave – it was her first try on the bar and the high wire – and for showing what she shouldn't. It was all for you, she promised him afterwards; only for you. And he had reddened with pleasure. He was, as she remembered him, a strangely innocent man.

She wondered, sometimes, if Ettore Bugatti might have treated her more respectfully if he had known with whom she was spending time that spring. The count was just the kind of client Ettore liked best, a rich amateur enthusiast whose victories, if he had any, would be credited to the marque, while his costs – and Bugattis were notoriously expensive cars to maintain – would be his own affair. Perhaps, if she had dropped Bruno's name into the conversation when she went back to Molsheim to collect her car that March, not long after the gala, things might have been different.

It never ceased to amaze her that, after all the initial courtesy, the effort she had put into her training, the publicity her success had won for his firm, Ettore had still expected her to put up three-quarters of the full price for a second-hand car.[4] The price was high – 40,000 francs was a lot of money. She had made a second journey to Molsheim not expecting to pay a cent. It was a shock. She remembered staring at Ettore's face, wondering what he had heard, what she was being punished for. No answer came, only a tranquil repetition of the arrangement. He looked not at her, but slightly to the side, over her shoulder. Correctly, she sensed an insult.

The car, it was true, had been shaped to her needs like a tailormade, ready for her first rally drive in Morocco the following month. But any expectation that she would be welcomed back to Molsheim as a friend, part of the team, was dashed on the first evening. She was shown into a tiny, stifling attic at the Pur Sang, and told that her meals would be paid for by the company. No invitation came to join the family, as she had fondly anticipated, no morning stroll around the estate was suggested. The only bright moment came at the end, after she had paid over the money and taken possession of the car. Jean, Ettore said, laying heavy emphasis on his son's name to indicate that he did not represent his own view, had suggested she might take part in the Bugatti Grand Prix at Le Mans that summer. She always had plenty to say to the press about her wish to compete against men in Grand Prix: well, here was her chance.

The April rally in Morocco was a plan which had been hatched with Bruno. He was, he said, tired of only seeing her for an hour a week; travelling separately from Marseille, they could meet up at Casablanca, enjoy a few days of sun and pleasure, drive down south to the Atlas Mountains, if she wanted a bit of climbing. The choice was hers; the princess had taken the children off to see their grandmother; he was free and at her disposal.

Hélène often went back to participate in races in France's North African colonies during the 1930s. Her albums thickened with photographs of mosques, gardens, palm trees, groups of waving children, carpet sellers and souks. The welcome was always hospitable; to a young woman who loved hot climates, the dry air and wide blue skies added to the pleasure of discovering a country which, while its language was familiar, was unimaginably remote from anything she had yet known. Looking at her pages of tiny snapshots, it is tempting to imbue them with romantic significance. All that exists other than these is a dried yellow flower, a map of the route and a list of the drivers.

The list of entrants for the Casablanca rally was impressive. Marcel Lehoux, the oldest at forty-one, was an Algerian garage owner, French-born, who began racing in 1924, and was among the best of the Bugatti drivers, especially on the North African courses. Philippe Etancelin (Phi-Phi) from Rouen had built his career on a fortune made selling wool and goosedown for bedding and upholstery and turned to racing in 1926. Fast and fearless, he had a wife as intrepid as himself who, when regulations permitted, raced beside him. Anne Itier, a newcomer to the Grand Prix circuits after years of rally driving and hill-climb competitions, was a small, redhaired woman whose ability to swear in Gaelic was a legacy from her unhappy marriage to a violent Scot named Rose. Any one of these more seasoned drivers might have shown a relative novice how to map the course, which stretched from Casablanca down to Mogador, east to Marrakech and back to the north by Settat; the result was preserved by Hélène, together with a note that she had covered 233 kilometres in just over seven hours on a trial run. For a first prize of 70,000 francs, careful preparation was a good investment.

Her endurance skills, the ones most needed for a drive notorious for its dust storms, were never tested. Two days before the race, Bruno took his Bugatti out for a fast practice run back to

Bruno d'Harcourt in Morocco, 1930.

Casablanca from Medronna. Coming into a fast bend, he misjudged and overshot the road. He was still fully conscious when they found him some hours later, trapped under the car with a fractured spine. He died in hospital two days later.

Hélène never discussed this relationship; her fellow racers had no idea of a connection between the doomed driver and the jaunty, tough little blonde. Some surprise was felt when she announced that she would be withdrawing and returning to Marseille. By the middle of April, she was back in Paris. In her scrapbooks, years later, she pasted her photographs of Bruno at the wheel of his car on to the same page which recorded the death of Henri de Courcelles, together with her preserved yellow flower. Below, and next to his obituary, she wrote simply that the photographs showed him on the day of the accident.

The weather was terrible in France in the summer of 1930. The Seine surged through doorways in the streets of Montparnasse; the main train from Paris to Brussels was stranded for a week in a metre of water; floods prevented Hélène taking off from Le Bourget on her first and well-publicized flying lesson. Bad weather has never defeated the French in their love of a day at the races and, despite the rain, the crowds turned out on 1 June for Ettore Bugatti's Third Grand Prix at Le Mans. The race was for amateurs, but perhaps with Jean's coercion, Hélène was allowed to have the use of Joseph Cecci, the Molsheim employee who had supervised her car for the Montlhéry trial. Cecci was a dour character, but he should have had no complaints to make that day. This was her first Grand Prix, and she brought the car home in 3rd place, after doing 32 laps, 566 kilometres, of the celebrated 24-hour course. Typically, Hélène only minded that the victor, Juan Zanelli, the elegant Vice-Consul of Chile in Nice, had beaten her by 28 kilometres. 'I'll do better next time,' she said afterwards. 'It's all I ever ask for, just to show what I can do, without a handicap, against men.' She took care to make the point that she would have been going in for the Swedish Grand Prix next, had they deigned to allow women to compete.[5]

Ettore and his son were both there to award Zanelli his prize of a T43. Both men were in poor shape, Ettore after a fall from one of his horses, Jean on crutches after crashing on a practice run at Molsheim. (The official story was that he had slipped on a staircase.) It was Jean who presented a filthy-faced, exhausted Hélène with her third prize and Jean, perhaps, who sent her the souvenir picture of the two of them which she liked enough to keep. One can see why. Confident, well-dressed, a little arrogant, the young car designer leans forward, crutches forgotten as he stares into the eyes which look up into his with beaming and undisguised joy. Ettore, although not visible, must have been comforting himself with the thought that she would be out of the country by the end of the summer, never, with any luck, to return. This was not the kind of match he had in mind for his brilliant heir.

To have come third in her first Grand Prix was a magnificent achievement, and not diminished by the fact that the five other entrants had failed to complete the course. To many of the actors and cabaret performers who braved atrocious weather for the Seventh Actors' Championships a few days later, it seemed grossly unfair that they should be expected to compete against a semi-professional. Blanche Montel, still smarting at having been robbed of both victory and publicity the previous year, announced that she would not be taking part in the same events as Miss Hellé Nice.

Torrential rain and shabby grandstands were blamed for the fact that spectator crowds were disappointingly small at Paris's Parc des Princes sports park for its last function before being revamped; the actors, nevertheless, put on a magnificent show. Sidney Chaplin, Charlie's older half-brother and a devastatingly funny performer in drag, turned up in a loud suit to help out his friend Georges Biscot when his baby Bugatti needed a push. Diana, calm and beautiful as always, drew applause as she drove sedately down the course in a green Delage which took first prize for elegant looks in the car show. Nadine Picard, a rising star in the Gaumont short films which many of Paris's music-hall stars made in their lunch-breaks, was there; so was her sister Gisèle, dressed as her twin in beautifully cut beige silk. André Roanne, Hélène's co-performer at the Actors' Gala of 1928 as the the third of 'Les Harrys', rolled up his shirt-sleeves and flexed his muscles at the crowd, miming his determination to win; the handsome young actor Raymond Maurel disqualified himself by jumping out of his car during the obstacle race to wave at the fans.

There were only two real stars that day. The first was a talented young female acrobat called Line Jack. Dressed in a white bodysuit which emphasized the grace of her movements, she presented herself as the bonnet-top mascot of a scarlet Mathis driven by Farwell, her actor-lover. Bending like a croquet hoop as the car slowly circled the track, she brought her head between her ankles, smiled to the cameras with her chin on the tall radiator, and raised her slender legs like twin arrows, toes pointing skywards.*

Line Jack contributed the grace that day and Hellé Nice the drama. Privately, she must have cursed the massive sports touring car, a Bugatti T43A, which she was driving and which a new mechanic had failed to conquer. Oh! What a fearsome machine! the sports writers exclaimed as smoke belched from the exhaust pipe and the gearbox clanked like a box of chains; oh! how terrified the other competitors must have been! An ill-prepared car didn't stop Hélène winning the gymkhana and the ladies' speed trial. She did so with a nonchalance which must have had Blanche Montel's nails bitten to the quick. The cartoonists, summing up the day's events in playful images for the sports pages of *Le Journal* and *L'Intransigeant*, showed their favourite heroine riding to victory – in very high heels – on a rocking-horse with a Bugatti pennant flying above her; the photographers paid tribute to her professionalism by photographing the champion in an uncharacteristically demure pose, knees out of sight, white blouse buttoned to the throat, sitting between the gigantic Grebon headlamps of her troublesome car.

The following month, Paris's theatre world reconvened at the Buffalo vélodrome at Montrouge for the last of the summer car shows. Hélène's T43 was still causing trouble, but it hardly seemed to matter in a day which became a one-woman promotional event, a hijacking of publicity which ended any remaining vestiges of friendship with her fellow stars. Her first coup was to jump on a motorbike for a duel against Arthur Honegger, the young Swiss

---

* A couple of photographs appear to show Hellé Nice performing similar feats on the car; as a newly fledged acrobat, she might have relished the challenge to show off her skills – and her shape.

*A stylish way to perform a lap on the bonnet of a
Mathis at the Actors' Championships of 1930.*

composer who was, at the time, the most commercially successful and celebrated of the group later known as Les Six. His music, Honegger said, was intended to reflect the mechanical age, the sounds of speeding trains and wailing taxis, the whine of high-speed cars. He was a fearless driver but his bike, on this occasion, was soundly beaten. Taking to the circuit again before rain brought an end to the day, Hélène demonstrated her biking skills on the dirt track normally reserved for cycling competitions and then, to cheers from under the dripping umbrellas, perched side-saddle on the back of a motorbike with the British sportsman Angus Dallimore and roared around again. The crowd gasped when the heavy bike skidded, sending her sprawling in the dust; they were delighted when she jumped up, dusted herself down, laughed, and gave them a bow.

This sudden love affair with dirt tracks was explained the following day when a newspaper article disclosed that France's most intrepid woman racer was off to America to compete against men on speedways and dirt tracks in a supercharged Miller, one of the world's fastest cars. 'Congratulations to the manager of the Miller company on his shrewd choice,' the journalist finished with a flourish, 'and congratulations to him on being so well-represented! Good luck to you, our charming ambassador!'[6]

The man who had prepared Hélène's programme at Buffalo with such skill was her new agent, a cheerful bespectacled man called Henri Lartigue, whose wife, Madeleine, shared Hélène's passion for shih-tzus and pugs. The name which appeared most prominently on Lartigue's business paper was that of the American William Morris, who had by 1930 become Hollywood's best-known film agent. This may have been what first drew Hélène to Lartigue; what she could not have known was that her new agent had never met Morris. His own American connections were to a much less glamorous outfit, Ralph Hankinson's Hot News Agency.

Hankinson, a tough veteran promoter of several of the East

Coast fairgrounds on which some of the most dangerous dirt-track driving in America took place, was seeking ways to bring crowds to the tracks. A good-looking French girl, a Parisian, no less, who had now beaten the women's world record for speed, struck him as a splendid promotional asset. Her background as a dancer and acrobat added to her marketability; Esso expressed an interest in an advertising campaign.

The bait held out to Hélène was a good regular salary of $200 for each appearance, the promise – it was not fulfilled – of all transport and hotel expenses being covered, the chance to drive one of the world's best-known cars, Ralph DePalma's supercharged Miller, and considerable publicity.

Hélène signed the contract with the Hot News Agency on 23 May, agreeing to arrive in New York by 3 August. The promised Miller had, by the time she put her name on the contract, been converted into an assurance that she would always be allowed to handle 'a first-class racing automobile': not quite the same. The disappointment was sweetened, however, by the news that she would, if successful, be given a renewal of her two-month contract, with a chance to renegotiate her payments.

It is possible that her ambitions reached beyond the dangerous thrills of dirt-track racing. She had, during her successful run in *Les Ailes de Paris*, been in daily contact with Maurice Chevalier, the show's star, and Chevalier had already left Paris to try his luck as a screen-star in Hollywood. It isn't even necessary to conjecture an affair with the shamelessly promiscuous Chevalier to see why Hélène might have wanted to try her luck in films. She had, throughout her dancing years, lived among people who had a second career as screen performers: André Roanne, Blanche Montel, Georges Biscot, Nadine Picard, Sidney Chaplin, Harry Pilcer, the Rocky Twins, the Dollys. It is hard, in fact, to find a music-hall star of that period who had not, at some point, gone to work at the Gaumont studios based so conveniently close to

Pigalle's theatres. Marie Bell, in 1930, appeared as a racing-car driver in the popular film *The Night is Ours*: Hélène must have thought that she could play the same part with more authority.

An interview which appeared in *Pathé Journal* on 1 August 1930, shortly after Hélène's departure for the United States from Le Havre, reported that the racing driver had just been taking voice and screen tests and that the result had been highly successful; a glorious film career was predicted. The article may have been a puff placed by Lartigue, but he could not have fabricated the taking

Hélène doing acrobatics on the beach at Le Touquet with an unknown friend, June 1930.

of tests. She must, at the least, have been considering a film career and yet, despite Lartigue's urgent reminders, she never contacted William Morris.

The money being offered for her American tour was good, the chance to spread her name abroad was unlikely to come so easily again. But the prospect of an adventure was the main attraction for Hélène. She was thirty years old, with nothing to tie her down. Hankinson had promised that she would be the first woman to drive on the dirt tracks and board tracks of America. She had seen the English sportswoman Gwenda Stewart driving a Miller 91 at Montlhéry, and had envied her. Let Stewart keep the dull Montlhéry circuit: how much more glorious it would be to drive such a car in America, to be a daredevil among dauntless men.

FLYING HIGH

9

RALPH'S HONEY

'Honey, Honey bless your heart
Honey that I love so well
I's done been true
My gal, to you
To my Honey that I love so well'

'LA CHANSON DE MR HANKINSON',
TYPED OUT FOR HELLÉ NICE'S SCRAPBOOK

Both the *France* and the *Paris*, liners which had been sturdily crossing the Atlantic throughout the 1920s, were of pre-war design. Efficient as carriers, they lacked the aura of glamour which surrounded the *Ile de France*. Built after the war, the new passenger-ship was decorated, as befitted an ocean-going advertisement for French design, with Art Deco fleur de lys, from the walls of its staterooms to the linen and tablecloths. The dining room allegedly stood comparison with the best restaurants in Paris. The liner's first voyage in June 1927 caused more of a press sensation in France and America than the news, three months later, that the great pioneer of modern dance, Isadora Duncan, had been strangled by a trailing scarf as she was driven along the

Promenade des Anglais at Nice by a handsome young man whom she nicknamed 'Bugatti'.*

Perhaps the company on the *Ile de France* went to Hélène's head (her travelling companions included a French marquis who was currently surviving marriage to Gloria Swanson; the handsome heavyweight boxing champion, Georges Carpentier; a Broadway producer; a couple of actresses; and the odious Harry K. Thaw, the Pittsburgh millionaire who famously shot his showgirl wife's lover and infamously escaped conviction). It was probably they who persuaded her that the only place to stay in New York was the Savoy Plaza, on Central Park. Arriving on 29 July, Hélène went straight to the city's most expensive hotel, took a suite, and sent a few telegrams. Henri Lartigue, when word reached him in Paris of her accommodation arrangements, was ready to faint with horror. Hadn't she been told that the Paramount had perfectly good rooms for $4 a night? Was she mad? Who did she think was going to pay? Softening, Lartigue admitted that she seemed to be making an excellent impression. Word had already reached him from the Hot News Agency that Hankinson, his partner, Frank Wirth, and their publicist, Harry Riggins, were all thrilled by her ('enchanté de toi').[1]

There is no doubt that the Hot News Agency were pleased with their new client. Publicity director Harry Riggins, a skinny, cheerful man with an endearing fondness for wearing baggy chequered knickerbockers and an oversized sports cap, thought she was gorgeous while his colleague Frank Wirth referred to himself as 'your most ardent applesauce admirer' and begged Lartigue to send over some of her friends. Even Hankinson, one of the toughest promoters in the sports world, was sufficiently charmed

---

* Benoît Falchetto went on to become a successful racing driver and a friend of Hélène's. The car in which Duncan was killed was an Amilcar. The fact that she referred to Falchetto as 'Bugatti' shows how impressively Ettore's marque had become identified with racing by 1927.

to insist, if everything worked out well, that she should come and spend some of the fall with his wife and children at the Daytona Hotel on the celebrated speed-trial beach.[2]

The invitation came as the sweetener at the end of an afternoon of harsh business talk. The Hot News Agency would not, Hélène was informed, cover her costs at the Savoy Plaza. Neither would they pay for her meals, her telegrams and telephone calls, or her shopping trips. Her contract would begin with a practice run out at Harrington, New Jersey, well away from the public eye; during her first week she would be expected to familiarize herself with

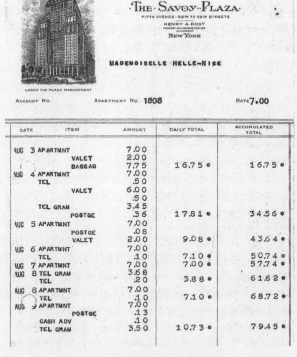

THE PLAZA · NEW YORK
THE COPLEY · PLAZA · BOSTON
THE GREENBRIER
WHITE SULPHUR SPRINGS, W.VA.

TELEPHONE
VOLUNTEER 2000
CABLE ADDRESS
SAVOYPLAZA · NEW YORK

·The·Savoy·Plaza·

FIFTH AVENUE · 58TH TO 59TH STREETS

HENRY A. ROST
PRESIDENT AND MANAGING DIRECTOR
NEW YORK

MADEMOISELLE HELLE-NISE

UNDER THE PLAZA MANAGEMENT

Account No.   Apartment No. 1503   Rate 7.00

DATE	ITEM	AMOUNT	DAILY TOTAL	ACCUMULATED TOTAL
AUG 3	APARTMNT	7.00		
	VALET	2.00		
	BAGGAG	7.75	16.75 ⦁	16.75 ⦁
AUG 4	APARTMNT	7.00		
	TEL	.50		
	VALET	6.00		
		.50		
	TEL GRAM	3.45		
	POSTGE	.36	17.81 ⦁	34.56 ⦁
AUG 5	APARTMNT	7.00		
	POSTGE	.08		
	VALET	2.00	9.08 ⦁	43.64 ⦁
AUG 6	APARTMNT	7.00		
	TEL	.10	7.10 ⦁	50.74 ⦁
AUG 7	APARTMNT	7.00	7.00 ⦁	57.74 ⦁
AUG 8	TEL GRAM	3.68		
	TEL	.20	3.88 ⦁	61.62 ⦁
AUG 8	APARTMNT	7.00		
	TEL	.10	7.10 ⦁	68.72 ⦁
AUG 9	APARTMNT	7.00		
	POSTGE	.13		
	CASH ADV	.10		
	TEL GRAM	3.50	10.73 ⦁	79.45 ⦁

Hélène's bill from the Savoy Plaza, New York.

driving on dirt tracks and wooden speed bowls. Her first appearance was set for 10 August at Woodbridge and she would receive $200 per appearance, before deductions, as agreed. This might not seem a large sum but she should bear in mind the very considerable expense that he, Ralph Hankinson, would be laying out on publicity and the acquisition, as always promised, of top cars for her use. Would she like to guess just how much Ralph DePalma, 'the Silver Fox', charged for loaning out his Miller 91? It was a pretty sizeable amount but he wasn't going to stint her. He knew the thrill she got out of driving the best cars and the best were what he planned to have her drive.

Hankinson saw no reason to explain yet to his client that he would be making the Miller available to her only at events where another driver had hired the same car for a feature race and would be glad to split the costs of paying the owner. Hélène, while disappointed by the modesty of her fee, was ready to forgo an increase of wealth for the thrill and challenge of speeding along some of the fastest tracks in the world. Familiar only with the dirt track at the Buffalo velodrome in Paris, she had no grasp of what a life-threatening experience she was about to face. Her promoter was in no hurry to tell her.

Depression was biting deep when Ralph Hankinson signed Hélène up for her American tour. Over 13 million workers had already lost their jobs; millions more faced the loss of their homes through inability to keep up their mortgage payments. Light entertainment has always proved a good source of revenue in an economic slump. Movie theatres were packed in 1930; taking on the notoriously dangerous Woodbridge speedbowl as its director-general for the new season, Hankinson was ready to use all the glamour he could recruit in order to persuade a ticket-paying public to keep spending. For his opening event in May, he hired Ralph DePalma and Barney Oldfield to appear, an expensive investment guaranteed to thrill all those who knew that DePalma's greatest triumph had been the day in 1914 when he beat the brilliant Oldfield to first place in the Vanderbilt Cup, run over the twisting roads of Santa Monica in California. Would Oldfield take revenge, twenty-six years later? Was the Silver Fox to be trounced at last? This was the kind of promotion at which Hankinson excelled.

It was with the same strategy in mind that Hankinson decided to proclaim his new client as the greatest woman driver in the world. Women were forbidden to participate in American championship races on either dirt or board tracks. Hélène, with her eyecatching background as a music-hall star and acrobat, would hit the headlines everywhere if she was presented as the first to break the rule. (In fact, she would be performing legitimately, as an exhibition driver whose stated intention would be to match or beat the fastest time made in a race that day.) She would drive notable cars and she would, if Hankinson had his way, drive them – as no man did – without a helmet, showing off her blonde curls. Any concern for the safety of his client was outweighed by the promoter's eagerness to attract a good crowd.

Hélène evidently believed Ralph Hankinson when he told her that no woman had ever before driven on the American dirt tracks. She was not the first, even though rules did not permit women to compete on them in races. Little record remains of Joan la Costa, who had also been described by her promoter as 'the greatest woman driver the world has ever seen'; her drive of a mile in 45.5 seconds was done on a dirt track in the 1920s, and she achieved the remarkable speed of 145 mph on what was then called a straightaway in Florida during the same period.[3] Earlier still, Elfreida Mais had been presented at Wichita, Kansas, in the summer of 1916, as an exhibition driver on dirt tracks who already held the woman's record for a mile in 53 seconds. (The daring Elfreida was killed in 1934 during a stunt which required her to crash through a burning wall.)

Left to right: Hermann Schurch, Ralph Hankinson, Billy Winn and Hélène in a very unusual customized car.

This does not diminish the challenge which was being presented to Hélène. La Costa and Mais do not appear to have been riding on especially difficult tracks, while she was scheduled to drive on some of the most notorious in the country. Langhorne, just north of Philadelphia, took twenty lives before it closed in the early 1970s; Woodbridge, the wooden speedbowl now also under Hankinson's direction, was another Charybdis, its history littered with corpses. The danger of the sport cannot be overstated. Dirt-tracking in those days was, in the view of one historian, 'the most hazardous form of a hazardous sport';[4] board tracks, while more widely used – Douglas Fairbanks* was, predictably, an enthusiast – were equally lethal. The fragile boards often trapped the wheels;

* Fairbanks drove on the Beverly Hills speedway, which thrived from 1919 to 1924. Superbly maintained, it caused no fatalities. Used by film companies for such forgettable features as *The Pace that Thrills* (1925) and *Racing for Life* (1924), the wooden oval was popular with Mary Pickford, Jean Harlow, Mack Sennett and Jackie Coogan, all keen drivers.

chunks of wood flew loose; parts of the track caught fire from the overheated machines. Deaths were frequent; prizes of up to $25,000 guaranteed that there would always be entrants ready to take that risk.

Hélène, restricted to a salaried role as an exhibition driver, could only dream of such rewards. Hers, other than the thrill of the experience, was to be in the form of massive publicity. As a woman who revelled in being the centre of attention, she must have been entranced both by the advance coverage she received for her sensational first appearance at Woodbridge, and by hearing that she would be conducted on to the track by a motorcycle escort and greeted by a band of forty drum and fife players, all in dress uniform. It seemed for a time as though she only had to open a paper to find her face smiling out of it. Here, they showed her as a ballet dancer; there, she beamed out of a racing car, the record-breaking world champion. Feature writers competed with each other in the extravagant superlatives they lavished on her past achievements.

Addressing readers to whom job security now meant everything, they emphasized the courage she had shown in abandoning a successful stage career – no mention was made of her nude dancing – for the risky and unpredictable life of a racer. But it had always been her dream. Even as she danced, they suggested, this graceful girl had been dreaming of the moment when she would break land speeds in a car. Since then, sitting at the wheel of her 'specially constructed' Bugatti racing car, she had achieved 'miraculous exploits'. The fact that all racing cars need some form of reconstruction to suit the requirements of the individual driver was presented as a homage paid uniquely to her by the manufacturer; much emphasis was laid on the fact that she had never before driven in the kind of conditions she now faced. 'Aviation has its Elinor Smiths and Amelia Earharts,' began one of these rhapsodic items:

Motor-boating has its Betty Carstairs, the brilliant and daring Englishwoman who has recently driven her boat at a speed approximating 90 miles an hour. For sheer dare-deviltry [sic] and reckless abandon, however, it has remained for Mlle Hellé Nice, a beautiful young Fresh [sic] woman to eclipse all her sisters in the flesh by abandoning the stage for a career on the automobile racing tracks of Europe and America. Both motorboating at high speeds and flying airplanes pale into comparative insignificance at the feats which Hellé Nice has performed on the racing courses of Europe.[5]

Sharp-eyed readers might have noticed a strange similarity in many of these articles; the old lady in her Nice attic must have laughed when she came to the page she had preserved from that time. Harry Riggins, the Hot News' publicity director, had let her have the scrawled draft, just as he wrote it: 'Aviation has its Elinor Smiths and Amelia Earharts . . .'

Hankinson and Riggins fed information to the papers; Hélène, meanwhile, was given a brutal introduction to the danger of the world she had stepped into. 'Wild' Bill Albertson, one of the most experienced drivers on dirt tracks and speedways, was the man Hankinson had chosen to act as her teacher. He taught her on the Harrington course and was there to watch her drive at Woodbridge the following week. On 16 August, only an hour after he had scrawled a portrait photo with an affectionate message 'To my racing pal Hellé Nice', Albertson was killed while driving on the Middletown track. Like most racing drivers, she was superstitious: Courcelles; Harcourt; Albertson. Who next?

Albertson's photograph was eventually stuck into the scrapbook, dated and annotated; his smiling face looked up at the old lady from what she decided to call the American page. Beside each face, ornamented with a personal dedication to herself, she set about writing a note or two to hint at their place in her affections.

impossible de regarder en face
je suis en plein soleil aussi
quelle binette.

Derrière moi au milieu Mr. Haw-
kinson mon "boss" en chemise noire
Herman Schurch (qui est arrivé 2.
au grand prix d'Indianapolis était 1. mais
a eu des ennuis de moteur à la fin) à
gauche Billy Winn, tous deux sont
2 des meilleurs conducteurs, Ce n° 6 est
une Clemons spéciale appartenant à
Herman mais conduite par Billy et
par moi quand la Miller de Ralph
de Palma n'est pas là, elle peut faire
245 k. à l'heure c'est aussi vite que
la Miller

J'ai pas de serre-tête ils veulent
voir mes cheveux.

Le gagnant d'Indianapolis
a gagné 53.000 dollars = 1.325.000 f.
c'est assez agréable.

A sample of Hélène's notes from her scrap albums; here, she describes
Schurch's car and explains that the accompanying photograph (see page
124) shows her at the wheel but with no helmet because the crowds
always liked to see her hair when she was driving.

Fred Frame had been a dashingly suave man who always wore a bow-tie and who had twenty victories on the Woodbridge oval to his credit; Billy Winn of Atlanta, Georgia, was a fearless driver with a notorious temper and an off-track record for womanizing, drinking and drug-taking. Billy was, she thought, the bravest of the drivers she had known: she remembered watching him on the Brockton track in September, covering two full laps with a missing wheel and in a hailstorm of clay clods, struggling to snatch the victory from Frame. He should have been killed; it was his own pit-stop attendants, scenting a share of the prize-money, who waved him on. She saw them do it.

The race at Brockton was won, not by Frame, but by Billy Winn's best friend, a handsome young Californian called Hermann Schurch who had already beaten Frame at Woodbridge in June and now looked set to become a champion in this risk-filled sport. Schurch, the wealthier of the two men, owned a sensationally fast machine called a Hoosier Pete* which Billy Winn often drove; Hélène was allowed to make free use of it whenever the DePalma Miller was not available. It went, she remembered, equally fast – 245 kilometres an hour, a speed which could easily be achieved on the slippery wooden bowls but which became impossible on the pitted clay ovals which had once served as trotting circles for horses at the state fairs.

Both of her new friends died young and on the track. Billy, having won a long war against alcohol, was killed driving at Springfield in 1938; Hermann crashed at Legion Ascot, California, in November 1931; it was where he had chalked up his first major victory the previous year. He had been married for just nineteen days. She looked down at the photographs and smoothed them absentmindedly with her fingers. She had enjoyed Billy's company;

---

* Also known as a Clemons Special, this was a modified car with a Clemons engine in a Ringling chassis.

her relationship with Hermann was more intense. Telegrams flew to and fro between the events of each week; photographs of her smiling at Hermann, sitting in his car, leaning over the side as he prepares for a race, tell their own story. His face looks open, boyish and kind. He also looks heartbreakingly young.

Her first appearance was to be made at Woodbridge on Sunday 10 August. Knowing her love of style, Billy promised to send a car and driver ('my boy') to the Savoy Plaza to take her to the track. The staff who worked downstairs at the hotel were treated to the spectacle of her dressed for action, a beret pulled low to shade her cornflower-blue eyes from the morning sun as she swaggered down the Plaza steps, to be greeted by a driver with a mustard-coloured sedan.

It was a three-and-a-half-hour drive out to Woodbridge and the last part of the journey was slow, as Billy's driver was trapped in a stream of cars, carts and old-fashioned carriages heading for the speedway. They arrived late, missing the first race of the day. The grandstand, unusual in that it provided the 10,000 spectators with a clear view of the entire oval of the high-banked track, was already packed. High above one of the stands, fluttering in the wind, she saw a giant image of her face, confident and smiling at the wheel, above the announcement: 'For championship performance give me ESSO.'

It was, Hankinson had decided, to be her day. Her face was in the programme, on the flags, and on the free leaflets which were being handed out with the admission tickets. She appeared, as promised, with a cavalcade of outriding motorcyclists, surrounding the Miller – not DePalma's on this occasion – that she would drive in a high-speed dash at the end of the day.[6]

The band played, a cannon was fired, the celebrity, pleasingly starlike in her white costume and with her Harlow-blonde hair, demonstrated her stage training by waving, blowing kisses and

Hélène appears in the 1930 Esso campaign.

making gestures of delight and admiration at the beauty of the car she was to drive. Since the elegant racing machines designed by Harry Miller were America's version of the Bugatti, seductive, powerful and successful – Millers won 71 of the 164 board-track races recorded between 1915 and 1931 – the crowd were ready to applaud her good taste.

None of Hélène's experiences in America can have been more testing than this first exhibition drive, closely watched by the man who had her under contract and who had already strongly objected to her extravagance. She knew the history of the Woodbridge track; no woman had driven on it before. Every newspaper report she read told her that it was lethal. Hermann Schurch, who had won here on 1 June, must have described his own first race here under Hankinson's directorship when, with a front wheel beginning to loosen from its moorings, he spun round three times on the track and plunged down into the dust before managing to right the car. A year earlier, a brilliant young driver had shot through the top barrier rail and into a nosedive of 35 feet. Like Henri de Courcelles, he died on the way to hospital.

Hankinson had a more recent tragedy in mind. Only two weeks before Hélène's appearance here, one of Woodbridge's most popular drivers, Bob Robinson, had swerved to avoid an out-of-control car and crashed through the barrier to his death. A shadow had been cast over the day. Tragedy was not good for business. Just before Hélène set out to make her exhibition speed run, Hankinson dropped a friendly hand on her shoulder and explained the situation. Make a nice gesture, sweetheart, he urged her; something to please the crowd; she'd worked audiences before this; she'd know what to do.

And then the pistol cracked the signal.

Drivers on the notorious Woodbridge speedbowl.

Driving on a near cliff-face of slippery, lightning-quick boards, she had no time for reflection; forcing the car up, she straightened it and pressed down hard, remembering DePalma's cheerful declaration that he could go round a speedway with his eyes closed, once the pace was right. Easily said; she could feel the wheels skidding and sliding, resisting her wishes. Faces flashed past like strips of white ribbon as she searched the rail and saw where Robinson's car had smashed through it. Pulling the scarf from around her neck, she managed to throw it so that it caught on the splintered rail. The crowd roared approval; on the last of her ten laps, she pulled off her white beret and tossed it out at the same spot. It skimmed over the barrier into the darkness of the drop in a second, perfect display of homage.

It hardly mattered, after that act of grace, that she came nowhere near to matching the time made by the fastest driver of the morning. The crowd was in love. The papers hailed her as 'The Speedbowl Queen'.[7]

Woodbridge was succeeded by a weekly procession of exhibition drives, sometimes in the DePalma Miller or the Miller which had belonged to the unlucky Bob Robinson, sometimes in Hermann Schurch's Hoosier Pete, and occasionally, after his death while driving at Middletown, in her former teacher's Duesenberg. Claims that she would break the records of the male drivers were not borne out; she still drove fast enough to delight crowds who were unfamiliar with the sight of a woman in a racing car, let alone a pretty, delicate-looking Frenchwoman who struck poses and had the radiant smile of a filmstar. Hankinson had promised an exotic attraction and Miss Helen, as she grew used to being addressed, fitted the bill perfectly. The drivers were entranced; she returned the compliment by telling journalists that she was enjoying being treated as a colleague, one of the boys. The telegrams from Hermann, lavishly peppered with 'love and kisses' and confessions of missing her 'very much' every time they were apart for as much as a week, show that she was not quite that.

It's a relief to know that the Hot News Agency men doted on her, and that she did have at least one steady relationship, and with a warm, affectionate man, to rely on; her life as she trailed from one dirt track to another, competing for attention against the regular state fair attractions of human cannon-fodder, acrobats, weightlifters and what were bluntly called freaks, was harsher and more lonely than any of her previous experiences.

The loneliness was part of the attraction. In interviews, she continued to emphasize her passion for solitude and to identify it with her love of skiing and mountaineering. 'I love being alone in a lively street, in a crowded town,' she told one interviewer, and added that she would much rather watch a crowd than go to a cinema.'[8]* She sounded strong and confident, but Teddie Caldwell, a lively New Jersey girl who was friendly with both Hermann Schurch and Billy Winn and who often joined them and Hélène in a foursome, was anxious about her. What Caldwell saw was a woman of violent mood swings who drove because racing had taken possession of her, like a drug, and who revelled in her ability to attract attention, to draw both men and women to her. It was, Caldwell thought, all very well for the moment, while she was driving at the peak of her powers and looking gorgeous enough to be seen as an attraction on any track, but what about when her looks started to fade, the strength to diminish?[9]

A hint of Hélène's darker moments can be found in a poem which she snipped from a newspaper and pasted into her journal. It is an epitaph and it suggests that she was piercingly aware of the price that she might one day pay for the independence she asserted with such pride.

---

* The cinema reference could be pique. It's always possible that she did make contact with William Morris and was given the brush-off.

When he died, nobody laughed, nobody cried.
Where he went, how he fares
Nobody knows, nobody cares.

Ralph Hankinson was so delighted by his client's performances
in her first eight weeks that he offered to renew her contract
immediately. The offer was made at Bloomsburg, the last
exhibition which she had agreed to give, on 26 September. The
racing, as so often at the state fairs, was wedged between vaudeville
acts; coming out to salute the crowd, Hélène was given a standing
ovation before she drove on to the track at the wheel of DePalma's
famous Miller. Returning to the local hotel with her contract
signed, she sent a wire to her father's brother Henri, asking if she
could come and visit him and her aunt up in Calgary for her
vacation. It is just possible that she had become pregnant and that
she wanted to remove herself from the public eye until she had
dealt with an inconvenient problem. It is more likely that she
wanted to be among familiar faces, to go climbing in the Rockies
and to indulge in the pleasure of talking in her own language. She
may have felt more lonely than pride allowed her to admit.

Hankinson's strategy was to keep his female attraction on the move,
ensuring that she would always have fresh press coverage and draw
new audiences; one reason for this was that she was unable to fulfil
the boast he had made that she would match or exceed existing
speed records. Her times were good, but they were not spectacular.

It was probably for this reason that the second half of Hélène's
American tour took her further south, starting on 11 October with
the dirt track at Winston-Salem in North Carolina. Neither
Schurch nor Billy Winn was on hand to give her advice about
handling a car on this notoriously tricky fairground oval or to
spend time, as one of them would often do, on giving her car a
last-minute check.

There had already been an accident, although not a fatal one, in the feature race of the day. The winner was Bob Sall, described by the local press as 'a rip-tearing demon of the dirt track' and enthusiastically cheered by a grandstand crowd of eight thousand for his time (12 minutes, 10 seconds over twenty laps of the mile-long track). Hélène's challenge was to beat the best timed trial of the day, a half-mile covered in 31·15 seconds.

The fuzzy photographs suggest that she was driving a Miller; a new touch had been added to her appearance by wearing short sleeves trimmed with a feminine bow; the photographs also show that she was wearing only a beret to protect her head. She performed three laps before speeding up for her attempt to match the record.

Accounts vary about the precise cause and nature of her accident; talking to a local journalist at the end of the day, she said that the steering wheel had not been correctly aligned. She had slightly dropped her speed for an approaching bend when she hit a pothole in the rough track. Swerving away from the spectators standing on the inner side of the track, she hit the barrier rail. The car overturned, hanging perilously above a high escarpment on the outer side of the track.

This was the moment in which Ralph Hankinson saw his client's remarkable professionalism. Crawling out from under the car, Hélène stood up, dusted herself down and ran back along the track towards the grandstand, waving her white beret and smiling. 'And then,' she told one of her interviewers, 'I thought I might as well give them a bit of a song. So I did!'[10] It was, the local papers declared, the biggest thrill of the day.

Back in her room at the Robert E. Lee Hotel, Hélène bathed, ordered drinks, went through her English exercise for the day – she was studying the treacherous verb 'to get' – and changed into a dress before she went off to find the other drivers and gather tips about the next track.

★

Looking back at her American tour after a gap of thirty years, she remembered it as life in a travelling circus. She remembered the smell of hot oil, the apprehension as she waited to start her run down another dusty track, wondering if she was going to survive it when each of them, at any moment, could end her life. Nothing, she said, could match the fear of death she had felt on those tracks, or the relief when she reached the finishing line.[11]

No record survives to tell us how she fared at Langhorne in Pennsylvania, America's most dangerous dirt track; the cuttings she preserved show that she thrilled a crowd – but where? – with her timed runs in a Miller Special belonging to red-headed Jimmy Paterson. 'Red' Paterson had replaced Hermann Schurch in her affections; a number of photographs taken at Kinston, North Carolina, on 24 October, show them arm-in-arm, looking well pleased with each other. Hellé Nice had, in this rough and ready masculine world, become almost like a mascot. When she ended her tour, she was presented with a silver cup carrying the signatures of all the men – Ralph DePalma was the exception – whose cars she had driven; it is anybody's guess how many of them had been her lovers. Painting slogans on car bonnets was a common habit – the one she drove at Wilson had 'Let Pete Do It To Perfection' emblazoned on its side; a 1930s Duesenberg kept at the Brooklands museum is boldly painted with the name 'Hellé'. It could be a sweetly crass declaration of love, or an act of homage to the only European woman who had the nerve to cross the Atlantic and drive on the world's most treacherous tracks. One thing is certain: there was only one Hellé who raced Duesenbergs in America in the thirties.[12]

And then what? As so often in Hellé Nice's career, the trail comes to an abrupt end – in this case with her appearance at Spartanburg, South Carolina, on 11 November. Giving an interview the following year, she said that she had spent four months in America and that she had been given a wonderful welcome in the twenty states which she visited. In 1961 she airily referred to having raced at St Louis, Santa Fe and Houston. No record of these appearances has survived; it is probable that she was embellishing the truth. In 1931, she had given a simpler account, explaining that her love of a hot climate had taken her down to Florida for the last weeks of her trip. Earlier still, she had hinted that further adventures were in store. 'I shall be coming back to Paris in the middle of November,' she told interviewer Maurice Berson in February 1931, shortly after her return to France. 'I will tell you everything I have seen and what I shall be doing,' she said and added tantalizingly that she would have to stop talking, 'because it is a big secret.'[13]

If there was a secret, it had lost any news value by the time she made her return to France towards the beginning of December 1930, after a long and happy vacation with Ralph Hankinson's wife and their daughters at Daytona Beach in Florida. She had not become a film star or married a millionaire; she had, on the other hand, raised her profile as the only Frenchwoman to have raced on the American board and dirt tracks, while her record run at Montlhéry remained unchallenged. Ahead lay the gruelling and peripatetic life of a Grand Prix racer, in a world which was dominated by men.

10

SEX AND CARS

'The only unnatural sexual behaviour is none at all.'

FREUD

'I was the only woman who raced in Grands Prix in a Formula 1 car,' Hélène Delangle boasted to a friend in 1977 long after her career on the circuits was over.[1] This was hyperbole. The term Grand Prix was freely used during the 1930s to describe many races, both on circuits and on public roads, which did not have international status; the term Formula 1 did not come into existence until after the Second World War. Of the 76 'Grand Prix' in which she allowed it to be proclaimed that she competed, several – Nîmes, Dieppe, Biella – justify the name only in the substantial amount of prize money they awarded. This should not obscure the fact that Hélène drove on Europe's most demanding courses and that she did her best to drive, without the concession of a handicap, against the best male drivers of the time.

A handful of women raced in the thirties; few had the guts and stamina to trespass on the masculine domain which lay beyond rally driving and record-breaking. Fiery, red-headed Anne Itier drove in several Grand Prix events, competing against men; other French women followed the English example, preferring to test their skills at races set on steep hills, or at endurance rallies and speed trials. Even Itier, when questioned about her ambitions, hoped only to see three English women drivers competing against three French women. Hélène, asked the same question, ignored her own sex, naming the great Tazio Nuvolari, Louis Chiron and Philippe Etancelin as the racers against whom she wanted to test herself. Her wish was granted and few of her contemporaries would have disputed the view of the German authority Erwin Tragatsch that she was, with Elizabeth Junek, the finest female racing driver in Europe between the wars – and Junek had left the field after seeing her husband killed on the Nürburgring in 1928.[2]

Supremely feminine in her extravagance, her love of pretty clothes and ornaments, and the flirtatiousness which had male interviewers (figuratively) eating out of her strong little hands, Hélène made regular appearances in articles which targeted a female audience. She was admired by her own sex; men, her chosen rivals, remained the companions of her choice.

Visitors to Paris in 1931 might have thought that the country was doing remarkably well. The huge and faintly absurd Colonial Exhibition out at Vincennes vaunted France's imperial strength, with an almost full-scale replica of the temple at Angkor Wat representing Indochina and gardens of date palms symbolizing North Africa. This looked good, but signs of prosperity, once the visitor strayed from the capital or the booming Riviera Coast, were scant. Towns like Pau and Vichy, blighted since the war by the loss of a whole generation of young men, were struggling, short of money and of visitors. Genteel travellers who came to taste the waters, to look at the architecture and be on their way, were of no value; what these towns needed to help their businesses thrive were big captive crowds. Nothing brought them in so reliably as a Grand

Prix weekend event, but the size of the crowd depended to a significant degree on the attractions they were offered. Hellé Nice, blonde, brave and fiery, superb at establishing a rapport with the spectators, was a driver worth her weight in gold to a town which was trying to establish its name in the Grand Prix season.

Among the most poignant of the relics that the old lady in Nice preserved were the sheets of paper on which, with meticulous care, she kept track of her racing invitations, the money offered and the expenses she would have to pay. They are poignant because, despite the fact that she was sometimes offered as much as 6,000 francs in start money – payable so long as she began the race – the struggle was always hard. 'Not enough!' she angrily wrote beside one offer of 2,000 francs, and, since she often had to cover the cost of transport, maintenance, finding a garage, paying a mechanic, licensing, new tyres – they seldom survived a race intact – the response seems reasonable.

The fact that she also had to maintain one of the world's most extravagant touring cars, a Hispano Suiza, probably added to the sense of urgency. But Hélène was lucky in some ways and resourceful in others. She must, since there are no references in her accounts to any expenses for a Bugatti, have been looked after by Molsheim to some degree; she also had a special arrangement with Marcel Mongin's garage, which allowed her to have special rates for repairs and maintenance. Her lovers were almost invariably well-off members of the racing community, and in a position to offer financial support.

It was rare for a lover to be able to influence the amount of money Hélène was offered to take part in a Grand Prix; the fact that she was receiving between 5,000 and 6,000 francs per race, a considerable sum in 1932 and again in 1934, can be tied to the fact that these were the years during which she established new records on the demanding hill climb at Mont Ventoux in Provence; with each major success, her start-money increased. Conversely, after an operation for a burst appendix had kept her away from racing and the public eye for five months at the beginning of 1933, her start-money suffered a sharp drop.

Negotiations were tough and not always to her liking; many mechanics resented working for a woman racer and the cost of keeping a car in peak racing condition was considerable. Occasionally, Hélène dropped her guard of breezy confidence to admit despair. Teddie Caldwell, the friend she acquired on her American tour, was a regular correspondent. Teddie kept Hélène up to date about Billy Winn's continuing battle against alcohol – he quit drinking in 1934 and achieved some of his greatest successes thereafter – and sent the news in 1931 of poor Hermann Schurch's death during a time-trial in California, 'a big shock to all of us', less than three weeks after his marriage.[3] In the autumn of 1933, Teddie received an uncharacteristically despondent letter from France. 'Yes, Hellé [Teddie pronounced it 'Ellie'], I suppose you do have it hard,' she wrote back, 'trying to meet expenses on what the promoters want to pay and once in the racing game, it gets into your blood and you just don't want it to stop. Maybe, next year things will be better.'[4] Happily, she was proved right; 1934 and 1935 were two of Hellé Nice's most successful years: 'I was,' she wrote later of her triumphant past, 'received like an ambassadress whenever I travelled abroad to race. They played the Marseillaise when I drove on to the track, honouring France in the welcome they gave me.'[5] But Teddie's observations were prescient. The thrill of competitive racing had become her friend's drug, as necessary to her as breathing. However tough the conditions this was her source of joy, her way of life. She would never, now, consider any other. She could not.

Few family letters have survived from the period after Hélène's return from America, but an old inhabitant of Sainte-Mesme remembers the sports celebrity making occasional visits to the old-fashioned family house on the main street in which the couple always known as M. and Mme Bernard had lived since 1926. Hélène's most regular escort on these visits was the man who may have already become her civil law husband. Solid, prosperous and good-humoured, Marcel Mongin was a good friend to the family. In Paris, he brightened Solange Delangle's drab life as a telegraph clerk by taking her out to supper and an occasional visit to the cinema; at Sainte-Mesme, he was ready to take a turn at pumping water from the well at the back of the house or to stroll, with a gun under his arm, through the glades and rides of the Rambouillet woods with Henri, the gentle, purposeless young man who was still little 'Didi' to his older sister.[6]

The contrasts in the family character had, with time, become marked. Henri, like Hélène, was usually cheerful and buoyant; all he lacked were her explosive rages and ambition.* Solange, intense and reserved, had inherited her mother's depressive streak. Increasingly nervous, and angry with a life which seemed to have bestowed all its gifts on her sister and none on her, she ate like a bird and behaved like one, picking fretfully at the bloody rashes of psoriasis which covered her arms and hands and legs. A curious photograph taken with Hélène's treasured Leica shows her mother and sister in the front parlour of the house at Sainte-Mesme. Solange, ghostly in her emaciation, stands by the window and stares out with the eyes of a prisoner; Alexandrine Delangle seems unwilling to confront the black eye of the smart little camera. Instead, she stares into the room, hands clasped on her lap. The good-looking young woman of twenty years earlier is hard to reconcile with this gloomy, monumental figure: it is not surprising to discover that this was when Hélène began to collect diet sheets.

* Evidence of her temper appears in a report of her behaviour when she lost to a local at the Klausen hill climb held in August 1932. Her fury was so extreme that a police officer threatened to shoot holes in her tyres. The crowd, however, enjoyed the spat.

1 Baby Hélène in 1900, sitting on her mother's lap outside a stable door at Aunay-sous-Auneau.

2 Hélène catches her friend, the artist and illustrator René Carrère, as he looks up from his bath.

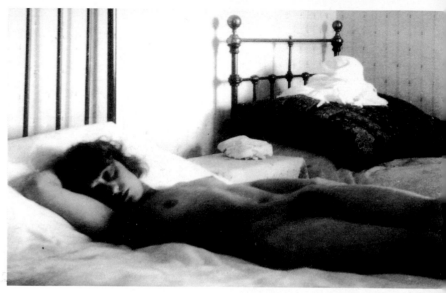

3 Resting on her hotel bed at
  Brighton in 1920. The photographer
  is probably Marcel Mongin.

4 During her first years in
  Paris, Hélène earned
  some money by posing
  for photographs like this.

5 In 1923, Hélène tried her hand at a self-portrait. This is the first documented appearance of the name 'Hellé Nice', used here as her signature.

6 This dapper couple are the Norwegian dancers who called themselves The Rocky Twins, who were good friends of Hélène's in her dancing years.

7 One of two photographs of herself as a promising young dancer which Hélène took care to preserve, and to display.

8 Hélène, front row, second left, relaxes with fellow-performers after an evening at the Hotel Miramar, Cannes.

9 Hélène gets to grips with a white dove while showing off her gorgeous smile, and a bit more.

10 Striking a pose before
    setting a new speed
    record at Montlhéry,
    1929.

11 Just before driving a
    Bugatti T43A at the
    Actors' Championship
    of 1930. She may be
    helping to publicize
    the car's new Grebon
    headlamps.

12 In triumphant pose on her T35 Bugatti in 1930.

13 Hélène is congratulated by an admiring Jean Bugatti after she takes third
place in the Bugatti GP on the Sarthe circuit at Le Mans, June 1930.

14 Hélène gets friendly
with her US publicist,
Harry Riggins of the
Hot News Agency,
during her 1930 tour.
Her scrapbook playfully
calls him 'my secretary'.

15 'Oh what a girl and
good scout. Send some
more over France.'
Frank Wirth of the Hot
News Agency pays
tribute to a great
sportswoman in 1930.

6 Left to right: unidentified friend, Mrs Hankinson, Hélène and the Hankinsons' youngest on Daytona's speed trial beach, September 1930.

A sedate Daytona speed trial, which took place during Hélène's 1930 holiday with the Hankinsons.

18 A drenched Hélène in shocking road conditions on the Dauphine Circuit for the
Grenoble GP, August 1931.

19 Hélène chats to fellow Bugatti driver Charles Grover ('Williams') before a race a
La Baule, September 1931.

0 Flat out at the wheel of a Rothschild Bugatti at La Baule, September 1931.

Not one of Hélène's best-chosen poses, at the Marseille GP, Miramas circuit, August 1933.

22 Hélène wears a racer's wind-helmet even when she's away from the wheel. Unidentified location, 1933.

23 After the drivers' meeting at Biella, early June 1935. Note Chiron's hostile arm language, second from right. Second from left, Tazio Nuvolari, Didi Trossi, Ton Brivio and, behind Hélène, Johnny Lurani.

24 Hélène takes a corner in her Alfa Monza at Montjuic Park, in the Penya Rhin GP, Barcelona, late June 1935.

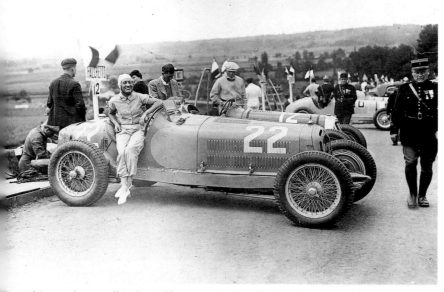

25 Taking a photo-call in her Alfa Monza before the Comminges GP at St Gaudens, August 1935.

26 Basco Béarnais, club president, congratulates her after the Pau GP, February 1935

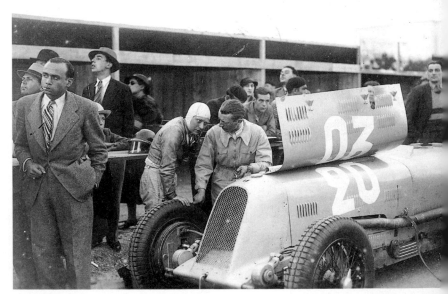

27 Hélène's scrapbook records her victory at La Turbie hillclimb, April 1936, despite mechanical problems at start.

28 One of Arnaldo Binelli's extraordinary set of photographs of Hélène's crash at São Paulo, 1936.

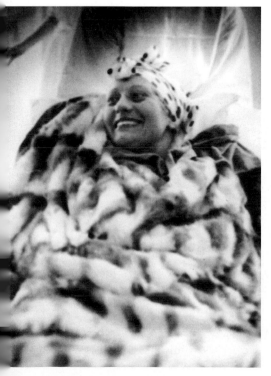

29 Her first public appearance after the São Paulo crash. Here she is leaving Santa Catarina hospital in September 1936.

30 At the wheel of 'Claire' before the Yacco trials, May 1937. Left to right: Simone des Forest, Odette Siko, Claire Descollas.

31 Hélène on the Montlhéry speedbowl during the Yacco trials, 1937.

*Madame Delangle and Solange at Sainte-Mesme, c. 1931,
photographed by Hélène.*

A racing driver needed to remain in peak condition and few – the exuberant, opera-singing Giuseppe Campari was among them – were overweight. Only 1·62 metres and 57 kilos in 1933, she worked hard to maintain her slight figure.

The photograph is strange enough to justify a little speculative deconstruction. It is puzzling, with such an attractive and successful daughter paying a visit, that Alexandrine Delangle refused to look at the camera. It is, perhaps, significant that only one terse note survived to the daughter she alone always addressed as Mariette. Had she – it would be understandable – disapproved of her daughter for flaunting her naked body on stage? Did she know, from Solange, if not from Hélène herself, about her carefree sexual life? Did she resent the fact that, while her older daughter was a postal clerk and her son a part-time upholsterer, Hélène had a cupboard full of furs, a flat near the centre of Paris and a circle of friends which included members of the richest families in France?

Even if the answer to all these questions is a cautious affirmative, another explanation for Madame Delangle's strange coolness should be considered. It is not clear at which point Jean Bernard entered the widow's life and made himself part of the family, but the pattern of Hélène's relationships, involving sometimes as many as three affairs at a time during the 1930s and many betrayals, is most easily interpreted as a reaction against early emotional damage. Playing the field, she escaped the risk of involvement and rejection; using her considerable sexual charisma as a weapon, she found it easy to draw lovers to her, to work from a position of power. Concentration on physical perfection and performance, when combined with a fear of sexual commitment, lest the flaws are discovered, is a primary behaviour pattern for cases of women who have suffered sexual abuse in childhood.

Supposing that this was the case, it becomes easier to understand why Hélène's voluminous collection of photographs and letters contains only one businesslike note and this uneasy photograph to connect her to her mother in adult life. It is tragically common for wives in such situations to allocate blame to the victimized child rather than the predator. If abuse did take place and if Alexandrine held her younger daughter responsible for seducing Jean Bernard, she would not have forgiven her.

'Poor little Didi was my only real friend in the family,' Hélène wrote later. 'Maman and Solange always sided together, and Solange was always jealous.'[7] Confirmation of this seems apparent in the fact that when Madame Delangle bought her second, considerably larger house in Sainte-Mesme in 1926, she used Solange as her witness and named Solange as her sole heir. French laws of inheritance favour equal division of property between the direct descendants. Hélène, living half-an-hour's drive away in Paris, was not hard to reach. This was not the act of a loving mother.

Visits home may have been lacking in joy, but two glorious photographs of a festival day at Nantes in 1931 show that Hélène was in good spirits after her return to France three months earlier. The high spot of the Nantes Mi-Carême carnival, held traditionally on Holy Thursday in the third week of Lent, was a pageant celebrating Joan of Arc's victory over the English at Orléans. Joan, crop-haired and radiant in her triumphal chariot drawn by a sturdy pair of dappled greys, was represented by Hélène, arms outstretched as she beamed at the camera over the helmeted heads of a genial gang of costumed medieval footsoldiers. Perhaps, happily boasting of her role as France's leading woman racer and ambassadress, she was seeing herself as

Hélène as Joan of Arc at Nantes, 1931.

Joan's descendant, championing her country against all foreign competition.

In June 1931 Hellé Nice carried off two prizes at the Women's Championship at Montlhéry; the following month, she met Marcel Lehoux at her first Grand Prix of the year.* Reims, with its long straight runs and only three sharp corners, was becoming popular as one of the fastest courses in Europe; she looked forward to a challenge. Beaten to first place in the day's Coupe des Dames by Anne Itier (they were the only two participants), she came 4th in the 2-litre class, against drivers who included Louis Chiron, René Dreyfus, Philippe Etancelin and the Parisian-based Polish aristocrat, Count Czaikowski. The champion of the day was Lehoux and Hélène found an opportunity to congratulate him when the local newspaper sponsored a champagne party in the pits. Lehoux was probably more impressed by her performance on the popular, pre-war course at Dieppe three weeks later when, despite torrential rain and a number of serious accidents† involving other drivers, she managed to come 7th, and 1st in the 2-litre class.

Lehoux, at forty-five, now began to share Marcel Mongin's role as a reliable father-figure in Hélène's life. Immensely popular and respected, he was a short, stocky man, known for his lack of ostentation, his generosity to rising young drivers and his professionalism. Born in France in the Loire valley, he lived in Algeria from the age of three and built up a successful garage business there which helped to subsidize a successful racing career. Hélène kept none of his letters, but their relationship was well-known in the racing community, especially since they often

* Lehoux had taken part in the Casablanca Rally of 1930, but Hélène was then fully occupied by her relationship with Bruno d'Harcourt and preparations for her first professional race.
† Jean-Pierre Wimille nearly ended his burgeoning career that day when his Bugatti spun off the road on a sharp corner and caught fire.

travelled to events together. Publicly taken photographs of them reveal their mutual affection; the usually reserved Lehoux often looks as though he has only just managed to stop laughing for the camera while Hélène, uncharacteristically, appears to be more interested in what her friend is telling her than in giving a good shot to the cameraman.

As a professional, Lehoux must have admired Hélène when he watched her driving her own Bugatti in August of 1931 on the spectacular and difficult mountain-encircled course at Comminges in the south of France, near Pau. This was one of the most popular French circuits and special trains had been laid on to bring some of the 15,000 grandstand spectators who were unwilling to face the crowded roads. It was Philippe Etancelin's day, in an Alfa Monza; Czaikowski took second place in a T51 Bugatti. Anne Itier crashed on her sixth lap; Hélène did well to come 9th. As always, she won the publicity race hands down, laughing at the cameramen as she perched on the blue torpedo-tail of the Bugatti, head thrown back, legs jauntily crossed. Three weeks later, she was the only woman entrant for the Monza Grand Prix near Milan where, after a disaster when Philippe Etancelin's car hit and killed three spectators, injuring ten others, the big race of the day began and was won by the fiery Italian driver Luigi Fagioli. A week later, she was back in France, speeding along the hard, flat sands of one of Europe's most beautiful beaches, La Baule, and racing against, among others, Marcel Lehoux. Here, she only lost 4th place when she was obliged to change spark plugs on the final lap. She was, the leading sports daily *L'Auto* declared in the following day's report on the race, 'une conductrice de valeur', a remarkably fine racing driver – for a woman.

The first event of 1932 was the Paris–Saint-Raphaël Féminine rally which had begun in 1929 and which later acquired the glamorous title of the 'Rally of Princesses' as it attracted an increasing number of aristocratic female competitors. It was a

*Hélène on her unsupercharged Bugatti 35
at Comminges, 1931, steals the show.*

demanding race of over a thousand kilometres, undertaken in
freezing weather and on icy roads which were often little better
than bumpy farm tracks. A victim that year was one of Hélène's
few close women friends, Renée Friderich, the pretty twenty-
year-old daughter of Ettore Bugatti's first engineer (he now ran the
Bugatti agency in Nice from which many first-class racers had
acquired their cars). Lively, dark-haired Renée had only been
driving competitively for a short time, but she was good enough
for Louis Delage to have tempted her away from what she must
have regarded as the family firm. She drove a Delage for the first
and last time in the Paris–Saint-Raphael rally; fatally, she tried to
handle it like the lighter, more flexible Bugatti, and crashed on the
steep and twisting ascent of Pougues. 'Pauvre petite Renée,
toujours gaie, toujours souriante,' lamented *L'Auto*, before
condoling with the father who had been summoned to identify

Renée Friderich

her crushed remains. Hélène, tightly swaddled in waterproof clothing, made the record time of the day, and of the entire event, on the same treacherous stretch of road.

The prospect of sunshine lured French drivers south in the spring of 1932 when their cars were winched up on to the steamers travelling from Marseille to Tunis for the two North African Grand Prix events. Lehoux was at the docks to meet Hélène and drive with her along the coast to Oran to prepare for her first Algerian Grand Prix.

'Oh, mornings in Oran!' Albert Camus wrote twenty years later in *Summer*. 'From high on the plateaux the swallows swoop down into the immense cauldron of simmering air. The whole coast is ready for departure, a thrill of adventure runs along it.' Almost Spanish in its hardness and in the brilliance of its light, the ugliness and poverty of Oran in the thirties made less impression on visitors than the beaches of fluttering asphodels and the towering, predatory crags of the Santa Cruz mountain which loomed above the city's yellow defence walls and dusty streets. Sheaves of photographs have survived to show that Hélène fell under the spell of Algeria's exotic combination of French and Arab ways, the silent crowds who lined the town beaches just before dusk, to watch a dark sea swallow the last fiery spikes of the sun, the graceful couples who lounged along the boulevards after dusk, the naked village children who, unused to cars, ran innocently towards the strange machines which emerged from the dust clouds like djinns from the desert sands.

Practising for a race is hard work. Notes have to be taken of all the places which might endanger the car; every corner must be memorized, every change of road surface recorded. The driving has to be fast for the notes to be of value; a bend taken safely at a slowish speed can prove lethal when the throttle is pressed down. Hélène was lucky in having Marcel Lehoux to monitor her; few drivers knew the North African circuits so well.

Familiarizing herself with the demanding Oran circuit in timed practice runs – it was said to be more difficult than any in France – Hélène met up with Lehoux's new protégé. Spanish by birth, like many Algerians, the tall and open-faced Guy Moll had recently started racing as a wealthy boy's hobby; he showed such uncommon aptitude that Lehoux loaned him a Bugatti to compete at Oran. Moll only missed victory after a mechanical failure while Hélène's hard work was rewarded when she came 2nd in the 2-litre class. Neither driver was so lucky at Casablanca a month later: a mechanical problem forced Moll to retire and Hélène's car failed to qualify; Lehoux, the middle-aged professional, took 1st place. Told by Lehoux that he had the ability to become one of the world's great drivers, Moll decided to accept the older man as his mentor. The three of them, Hélène, Lehoux and Moll, often shared the expense of transport trailers on the arduous slogs from one European Grand Prix to another; it seems probable that Guy Moll was the 'blond Spaniard' of whom Hélène sent rapturous accounts to Teddie Caldwell in the summer of 1933. Teddie was unacquainted with any blond Spaniards herself and had a mild prejudice against the nation; she confined herself to the cautious comment 'but if you say that he is nice . . .'[8]

Nobody ever described Philippe de Rothschild as nice and nobody supposed that he was regularly lending Hellé Nice the supercharged Bugatti T35 she called 'Yoyo' – it was the new craze in Paris for ladies to dangle these little weighted wheels from gloved fingers while walking along the street – out of altruism. Hélène first drove her sporty 'Yoyo' on the sands of La Baule in the autumn of 1931; she was in it again the following summer on the hill climb of Pougues which formed part of the Paris–Saint-Raphaël rally and at Mont Ventoux in Provence, where she set a new Ladies' record before driving west to the dreary oval plateau of Miramas where the first Grand Prix of Marseille was taking place in September. She had long since parted with the Bugatti in which she had made her record-breaking drive at Montlhéry in 1929; and later, in 1932, she sold a second one.[9] Rothschild's car became, during the year of their affair, a welcome substitute, freeing her from the expense of maintenance.

The theatre director Joan Littlewood, who compiled Philippe de Rothschild's lively autobiography from her many conversations with him during the 1980s, made no reference to a racing driver among his multitudinous sexual partners. When interviewed, however, she remembered that Philippe had mentioned a sporty and gamine blonde ex-dancer among the impressive file of film stars, society women and models who visited his bachelor flat on rue Cortambert for brisk sexual tussles after a light meal served by an obligingly discreet valet.[10]

Two years younger than Hellé Nice and not much taller – he was five foot eight in his socks – Philippe de Rothschild could have

Philippe de Rothschild at the wheel of a Bugatti.

first met her either at Molsheim or in Paris, when he was running the Théâtre Pigalle designed by Charles Siclis for his father. An exceptionally shrewd and competitive young man, he took over the reorganization of his family's superb but dilapidated wine estate at Mouton when he was only twenty. By 1929, while his father frolicked around the Mediterranean on a yacht called *Eros*, Philippe was combining management of the vineyards with racing his own Bugattis, running a Paris night club, importing banned Soviet films and having an affair with Yvonne Printemps, the actress who was appearing with her husband, Sacha Guitry, at the Théâtre Pigalle. In 1931, by which time Baron de Rothschild had decamped to Hollywood with an attractive French actress, Philippe squeezed an enjoyable affair with Hélène Delangle into the months left over from a tour of the East and a spot of tiger-shooting.

Philippe was, according to his friends, clever, compulsively energetic and excellent company, 'radiating a supreme self-confidence in his ability to solve almost any problem'.[11] Brought up in considerable luxury by a father who financed a car factory (Unic*), a mustard factory (Maille) and a soapworks (Monsavon) in between writing plays, practising medicine and inventing a successful treatment for burns, Philippe was equally remarkable in the breadth of his interests, from designing the first form of windscreen wiper to translating Elizabethan poetry. The fact that Hélène began to read French and English poetry, plays and novels at this time owed much to his influence; so, perhaps, did her choice of a new, flamboyantly modern Paris home.

Late in 1932, she left her old apartment on rue Saint-Senoch for more spacious accommodation in an exuberantly curvaceous building newly designed by Bassompierre de Rutte Sirvin. The building, still standing at Rondpoint Mirabeau beside the Seine, is a splendid relic of thirties style; beside it, the Métro stop André Citroën marks the former site of France's largest car factory, spread at the foot of the Eiffel Tower around the top of which Citroën used to flash his name in lights, proclaiming his reign over Paris. Looking through her vast convex windows on the sixth floor, Hellé Nice had one of the finest views in Paris, stretching out, almost, to Vincennes; inside, five handsome rooms were rapidly filled with the unexpectedly ornate furniture and delicate water-colour landscape sketches which she collected with acquisitive pleasure. Here, and in the overdressed porcelain dolls

---

*Unic taxis became ubiquitous in the early twentieth century; Proust made use of them on the pilgrimages to Cabourg where he began his own love affair with cars, and with the dedicated young chauffeurs he employed to drive them.

which, with her little dogs, assumed the place of the children she would never have, she expressed her own taste, not Philippe's. An unkind visitor might have seen the apartment's interior as more suited to a music-hall star's dressing-room than to France's most dashing female racing-driver. Hélène, indifferent to criticism, adored it.

It seems unlikely that Hélène cared much for the elegant social world which Philippe de Rothschild entered and left at will; of rumba dancing in the white room at Ciro's, of attending, in full fancy dress, the fabulously expensive, and absurd, balls presided over by Elsa Maxwell and Count Etienne de Beaumont. There is no doubt, however, that she liked a title. She had a short affair with the dashing Prince Nicolas of Romania, a racing friend of Philippe's, and it wasn't admiration for the ruthless way in which the young Spaniard Count José de Villapadierna had stolen his grandmother's jewels to buy his first race car that attracted her when they had an affair the following year, in 1935.

The list of lovers, aristocratic and otherwise, who became involved with Hellé Nice during the 1930s is almost as long as the list of races in which she took part; fortunately for us, she had the helpful habit of marking their names with an 'X' in her new black address book. Racing at Nîmes, where her car broke down, in May 1932, she was comforted not only by two charming married friends from Marseille, Jean and Andrée Marquand, who had come to cheer her on, but by a dashing fellow competitor who posed for her in his car, a cigarette clenched Spanish-style, like a rose-stem, in his teeth. He signed himself 'Georges' and assured her that his fierce smile owed everything to the presence of his 'chérie'. Georges d'Arnoux was in evidence again at the Grand Prix of Marseille of that autumn, for which he shared lodgings with Hélène at Aix. The lodging may have been a family home; her photograph shows him on the steps leading up to a chateau, white handkerchief perfectly folded in his breast pocket, hand lifted to point out some interesting feature in the distance to an unrecognizably elegant Hélène, hair upswept and feet fashionably shod.* Within a few months, she had added another lover, Henri Thouvenet, to her list. Thouvenet, visible only as a muscular torso in an extraordinary beefcake beach photograph taken by Hélène in 1933, was a wealthy and hot-tempered young Parisian. His letters show that he doted on 'M'amie', pining in her absences, reminding her that his love, however frequently they quarrelled, was deeper than she could ever imagine.

Beach boys, Ste. Maxime, Riviera, 1933, photographed by Hélène. Left to right: standing, 'x' and Henri Thouvenet; centre right, Dr Pierre Chambret; foreground, Fred Arra, Antoine Molinvaud.

* Here he is identified as Georges d'Arnoux; confusingly, another Georges, 'Lolo' Caruana, seems to have been her lover when they both competed in the 1934 Moroccan Grand Prix.

Deeper, perhaps, than she wished it to be. The inventory of her lovers could be expanded. Whatever the nature of her relationship with Mongin, she continued to sleep, on and off, with Lehoux, Moll, Thouvenet, the racing driver René Carrière and his near namesake, the artist, René Carrère, throughout the early thirties. Security, for this woman who spoke with such consistent passion of her love of solitude, lay in numbers, reassurance in the sense of being adored by a multitude.

1933, the year during which Hélène stopped racing in Bugattis, marked a turning-point in France's fortunes. Plunging always deeper into economic depression, the country remained paralysed by the growing threat of another war; her sufferings in the last had been too terrible for another to bear contemplation. A decision not to devalue, as other countries had done during the depression, kept the franc untenably high. Tourists retreated; French products were outpriced by foreign competitors; wages were cut and French defence, largely based on faith in the limited security provided by the Maginot Line, became a subject for sour jokes. In 1914–18 France's major advances in technology had come from money poured into the aircraft industry; now, while Hitler and Mussolini focused all efforts on the production of super-efficient machines, French expenditure was pared to the minimum.

France's triumphs on the racing circuits had been a demoralizing experience for her bankrupt neighbours in the mid-twenties. Defeat had taught them the value of racing as a propaganda tool; Mussolini lavished money on the state holding company that rescued Alfa Romeo from its creditors in the early 1930s and honoured Enzo Ferrari's team of Alfa-driving champions; Hitler was ready to give half a million reichmarks to the company who could produce the first successful German car. Auto-Union and Mercedes met the challenge and, during their remarkable string of victories in the mid-thirties, changed the nature of racing. Until now, a brilliant driver like Tazio Nuvolari had been able to demonstrate that a race could be won by expertise and tenacity, even when the car was not the latest model; the Germans, bringing teams of mechanics, engineers and scientists to the track, put the car and its support team on a par with, if not above, the driver. By 1935, the age of the ace and the independent driver was virtually over; France, the country which had invented Grand Prix racing and excelled at it, now suffered the humiliation of seeing its finest drivers consistently defeated by Italian and German competitors. Grace was maintained, in the French sporting press's reports of these events, with evident and increasing difficulty.

Racing drivers are not, in normal circumstances, political animals; Hélène was not being intentionally disloyal to France when she began to take an interest in driving an Alfa Romeo.* She had loved driving Bugattis; her 35Cs were beautiful, lively and responsive, cars of a character which is unimaginable to the modern driver. But the newly designed 59 was too heavy for her to handle and the 35C could no longer match the more powerful Alfa Romeo which had been known as the 'Monza' since Tazio Nuvolari drove one to victory on the circuit of the same name, north of Milan, in 1931. Marcel Lehoux fostered her new enthusiasm; in August 1933, he invested in an Alfa Monza and gave it to his girlfriend to try before they both took it to the Milan circuit in September. The car, strikingly painted with a triple stripe along the side, was heavier to handle than the Bugatti and the

* ALFA (Anonima Lombarda Fabbrica Automobili) took the second part of its name from Nicola Romeo, a mathematics professor who bought the Milan-based munitions and truck maker in 1915, and began to develop racing machines after the war.
† Possibly because she had already acquired a less exciting 1750 Alfa, of which she kept some maintenance records. But she had also kept a third Bugatti which she sold to an English driver, Freddie Clifford, at Dieppe in 1934 ('Les Souvenirs Sportifs d'un pilot amateur', in *Le Fanatique de L'Automobile* (Editions Larivière SA, No. 119, p. 38).

pedals were differently laid out, with the throttle in the centre. Hélène mastered it with ease.[†] Delighted by the surge of power which she had been missing in the Bugatti and shrewdly aware that a more modern car would increase her value to sponsors, she agreed to a deal with Lehoux. There must, nevertheless, have been a moment when the brutal, squared-off lines of the Monza seemed a poor substitute for the spirited elegance and grace of the Bugatti in which she had driven with such pleasure at it its verve and almost animal response to her lightest touch.

Hélène had been having a successful summer. In June 1933 she took the Woman's Grand Prix title at Montlhéry and made the best speed of the day in a closed car competition of Peugeot 301s for the annual Championnat Féminin. (Perfect photographic opportunities presented themselves, as they always did when Hélène was around, as she kissed the lucky policeman who had won himself a Peugeot in the day's lottery.) The photographers were there again when she came third out of 121 entries in the demanding Coupe des Alpes in July, co-driving a sporty T51 Grand Prix Bugatti with a new lover, Roger Bonnet, a Neuilly garage owner whom she had met through Marcel Mongin. The event, which made no allowances for sleep or nourishment, began and ended on the Riviera coast. Hélène, sexily dressed in silk harem pants and a tight striped jersey, struck a champion's pose beside the car, while Bonnet discreetly absented himself from view. Two months later she and Lehoux drove to north Italy for their next Grand Prix.

A challenge, the old lady gallantly wrote from her attic, was what she had always enjoyed most: she had no hesitation about accepting an invitation to try out the new Alfa in September 1933 on the track it was named after. The Monza circuit, created during the twenties from a beautiful private park north of Milan, was one of the toughest in Europe. A rough surface on shallow banking pulled the racers up before they roared down to a

Marcel Lehoux, left, and Hélène at Monza, September 1933. Note the bows on short sleeves which had become her trademark.

winding, wood-bordered route and out into open country. All the great drivers had gathered at what French newspapers described with innocent good cheer as Fascism's true home: Nuvolari, Chiron, Fagioli, Zehender, Pellegrini, Lehoux, Earl Howe and the American-born Whitney Straight who had made his home in England. Among them, and attracting considerable attention, Hellé Nice was the sole woman racer of the day. She was also the only driver with the presence of mind afterwards to provide a detailed telephone report to French newspapers of the most tragic day in Italy's racing history.

The trouble, according to her, began when a Duesenberg driven by dashing Count Didi Trossi, President of the Monza Grand Prix, spilt oil at a corner during the morning race. Guy Moll, she was eager to stress, had been the first to point out the danger after coming through the corner in a life-threatening full-turn skid. Sand should be spread on the surface, Moll insisted; instead, cautions were issued to the seven drivers in the afternoon races. Charming, lighthearted Giuseppe Campari, defying the stewards' warnings with the statement that they all knew how to drive, reassured his fans that this was absolutely the last Grand Prix in which he would compete before he left the race circuits for the concert platform and his kitchen (Campari was a superb cook). It was a good moment to quit; a glorious year had culminated in his snatching the ACF French Grand Prix victory from Philippe Etancelin. Neither Borzacchini nor the Polish Czaikowski, who had also been racing well that year, had any such plans for retirement. Madame Czaikowski, an elegant woman who sometimes raced herself, had come, as she often did, to act as her husband's timekeeper in the pits.

The first disaster took place when Campari, driving at full speed, skidded on the oil-drenched corner of South Curve and shot into space over the high banking. Coming up alongside him, Borzacchini's car overturned, trapping the driver underneath. Both men died and two more potential victims were lucky to escape with a few cuts; Hélène, skilfully avoiding the treacherous oil slick, brought the Alfa Monza home in 3rd place. Astonishingly, after further consultation and an attempt to mop up some of the oil, the afternoon's races continued. In the last heat of the day, Count Czaikowski's engine caught fire; spraying burning petrol back into the car, it blinded him. The car skidded, flipped over and went up in flames; the driver, paralysed by a broken back, was burned to death.

It was a day of hideous tragedy. Another woman might have paused to reflect on the dangers of a career in which death could come with such cruel ease. Even Hélène, thriving on the adrenalin-rush of a life which was always poised on the brink of death, was briefly shaken. By the following day, however, she was feeling sufficiently collected to drive back to France, deliver a detailed report of the disasters to the sports papers for a substantial fee, and to begin preparing herself to take the Monza south for the San Sebastián Grand Prix at the end of September. As the car's new owner, she banished Lehoux's tricolour stripe and had the car patriotically repainted in two shades of French blue.

During 1933 she lost one of her first mentors, Count Guy Bouriat, the Bugatti driver who had helped prepare her for the record-breaking drive at Montlhéry in 1929; Bouriat was killed at the Grand Prix of Picardy when his Alfa Romeo's wheel clashed with another car, throwing him into a skid which ended when the car hit a tree and caught fire. In 1934 the brilliant young Guy Moll, driving an Alfa as part of the Ferrari works team in the Coppa Acerbo on the beautiful Pescara circuit, was overtaking a silver Auto-Union at 266 kph when he lost control in a gust of wind. Trapped in a ditch for 50 yards, the car smashed into the supporting pillar of a stone bridge before, careering on, it hit the side of a house. Moll, who had already built up a reputation as one of the great drivers of all time, even beating Louis Chiron once on his home turf at Monaco, was killed outright when his flying body hit a concrete post.

Moll had just taken part, during a weekend of blistering heat, in a Pescara event which was regarded as the toughest of all the '24-hour' races, the Targa Abruzzo. This followed the Le Mans pattern in starting with all the drivers running across the track the moment Air Marshal Italo Balbo dropped his flag. Balbo, famously, had an eye for a pretty woman and the newspapers were full of pictures of the celebrated pilot beaming at Hélène, who had brought her new Alfa Monza to Pescara to co-drive it in the Targa Abruzzo with Marcel Mongin. (She had been invited independently and was paid

6,500 francs and 5,000 lire for this appearance; Guy Moll, by comparison, was still driving on a retainer fee of 1,500 lire a month from Ferrari.)

She was out of luck on this occasion; the Alfa's fuel tank came apart during the race and the Mongin–Hellé Nice team was forced to withdraw. This was, nevertheless, one of her most successful years and one in which, despite the emergence of Germany's powerful spaceship-style Auto-Union cars and a futuristic, exquisitely streamlined W25 Mercedes, the Alfas continued to hold their own. Hélène had started the year by joining Odette Siko, one of the best – and sweetest – of her female competitors, for the Paris–Saint-Raphaël rally, driving an Alfa before she headed south to take her car by sea to Morocco. Lehoux was at the docks to see her being decked with garlands of flowers, a tribute which was not extended to the only other woman racing in the Casablanca Grand Prix, Albertine Derancourt. But Hélène, known to be Lehoux's companion and protégée, could expect to enjoy special treatment in his home territory; Derancourt must have seethed on the day of the race when the photographers pushed past her to reach the Ferrari pitstop where Hélène, sporting her usual short sleeves tied up with bows, was sharing a joke with Lehoux and their mutual friend Madame Brunet before sauntering off to climb into the two-tone Alfa Monza which she had nicknamed Bidon, or petrol can. But it was ever so, and Derancourt was not the only driver to detest the blonde girl with the glorious smile who always took the star's role, whatever the quality of her performance.

The King of Morocco was passionate about cars and large sums of money had been spent on improving the Casablanca course; even royalty could not control the weather and a cyclone was predicted for the day of the race. It was not the route or the weather but a humped bridge taken at too great a speed, smashing the rear axle, which knocked Hélène out of the race on this occasion. Her subsequent performances that summer at the Grand

*Hélène's Monza being loaded at Marseille for
the Casablanca Grand Prix.*

Prix of Picardy and at Vichy, in driving rain, were not remarkable, although she was paid good start money to drive in both races; much more impressive was the fact that she was the only woman invited, and paid, to take part that June in the Eifelrennen on the Nürburgring. She failed to complete the German race, but this was a cruelly demanding course, a high and fiercely convoluted route through densely wooded hillscape, allowing the drivers no moment of respite. Many considered it to be the greatest test in Europe of a racing-driver's skills.

The weather improved, at last, when she arrived at Dieppe for the July Grand Prix of 1934, a race which always brought a flood of English drivers across the Channel. Driving in the second of the preliminary heats, she witnessed one of the tragedies which litter the annals of pre-war racing, when her friend Jean Gaupillat, a handsome and kindly middle-aged man with a Légion d'Honneur for military achievements, hit a tree while trying to pass the British driver, Earl Howe. Perhaps in recognition of her friendship with the victim – Gaupillat died of his injuries at the local hospital that day – a rare concession was made and accepted. Having failed to reach the agreed average time in the heat, Hélène was still allowed to participate in the afternoon race; she came 7th in an all-male field which included Louis Chiron, Lehoux, Etancelin and Earl Howe. Racing at Comminges a week later, she was praised by *L'Auto* for having achieved some of the best laps of the day in a car which was relatively underpowered. This, from the chauvinistic *L'Auto*, was high praise.

Hélène with Mme Brunet, second from left, and an unidentified friend at the Casablanca Grand Prix, 1934.

Germany was victorious once more at the Mont Ventoux hill climb in September, when Hans Stuck's Auto-Union took first place. Here, once again, Hélène was the only woman participant, coming 2nd in the sports-car class as she roared up the precipitous bends to set a new women's record. At the Algerian Grand Prix, the last race of the year for her, she came 7th while Jean-Pierre Wimille took the winner's prize in a Bugatti.

'Hellé Nice drove with flawless skill,' the admiring correspondent from *L'Auto* wrote after watching her race in the Picardy Grand Prix at Péronne in the summer of 1935; Anne Itier, meanwhile, was given the cool compliment of having managed to bring a relatively modest car to the finishing line without breaking down. Hélène had achieved her goal. She was now acknowledged as the most professional and competitive of the tiny band of female racers; her start fees escalated again and her former agent, Henri Lartigue, planning to set up a new Grand Prix himself, wrote to suggest that she, with her influence and reputation, might be able to help him. Writing to her on 30 March, Lartigue reproached her for being so continuously engaged on the telephone that he had been reduced to using the mail for his important – and highly confidential – proposals. Her telephone bills were, indeed, enormous, sometimes almost matching the upkeep of her cars. For a woman who liked to have several love affairs on the go at once and hated writing letters, the telephone was no luxury but one of life's most essential ingredients. Her skill at flirting down the wire was legendary. Many a dazed interviewer could testify to that.

In March 1935 Hélène had just arrived back in chilly Paris from a sunny week at Pau near the Pyrenees where she had done well to come 8th against, among others, the brilliant Nuvolari, René Dreyfus and Benoît Falchetto, the driver who, as a young man, had been unlucky enough to be driving the car in which Isadora Duncan was killed. In a fortnight, Hélène would be driving south again, to compete on the steep ascent to La Turbie, a beautiful and ancient village perched high on the Riviera heights above Nice; in the meantime, Lartigue wanted her assistance.

Lartigue had used his own connections to become a successful impresario who provided star performers for cabarets and theatres at Biarritz, where he and his wife, Madeleine, had been living for some years. He was well placed to promote a new Grand Prix; what he wanted Hélène to do was to approach the great drivers of the racing world and persuade them to come to the opening race. Lartigue had a high opinion of his friend's negotiating skills; he also thought she might persuade the Bugatti factory to send their new sports variation of the T57, the sensationally beautiful touring car designed by Jean which had dazzled visitors to the Paris Automobile Show in the autumn of 1933. If she could pull this off, Lartigue told her, he would see that she was well-rewarded.[12]

Hellé Nice was interested, sufficiently so to put forward several practical suggestions as to how the event should be set up; for reasons which are unclear, however, the Biarritz Grand Prix failed to make it to the international calendar of racing events. There may have been a dispute; Hélène could have felt that too much was being asked of her for too little gain. The Lartigues disappeared from her life after the summer of 1935, never to be mentioned again.

The new Alfa served her well at the steep 17-kilometre La Turbie hill climb, where she came 2nd in her class, and at Péronne, where she had the pleasure of beating her nearest rival, Anne Itier, in the Picardy Grand Prix. It was for Biella in northern Italy, however, where she was again the only woman racer, that Hélène would remember the year 1935. The grandstands were crowded, the weather was glorious and she was given a warm welcome by the Duke of Spoleto and Prince of Savoy, the president of the track, who was enthralled to discover that the charming woman he had drunk cocktails with in Monaco was a French racing

Hélène racing at Biella, 1935.

champion. Hélène was quick to tell the papers that she and the Duke were old friends, but it was not on this account that photographs taken at Biella show her suddenly looking about ten years younger than her age – she was thirty-five – and appealingly vulnerable. The giveaway is a publicity shot of her sitting at the wheel of the Alfa. She signed it, with a flourish, to Arnaldo.

Arnaldo Binelli was the Italian-speaking son of a Zürich-based family. Considerably younger than Hélène, he had thick curly dark hair, almond-shaped eyes, a lean body and a manner which charmed all who met him. Lacking any ambition to become a driver, he was in love with speed. He had plans for improving the designs of engines; he had pockets filled with drawings of electric bicycles, power-driven skis, mechanized trailers. He came to Biella to watch the race and to find a backer for his schemes; he left as Hélène's lover. To the other men in her life, she said no more than that she had found and appointed a new mechanic who would be travelling to races with her from now on; neither Marcel Mongin nor Henri Thouvenet appears to have been aware that there was a more intimate side to the relationship, although they may have wondered why she suddenly decided to eschew the free use of Marcel Lehoux's excellent young Algerian mechanic. Her reticence was self-interested: Thouvenet was a prosperous businessman and Mongin, who had now joined the Delahaye factory, was invaluable as a supplier of cars and connections. They were too useful for her to risk the loss of their friendship.

New happiness went hand in hand with good fortune. Racing, again as the only woman, at Barcelona three weeks later, and enjoying a brief flirtation with one of her fellow racers and transport provider, young José de Villapadierna, she was on her fifty-fourth lap when a mechanical problem forced her to retire. At Comminges, she again came in ahead of Anne Itier before taking part in the Côte de Lectoure hill climb in the Pyrenees. Her placing in the second South African Grand Prix at East London, early in January 1936, is not established.* Later that month she had one of her greatest triumphs when she and the fearsomely hardy Russian driver Madame Marinovitch won the Ladies' Cup in the Monte Carlo Rally after driving 4,000 kilometres in deep winter from Tallinn to a rain-drenched Monte Carlo. Only twenty-two competitors had opted for this, the toughest of all the routes – others wound back to Monte Carlo from Athens and Palermo – with only five days allowed for the completion of the run. Praise was given, in particular, to the fact that their powerful Matford Ford had been delivered to them just before the start of the Rally,

---

* It is not certain that she accepted the invitation; no mention is made of her in memoirs of the race, although interviews given to South African papers suggest that she may have travelled there.

allowing for no practice and no alterations to the car. This was the old-fashioned kind of competitive driving Hélène liked best, when expertise, stamina and guts counted for everything. It began with a headlong rush along the glassy roads of Estonia, black ice all the way. Headlights flaring into the mist, the women drove as if possessed, often having to rely on what could be seen by holding the passenger door open and shouting directions to the driver. Sleep was grabbed whenever five minutes could be spared; food was devoured at the wheel. The press shots of their beaming, oil-smirched exhausted faces – all repairs on the journey had to be undertaken by the two of them – show how worth the struggle it had been.

Further success lay ahead, when Hellé Nice came 1st in her class on the difficult La Turbie hill climb; again, the only secrets were skill, determination and her regular practice runs on the twisting, dizzily ascending Riviera roads.

But skill, by 1935, was no guarantee of success on the racing circuits, and her car was out of date. Even at Barcelona, a few rude remarks had been made about the fact that the beautiful Elli Nici was driving a Monza, a car which now had to struggle to find a place against newer, more dynamic models; at the Grand Prix of Pau, her last French race of 1936, she was hopelessly outclassed by the powerful machines which her competitors were driving and was forced to retire after only two laps with engine trouble. Philippe Etancelin won the race.

France, in 1936, remained fearful of taking any action that might provoke her powerful neighbours to retaliate. Reluctantly, she upheld the League of Nations in imposing economic sanctions on Italy, in order to register disapproval of Mussolini's invasion of Abyssinia. Ferment in Spain threatened her from the south; on the east, Hitler's occupation of the Rhineland made headlines in March. Rejecting Poland's offer to join forces and make some aggressive show of strength, France clung to the hope of preserving peace, at whatever cost. To many, invasion by Hitler seemed preferable to war. At home, the new left-wing Prime Minister, Léon Blum, was confronted by increasingly strident demands for better working conditions, more pay, less hours. For the oppressed French workers, including underpaid employees in the car factories, the time for a change was long overdue. Seeking reforms which would improve their own welfare, few workers shared Blum's concern about Germany's increasingly militant stance. It was not their concern.

And yet the warnings were all there; Hélène's favourite new song, 'Madame la Marquise', told of a lady who learns, by slow degrees, that her country estate has been destroyed. Each verse makes the news a little bit worse than the last, until absolute devastation is revealed in the final lines. The French loved the song, seemingly unaware that the Marquise represented their defiant blindness to the dangers which threatened them from every side. When they grumbled, it was about the expense of everything, the pay cuts, the jobs which they saw being snatched from them by a tide of recently dispossessed German-Jewish immigrants.

The clearest of all the warnings came from the heart of the automobile industry. Charles Faroux, the influential editor of *L'Auto*, visited Germany to inspect the Mercedes factories in the spring of 1936. What he saw terrified him. France, he wrote for his paper on 25 April, must make an immediate industrial commitment; it was crucial that the government should provide funds to this end. Even so, he concluded, the time might already have passed; no country could hope now to compete against the sophisticated technology of the Reich. To do so, Faroux estimated, would take a minimum of four years. His column was earnest in tone and eerie in its accuracy, but it made no impact on a troubled and divided government.

Given the state of gloom which prevailed in the car industry, and her eagerness to spend as much time as possible with her handsome young lover, it is not surprising that Hélène was delighted by an invitation★ to spend the summer racing in South America, and being paid for it. At the beginning of June, the Alfa Monza was winched into the hold of the *Augustus*, sailing from Italy, via Boulogne, for Rio de Janeiro. On board were its owner and her lover.

★ The invitation, and the almost royal level of her reception in Brazil, may have had something to do with Hellé Nice's friendship with the distinguished Souza Dantos family. Luis Martinez de Souza Dantos, the Brazilian ambassador in Paris from 1922 to 1940, was listed in her address book and had a reputation for dalliances with French actresses. In later years Souza Dantos saved over 800 lives during the Occupation by providing exit documents, work permits and identity passes.

FALLING

11

1936: 'L'ANNÉE MALHEUREUSE'

'Racing was what she lived for, racing and the sun.'

JANALLA JARNACH
(IN INTERVIEW)

The Year of Bad Luck was how she described it later. But how could she have known that it would be remembered like this, that she would come to curse the day she had accepted the invitation to drive in Brazil?

On board the *Augustus*, sailing west at a leisurely pace, Hélène and Arnaldo Binelli sunned themselves, read, drank and made love; other passengers, seeing how tenderly they photographed each other, must have assumed they had a couple of honeymooners on board, off for a long holiday or to start a new life away from troubled France. It would not have been easy to persuade them that this vivacious, intensely Parisian woman with her scarlet fingernails, high-heeled shoes and fashionably blonde curls was currently regarded as the top woman racing driver in France. Not, that is, until she took off her jacket and they saw her muscular arms, bronzed from years of driving in short sleeves. Questioned, she explained that she was planning to compete in the Rio Grand Prix on the Gavea circuit, one of the most dangerous in the world. Told that South American drivers were ferociously macho, treating the racecourse as a bullfighter would the ring, she must have laughed: nothing new about that to anybody who had survived the war games fought on the dirt tracks of New Jersey.

Arriving at Rio, she heard that President Vargas wished to meet the first Frenchwoman to compete in their Grand Prix and to introduce her to his family. As a sincere admirer of Mussolini's state, he was delighted to know that Mademoiselle Hellé Nice drove an Italian car and had chosen to come out on an Italian ship; there was no need for him to be told that the choice of shipping line had been a strategy to escape registering the car for customs. Wearing her best straw hat and cotton gloves, Hellé Nice was the perfect lady, posing beside the Vargas daughters and complimenting them on their beautiful country as she sipped better coffee than she had ever tasted in Paris. Despite the friendship extended to her by Vargas, it is unlikely that either Hélène or Arnaldo took a close interest in the complicated politics of Brazil in the 1930s. To them, as to most urban Europeans, Brazil was where coffee came from until the Depression damped down demand for Brazil's most valuable commodity. Coffee and rubber exports had been the basis for Brazil's phenomenal rate of expansion in the twenties; now, seeking industrial clout and ways to build up a powerful military force, Vargas found a supporter in Adolf Hitler, another of his heroes. By 1936 Nazi Germany had become Brazil's biggest supplier of the machinery needed to create a military superstate.

France, in 1936, was useless as a supplier of modern technology; her power was in her legend. Many of the Brazilians Hélène met had never left South America, but they had heard of André Breton and Jean Cocteau, studied photographs of Schiaparelli's newest German factory worker-style frocks, watched Henri Garat and Jean Gabin on screen. They spoke of evenings at Ciro's, of Django at the Hot Club, with all the authority of true Parisians. Economically, France was on its knees, but its charm never ceased to fascinate; who could better represent the true France than a blonde-curled former dancer who had known Chevalier and Mistinguett, who lived between Paris and the dazzlingly glamorous Riviera and who raced in France's colours? Brazil adored her and Hélène became conscious of her function as an ambassadress. When she performed on the circuits of other countries, she told reporters, she sought success for herself and glory – la gloire – for France. New blue overalls, chosen to match the sky tint in the two-tone Monza, proclaimed her allegiance.

Letters awaiting her arrival at the Rio Car Club reminded her how wise she had been to take a summer away from France. Her two chief correspondents, Marcel Mongin and Henri Thouvenet, knew each other well. Each was devoted to her; neither knew her real plans, nor the romantic role that Arnaldo Binelli was playing in her life. Mongin wrote in an almost illegible scrawl, sending details of strikes in all the car factories, including Delahaye, for which he had recently become a works driver. You might, studying the well-known photograph of French strikers doing country dances in women's clothes, stripey dresses and petticoats, while they occupied a factory and forced a shut-down, be fooled into thinking they were lighthearted. The fact was, as an apprehensive Mongin told Hélène, that the situation was desperate; Léon Blum, the newly appointed President from the Left, was at his wits' end to know how to appease his supporters. Even Ettore Bugatti's loyal Alsatian team had downed tools and taken over 'le Patron's' Renaissance-style workshops. Word was that Jean Bugatti had been left to reason with them while EB had returned to Paris in a sulk, outraged by such disloyalty. The weather was foul, Mongin wrote; two weeks of incessant rain had lifted only for the Sunday of the French Grand Prix in which Jean-Pierre Wimille had just beaten him to second place. Allusions to visiting Marcel Lehoux's friends, the Brunets – Robert Brunet did a lot of business deals with Mongin – and plans to go to the Marne Grand Prix at Reims with Henri Thouvenet show what a tightly knit circle of friends this was.

The domestic side of Mongin's letters shows him functioning as a surprisingly tame house-husband to Hélène. He sent news of the dogs, Nono and Mimite, and of how well they were being looked after by himself and his sister Nelly; he warned her that the new cleaner at the Rondpoint Mirabeau apartment didn't deserve the title. For a spouse, however, he was a little detached. He mentioned plans for taking a holiday home for the two of them in the Midi, but urged her not to hurry back if she had the chance of getting down to Buenos Aires, where Hispano Suiza had an agency and might have a good offer to make to such a well-known devotee of their cars. Requests for precise details of her race results make him sound more of a manager than a lover; his joking injunctions to her to live it up on her holiday ('Au revoir, mon Poucet, sois sage toi aussi! Reviens en bonne santé et amuse-toi bien.') convey no hint of jealousy.[1]

Henri Thouvenet was more passsionate. 'M'amie chou je pense et j'ai pensé beaucoup à toi,' he wrote, 'et j'ai toujours attendu tes lettres avec une grande impatience.' He had heard that she was due to arrive back on 27 July, docking at Villefranche. How would it be, he asked, if he came and met her off the boat and they spent a couple of weeks together? (He seems to have been unaware that Marcel Mongin was making an almost identical proposal.) Uninformed of the new relationship with Binelli, Thouvenet was evidently aware that their own affair needed some repairwork and he was willing to make the required effort.

> OK M'amie, I admit it. I miss you. Neither of us is exactly perfect but I think I even miss our bust-ups. The bottom line of it is that I love you, M'amie sweetheart, and I think you're fond of me . . . I'm pretty sure of that. Anyway, write and tell me

what you think of our spending some time together [in the Midi, at a house he would rent] because we really haven't made enough time this year, what with the Monte Carlo rally, your holidays at Beaulieu, my work with the elections* and now your trip to Latin America. We might as well be the nightwatchman and the daily cleaner, with the kind of relationship we seem to have got into.[2]

The reluctance of 'M'amie chou' to come clean about her new relationship or even to admit that she was planning to stay on for another month in Brazil becomes more understandable when we see what Henri Thouvenet has to say at the end of his letter. Like Mongin, he evidently believed in mixing business and pleasure; after suggesting that they make more effort to spend time together, he turned to the subject of a new Grand Prix being run in July at Deauville. 'I got you a good offer in start money,' he told her; '4,000 francs. The mayor is quite a friend of Marcel [Mongin's] and mine. Still, that will keep for another year and you'll probably get 5,000 if you stay on to race at São Paulo, and a much better chance of winning a prize; all the big boys are going to be running at Deauville.[3] She might even, he added, use the prize money to get herself a more modern car after three years of driving a second-hand Alfa Monza.

With friends as useful as this to look after her interests, Hélène saw no value in disclosing more than was strictly necessary about Arnaldo. Her letters were carefully vague; to Henri Thouvenet, she

* References in Thouvenet's letters to the elections and to what goes on at meetings between the strike leaders and ministers suggest that he had political connections; a reference to the payment of a libel fine for violating the laws of the press raises the possibility that he was a political journalist. Disgusted comments on the Reds and on strikers taking orders from Moscow show his political colour, as does his tart observation that the only available newspapers have become – of all things – *L'Humanité*, *Le Populaire* and *L'Action Française*. All three papers were radical in outlook, openly endorsing the workers in their rebellion.

said only that she would stay on to compete at São Paulo; to Mongin, she wrote asking if he might be able to give her new mechanic some work with Delahaye when he came back to France. And Mongin, failing to register that Binelli had any significance, said kindly: why not? Arnaldo could work with his own mechanic, Fernand; Mongin would even let the young man handle a few of his own clients.[4]

Hélène, pleased to have taken care of her lover's future, continued to enjoy herself. She and Arnaldo went swimming and dancing together; they hired a couple of horses and went riding in the hills behind Ipanema. The president, charmed by Brazil's most attractive visiting racer, gave a dinner in her honour; Arnaldo, uninvited, stayed behind at the hotel. Possibly, he took it out on her later; Hélène's letters make it clear that he had a violent streak and was capable of being fiercely jealous. This added to his charm

Hélène riding with Arnaldo in Brazil.

for a woman with a temper of her own; years later, she rudely undercut his sexual prowess by nicknaming him 'Mr Three Minutes', but in the summer of 1936 she was under his spell.

Love affairs never undermined her professionalism; in the run-up week for the Rio Grand Prix on 7 June, Hélène was out practising on the circuit every morning. Practice was even more vital than usual; known as 'The Devil's Springboard', the circuit began on cobblestones and tramlines in the hill-town of Gavea before heading down to a narrow strip of road overhanging the sea and back into the mountains in a tortuous series of hairpin bends. It was just the kind of challenge that Hélène most relished; a personal photograph taken just before the race shows, not the camera-conscious star but a professional sportswoman, taking a quick drag on a cigarette and narrowing her eyes as she focuses on the circuit which she has already committed to memory. Here, as in a photograph taken at Biella of her holding out blistered hands

Hélène enjoys a quick drag before taking part in the 1936 Rio de Janeiro Grand Prix on the 'Devil's Trampoline'.

after the race, we can see why admiring reporters often simply said: 'Elle a du cran! (The girl's got guts).'

Most of the South American drivers had arrived with sturdy Ford V8s, the only cars they were able to get, reduced to their metal bones for speed. The V8 referred to the layout of the eight-cylinder engine, the first to be mass-produced. Two Italian drivers, Carlo Pintacuda and Attilio Marinoni, came with stripped-down Alfa sports cars from the Ferrari stable; Vittorio Coppoli, from the Bugatti agency at Buenos Aires, was driving a Bugatti, along with the Brazilian favourite, tall, glamorous Manuel de Teffe. Spectators were everywhere, and seemingly unaware that the start signal required them to keep away from the cars. Photographs taken at the beginning of the Gavea race show no barrier ropes; the drivers, as the Europeans must have realized with some alarm, were expected to take their chances in finding a safe way through.

It seemed to be her lucky year. For the first hours of the race, she held her place at the head of the pack; Vittorio Coppoli won but the crowd were almost as loud in their shouts for the only female competitor, who had driven her old Alfa Monza with such skill and panache on the country's most dangerous circuit. The news that she was to compete at the São Paulo Grand Prix the following month was enthusiastically reported in the local Brazilian press.

The race was to be the biggest in São Paulo's history. At nine in the morning, the broad streets of the city's sophisticated Jardim America district were already crowded with well-dressed *paulistanas* who had come to cheer on their home champion, Manuel de Teffe. Arnaldo Binelli, having helped to check the car, left Hélène chatting with her fellow racers outside the elegant building which housed the city's Car Club while he pushed through the throng towards the finishing line from which he planned to film the event. Above his head, speakers blared warnings to the crowds of pedestrians to keep away from the cars. A few strategically placed straw bales on sharp corners were the only gesture which had been made towards safety; instead, large numbers of policemen lined the sides of the track.

At 9.30 the mayor, visibly sweating in the full uniform he was obliged to wear for the occasion, gave the start signal; Hellé Nice was lying in third place as she roared into the view of Binelli's camera for the first time. By the fifth lap, she had moved up to lie second, with Teffe on her tail. She was in perfect control; Arnaldo told her later that he had never seen her drive so well. Coppoli, the champion of the Gavea circuit, dropped out on the thirteenth lap. Hellé Nice was forced to make a stop when papers blew down from an official's box and glued themselves to the front of the Monza, smothering the radiator grille; a couple of laps later she had regained fourth place. Arnaldo, bracing himself not to be pushed on to the track by the surge of bodies at his back, caught her in a familiar pose, lips parted to suck air like nicotine as she took a tricky corner. On lap fifty, she stopped to refuel, long enough to lose third place to the tall Brazilian; eight laps later, two from the finish, Arnaldo saw with delight that she had caught up again. Pintacuda had already passed the finishing post at record speed and entered Brazilian legend; Marinoni was coming up fast, but Hellé Nice was fighting Manuel de Teffe neck and neck for 2nd place, tearing along the straight avenues, sliding round the corners in a cloud of dust.

Arnaldo had trained his camera on the last straight. All around him, the Brazilians were screaming for de Teffe, their hero; from the corner of his eye, he could see them pushing out, a spill of colour flooding on to the track. What he couldn't see was whether the bale that suddenly appeared in the middle of the track directly ahead of the distant, speeding Monza, had been pushed, or thrown. A policeman broke through the crowd, stooped to lift it. But she wouldn't have time to see the bale, or the policeman. Coming round the corner at 150 kph, all she could possibly see was that de Teffe had left just enough of a space for her to squeeze through and take the lead.

Hélène's crash at São Paulo.

The camera caught her as she hit the bale. A body flew up, cartwheeling through a cloud of dust. The car jerked, spun and flung another body up, high over the screaming crowd, before it smashed into the jostling front line of spectators. They were too tightly packed for flight. They went down like reeds to a scythe.

Afterwards, when they lifted her unconscious body off the corpse of the man who buffered her – his head had been cracked open by the force with which hers had struck it when she was hurled from the car – they laid her out with the dead at the roadside. The first count said that forty people had been killed. Later, it was established that six were already dead and thirty-four more were receiving emergency treatment at the local hospital. It was the worst incident in the history of South American motor racing.[5]

Hélène was among those who had been taken to the Santa Caterina Hospital. Arnaldo, frantic with alarm, was told that she was in a deep coma. The doctors held out little hope that she would recover consciousness before she died.

12

THE ROAD BACK

Excerpts from a letter written by Solange to her sister Hélène
Delangle, 17 July 1936:[1]

My dear Hellé . . .
Well, I don't need to say what a state we were in at Sainte-
Mesme on 13 July. Monsieur Père* woke me at 8 in the
morning, after he got the news from our neighbours on Sunday
night's radio. As the bulletin said you had a fractured skull and
were in a hopeless condition, they decided to give us a night
off . . .

   Now I imagine you must be getting better, but you certainly
had a lucky escape. The accident seems not to have been your
fault, but Henri [Thouvenet] will be discussing that with you as
I don't really understand it. I'm just thankful you don't have to

---

* Jean Bernard, their common-law stepfather.

take responsibility for killing four [*sic*] people and injuring another thirty [*sic*].

Henri gave me supper last night, just for the two of us, and Arnaldo's telegram came while I was there. Pity it was so short. Henri took me home and we had a good gossip along the way. The weather's stifling in Paris. It's past midnight and pouring with rain, thunder rumbling away. It's been like this for a month . . .

Well that's about it, except that I'm fine, although my acne's come back. I'm pleased with the new apartment; two minutes to get to my desk, and that's including the lift.

Love, and get well soon

Your Totote
(10 rue Armand Moisant, Paris XV)

No great interpretative skills are needed to see the unpleasantness of this letter. Her sister had, through no fault of her own, been involved in one of the worst racing incidents of the century; Solange Delangle's response was to complain about the worry it had caused them, to nag her sister about her failure to communicate ('We're glad of good news, but we'd like it from you . . . I hope you're going to write to our mother,' she wrote in another part of this letter), to underline the horror of the death toll and injuries, and to stir up trouble with hints of the 'good gossip' she had enjoyed with Hélène's lover after an intimate dinner with him.

Marcel Mongin was, by contrast, tender and full of concern. 'You can't imagine the joy it gave me to see your own writing on the envelope,' he told Hélène a week later. 'You seem awfully low, but don't be: everybody's thinking of you and feeling so sorry for you. I've sent you some telegrams and you should have had a letter with two little flowers!'[2] The 'deux petites fleurs' seem to have been a present of some kind, possibly some money.

Arnaldo Binelli was too inexperienced to know what to do for the best; the man who took charge of Hélène's affairs at the time was Henri Thouvenet. Still unaware of the non-professional nature of her relationship with Arnaldo, he was touched by a stream of uncharacteristically needy letters in which she begged for reassurances of his love, to know that she was not forgotten, that she would be taken care of if things went wrong. Thouvenet, a man who seems to have had considerable influence, pulled every string in reach to ensure that the Brazilians took appropriate measures. They had, for two days, tried to lay the blame for the accident on her driving; with Thouvenet's help, the French Consulate was brought into play, lawyers were hired, meetings held. Arnaldo's film was produced, offering incontrovertible evidence that excited and unwary spectators had run out on to the track ahead of the Alfa Monza* as they cheered on the home champion, de Teffe. No fault could be found with her driving; now, as Thouvenet lovingly explained in a series of long, carefully worded letters, it was essential that proper compensation should be made. 'Please don't think I'm asking you to attack people who are now being very kind to you,' he wrote:

> But you *must* think of yourself. Your car is your investment, your breadwinner. Now it's wrecked and you have nearly been killed, and it certainly wasn't your fault . . . I don't know when you plan to come back, but, even though I'm longing to see you, don't push yourself. Get your strength back. Think about the compensation owed to you . . . Remember I love you more than you can ever imagine and that I'm hugging you as hard as I can from so far away. I adore you, M'amie.[3]

---

* See Appendix 1 for text of a letter written by Binelli about the accident and its causes to *L'Auto* magazine. The film, a close sequence of shots of the final moments before the accident, and of the crash, survives in the Agostinucci collection.

It is not clear which wellwisher – her sister? – decided that she ought to be informed of another crash, a fatal one; the number of French cuttings about it which are pasted into the Hellé Nice scrap albums show that she was provided with a dossier of material. On 19 July, in the same week as her own terrible accident, Marcel Lehoux had been killed after colliding with another car in the minor Grand Prix held at Deauville, the very race which Thouvenet had been urging her to enter on her return. Just fifty, Lehoux was praised in his obituaries as one of the most respected and courageous drivers of his generation; his loss, they wrote, would be deeply felt by the many racers who had benefited from his readiness to pass on his skills. When the inexperienced young Duke of Grafton burned to death in his newly acquired Bugatti at Limerick the following month and eight spectators were massacred by a swerving Riley at the Irish Tourist Trophy in September – Marcel Mongin narrowly escaped death in a collision during the same race – it became apparent that 1936 was going to be remembered as an unusually black year.

No disaster compared with the awfulness of the accident on the São Paulo course. Few of the thirty-four injured made a complete recovery and six were dead. Hélène herself was in a coma for three days; when consciousness returned, she had lost all memory of the accident. It pleased her, however, to be told that she had been given third place, after one of the leading competitors – Marinoni – was disqualified. 'I would have been first across the finishing line, because the two drivers ahead of me were disqualified,' she noted many years later in her private record of her racing history. The fact that Carlos Pintacuda had won by a full two laps was somehow overlooked.[4]

Sympathy for the injured woman racer was widespread; stacks of letters and cables were delivered to the hospital, many from Brazilians who had been milling in the São Paulo crowds. Arnaldo

Binelli, following Henri Thouvenet's detailed instructions, was able to tell Hélène that a fund had been set up and that, rather gruesomely, miniature models of the wrecked Monza were being sold by subscription to help raise money for her. President Vargas visited the San Caterina hospital with his family and promised the patient that she would be allowed to stay there for as long as was needed, without charge; an invitation to race in the Argentine in September was a further indication that no blame now attached to her.

The invitation was declined; seven weeks after her crash Hélène was still bed-bound at the hospital, weak and in low spirits. Writing a few trembling lines in pencil to thank Henri Thouvenet for all his help, she told him that sleep had become impossible; in her dreams and every waking moment, she was haunted by the thought of the devastation she had caused, and of which she herself now had no recollection. 'Don't be so sad, dearest Mie [*sic*],' Henri Thouvenet pleaded. 'You must stop blaming yourself. Nobody in the French and German papers, or even the Brazilian ones after the first two days, ever said it was your fault. Don't think about it. Try not to be so sad.'[5]

Thouvenet was feeling fairly low himself as he faced the possibility of seeing his car firm at Nancy nationalized by France's new left-wing government.* He wrote to the São Paulo hospital on 21 August, partly to apologize for the fact that the political situation made it impossible for him to come out to Brazil, partly to express relief that adequate compensation had been raised to buy

---

* Henri Thouvenet's references to Nancy lead me to conclude that he was working with the firm formerly known as Lorraine-De Dietrich. The company, as Lorraine, was producing railway cars and military vehicles at Lunéville, close to Nancy, in 1936; since Henri de Courcelles and Marcel Mongin drove a Lorraine-De Dietrich to second place at Le Mans in 1926, this would fit well with the fact that most of Hélène's lovers and friends seem to have had close professional ties.

a new car.* (Arnaldo, meanwhile, had managed to sell the twisted
carcase of the Monza to a São Paulo garage; all machinery was
welcome in an impoverished country, even from a wreck.†)
Mongin, too, wrote comfortingly on 21 August to ask his 'little
Apple' to 'come back quick so I can cheer you up and give you a
hug'. But her sadness was unassailable. A sharp pain in her jaw
provided a daily reminder of the man who had been killed by the
force of her flying body; over the years, she never ceased to refer
to this aspect of the crash, always with a sense of piercing guilt. 'I
killed a poor man with my head, and his death saved my life. I
broke his skull.'[6]

In September, after almost three months in Brazil, Arnaldo Binelli
and a noticeably agitated – 'perturbée' would be the word most
frequently used to describe her from now on – Hélène sailed back
to France on a Hamburg-bound steamer. With them, they took
her compensation payment and a handsome silver trophy plate. In
Brazil, once it was understood that no blame was going to be
attached to their adored Manuel de Teffe for the crash, the French
driver was remembered with sympathy and affection. Several baby
girls who were born in the winter of 1936–7 were named

* A note in the Agostinucci collection, dated 11 August 1936, gives the
compensation sum as 31 contos, 392,000 milreis, equivalent at the time to 23,000
francs. This seems surprisingly modest, especially since a lawyer had been retained
to argue her case. If her Bugatti, second-hand, had cost 40,000 francs, half that
sum would not have gone far towards purchasing a sophisticated racing machine
in 1936. But the sum mentioned may be misleading: many years later, Hélène
Delangle wrote to her friend Madame Janalla Jarnach of having been given five
or six million francs. All that can be confidently established is that the
compensation was sufficient to subsidize her life with Binelli for almost twenty
years. It is possible that the full amount was never officially declared.
† The Monza was bought and successfully raced the following year by a Brazilian,
Benedetto Lopez. Hélène later accused Binelli of having kept the money from this
sale for himself.

'Ellenice' in her honour; money was raised to build a new race circuit for São Paulo and invitations were issued for her to come back and open it. Understandably, perhaps, she decided against doing so.

Temporarily, at least, she had lost her confidence. A friendly invitation arrived in January 1937, asking her to compete in the Algiers Grand Prix in the spring of 1937, together with another minor event. It was declined, even though the letter writer, a flirt who dwelt less on her professional skill than on the joy it would give his fellow sportsmen to see her trim figure ('votre agréable physique'), had offered the services of Lehoux's former mechanic, 'le petit Bidon que vous connaissez', free of charge.[7] Instead, according to one account which appeared in a Parisian newspaper the following year, Hellé Nice simply went to ground on the Riviera, sunning herself and resting until she felt mentally and physically strong enough for rally-driving, and perhaps, for Grands Prix.

A dearth of material during this period makes it difficult to reconstruct a clear picture of Hélène's life. Some of her compensation money was spent on renting a new and even grander house in Beaulieu sur Mer, the Villa des Agaves on the steep boulevard Edward VII, next to the summer home of the Prince of Bourbon, Sicily. The prince, a sportsman who had once worked as a sales rep at the Bugatti showroom in Paris, was friendly, but Arnaldo and Hélène appear to have kept to themselves for much of the time; the photographs taken with her Leica camera leave little doubt that they were happy. Arnaldo, delicate-featured and dark-eyed, appears in shot after shot, playing with dogs, caressing a pet kitten, smiling at her across a sofa, marching purposefully down to the beach, or waving as he bicycles towards her. She had, for the first time in her life, found happiness in an exclusive relationship; at Arnaldo's wish or by her own choice, Marcel Mongin and Henri Thouvenet were ruthlessly and thoroughly

Arnaldo, with pet, at Villa des Agaves, c. 1937.

dropped. A couple of shots of a sour-faced Solange at Beaulieu offer a clue as to who brought the dogs down from the Paris apartment to be reunited with their mistress. Capricious though Hélène could be in her relationships with men, she was unswervingly devoted to her pets.

It must have been a bitter blow, at a time when she was still haunted by the deaths at São Paulo, to learn that she was to be summoned to court for car-smuggling. The first indication that a group of well-known drivers were being investigated had come just before the July race at Deauville in which Marcel Lehoux was killed; in the autumn of 1936, the news broke in the press. 'L'affaire de Menton', as it was generally called, focused on a number of celebrated racing drivers who had been making a suspiciously large number of journeys through the borderpost in a variety of cars. The charge was that they had been acting as transporters for vehicles which were then sold without import duty having been paid. Hélène's passport shows that she visited Italy more than twenty times during the period under investigation. The public were on the drivers' side; nevertheless, Hélène, along with her racing colleagues, Robert Brunet, Philippe Etancelin, Benoît Falchetto and Raymond Sommer, was summoned to court and each of them was found guilty and given a substantial fine, a thousand pounds.* In France, the news temporarily overshadowed the announcement of Edward VIII's enforced abdication and his plans to move himself, his Buick and his mistress – they married the following year – across the Channel.

In January 1937, at the time of the trial, Hélène was feeling too depressed to contemplate even a minor race in Algeria. It speaks volumes for her stamina and resilience that she was ready, only two months later, to contemplate entering some of the most challenging events in the racing calendar. Visiting Italy, she

---

* It is likely that Marcel Lehoux, Hélène's regular companion on many of these journeys, was also on the original list of drivers who were to be charged. Apprehension might have unsettled him and affected his driving in what proved to be his last race. The detailed list of mechanics and contact numbers at the Ferrari works in Italy preserved by Hélène reinforces the likelihood that both she and Lehoux were involved in bringing Alfas from the Ferrari factory into France. Lehoux was employed by Ferrari in his final driving years.

announced her plans in an article written for the popular evening paper, *Gazzetta del Popolo della Sera*. Opening with an account of the hundreds of devoted Brazilians who came from distant villages to visit 'la prima vittima' of the São Paulo acccident during her stay in hospital, she saved her surprise for the end:

> Now I have come to Italy to prepare for the new racing season: the Mille Miglia, the Grand Prix of Turin, Pescara, Monza and Tripoli. I'm especially keen to take part in the XI Mille Miglia, the longest speed-race on open roads in the world. But I always feel at home in your wonderful country. All your finest drivers are my friends, true friends of the best sort.[8]

Teddie Caldwell had been prescient when she wrote that Hélène had racing in her blood. Some might call it foolhardy; this was also a display of uncommon, and superb, courage. Eight months earlier, she had been involved in one of the worst accidents in the history of racing. Now, she proposed to enter the most demanding races which Italy could offer, yet she had no car and, at the time of writing, no invitation to any of the events she so optimistically mentioned. Perhaps, by announcing her availability in this way, she aimed to proclaim her return to health and attract offers from a racing stable such as Ferrari. If this was the case, the ploy failed. No manufacturer wanted to risk engaging a driver who had recently suffered serious head injuries and loss of memory; the risk of calamity and bad publicity was too great. She came back to her home at Beaulieu sur Mer empty-handed and began to plan other ways of staging a triumphant public return to the circuits she loved. An opportunity arose almost immediately, when she was approached by the marketing team for Yacco Oil.

Yacco then, as now, promoted itself as the oil used for demanding driving. Women were always good for publicity and it had become apparent by 1937 that women did better than men as drivers in trials of endurance. Eager to demonstrate that a car using their oil could outrun and outlast all competitive makes, Yacco were recruiting an all-female team to drive at Montlhéry with the aim of breaking as many world records as possible. They were to drive in relays over a period of ten days, without halt. The car they were to drive was a 3.621-litre monster, the first Matford V8 to be produced in France after Ford joined up with Ettore Bugatti's old colleague, Mathis of Alsace: thus Mat-Ford.

It is not clear how the four drivers were selected or whether the Matford received its nickname of 'Claire' from Madame Claire Descollas, a member of the team. Simone des Forest, the youngest, was a tiny and fiercely competitive aristocrat who had already proved herself on the Monte Carlo Rally and in the 1934 Rallye du Maroc, winding back to Casablanca from Rome. Interviewed for this book in 2002, Madame des Forest still found it difficult to withhold her dislike of Hélène Delangle. She had, she remembered, the manners of a film star; everybody was expected to stand around in the shadows while she posed for the camera. Not that she was anything so special to look at. Yes, she drove well, but the obsession she had with men: 'it was ridiculous, the way she went on. Frankly, I don't believe she ever thought about anything but sex and showing off.'[9]

Smoothing over what sounds to have been a difficult relationship were Claire Descollas and the team's famously charming captain, Odette Siko, another Alfa driver to have survived a serious crash when her car skidded off the Le Mans circuit in 1933. Siko had partnered Hélène in the Paris–Saint-Raphaël rally of 1934, and driven with Simone des Forest the following year in the Monte Carlo Rally. She, if anyone, must have been able to keep the peace.

Siding with des Forest and against Hélène was César Marchand, Yacco's highly experienced mechanic. Recalling the Yacco trials forty-two years later, Marchand still remembered the pleasure it gave him, now and again, to make a little slip while pouring oil, just enough to get a good splash of black viscous liquid onto Madame Hellé's over-displayed legs. That, he thought, was the way to treat a woman who was always grinning at cameras, making sure she had the most prominent place in every shot.[10]

It's hard to see how any participant in such an event could have provoked such rancour, for there was nothing glamorous about the Yacco endurance trials. The four women were dressed for warmth, leather jackets tightly belted over heavy woollen checked shirts, thick shooting socks pulled up under sturdy calf-length knickerbockers. Leather wind-caps kept their hair out of their eyes; goggles and a minute strip of glass shield above the wheel would help to prevent them from being struck and possibly blinded by stones. The only safety straps in the car were those which held down the Matford's massive bonnet; the broad leather driving seat was unsprung and hard as a box.

Rivalry was set aside as the drivers shook hands on the morning of 7 May and posed for the press before setting out to meet and perhaps exceed Yacco's high expectations. Odette Siko, as captain, had picked one of the trickiest driving times for herself, sunrise, when low rays dazzled along the Matford's bonnet, making visibility a matter of guesswork; Hélène took the equally treacherous hours of twilight before handing over to the younger and less experienced des Forest. Descollas sweated out the long afternoons. Each driver was expected to stay at the wheel for three hours; the speed was never allowed to drop below 140 kph. This relentless schedule was to continue without a break except for a lightning exchange of drivers, for ten days and ten nights. Marchand's expertise guaranteed that the Matford did not let them down; all the women had to do was drive around the high-banked Montlhéry bowl, and endure.

The authorities have, with one exception, failed to note one singular fact about the Yacco speed trials.[11] The first attempt failed. After three days, Claire Descollas pulled out and the trials were quietly called off. Yacco offered no further sweeteners, but on 19 May the team gallantly set off again in an attempt to make the ten-day record.

Hélène had always spoken candidly to the press about her hatred of the rat-in-a-cage experience of circling speed bowls. The one dramatically angled photograph of her at the wheel of the Matford shows that she was completely at ease and in control; other Montlhéry regulars had seen her training hard at the circuit during the month leading up to the trial. Still, it was just as well that it was Simone des Forest and not she who had the terrifying experience, while doing a trial lap at 180 kph, of seeing a photographer spreadeagled on the cement, his body directly in line with her speeding car. 'If he'd moved one inch,' des Forest remembered later, 'he would have been done for and so would I. I just had to hope he was too scared – and he was.'[12] For a woman whose car had scythed down a huddle of bodies less than a year earlier, the experience would have been traumatic.

By 29 May the exhausted team had notched up no fewer than twenty-six new records. It was an incredible achievement (see Appendix 2). Yacco showed their gratitude with ruby and diamond-brilliants brooches, shaped in the 'V' of the Matford's great engine; Hélène made a present of hers to her last benefactor, who still wears it with pride.[13] The French press hailed the women as champions; news of their success was reported in Britain and the United States but not in Italy or Germany, where foreign triumphs were of little interest. Most of the records achieved during the Yacco trials remain unbroken to this day.

Yacco's triumph came at a time when France was badly in need of a morale boost. Paris was playing host to the World Expo fair and looking glorious, with giant shafts of lights playing over the Eiffel

Yacco certificate recording the ten-day trials.

Tower and transforming the Seine into a river of liquid gold. It was, however, difficult to ignore the fact that the only national pavilions to have been finished on time were produced by Germany, Soviet Russia and, with vigorous support from a communist workforce, Spain. Picasso's passionate response to the atrocity of Guernica a month earlier drew less attention at the time than a megalithic sculpture in steel of two heroic workers holding the hammer and sickle flag high above the Soviet pavilion. 'Hurrying to the Lubyanka' was the disrespectful nickname given to it by cynical Parisians, but there were no jokes about a gigantic marble map of industrial Russia, marking its resource-sites with fabulous jewels. The German pavilion designed by Albert Speer offered a more chilling glimpse of the future; a tower, 170 foot high, was topped by a golden eagle with the emblem of the swastika held in its claws.

This was the symbol which presided over Paris in the summer of 1937. Hélène, looking out from the curving windows of her apartment above Rondpoint Mirabeau, could see it clearly. The bird's brazen wings glowed in the summer light, matching the sheen of her carefully polished row of trophy cups.

How ominous did Speer's pavilion seem in the summer of 1937? Some, like the writer Julien Green, had been conscious for several years of what Green described as an insidious general sense of apprehension.[14] Hitler, having repossessed himself of the Rhineland which flanked France's eastern borders in 1936, was focusing his attention on Austria and the Sudetenland, the German side of Czechoslovakia. French newspapers had started to carry advertisements for gas masks; discussions were held about the best locations for air-raid shelters; warning sirens were demonstrated at the Expo's Pavilion of Passive Defence. For most people, however, the fear of provoking Hitler was far greater than any sense of alarm at his territorial acquisitiveness. The fact that Germany was producing over 300 planes every month to France's modest 45 was reported in the press, but no suggestion was made that France should try to compete. Hitler, it was widely believed, would leave the French in peace so long as nothing was done to attract his attention. Lying very still and very low, France might escape harm. Safety was the great thing, protection from the carnage which had destroyed a whole generation of the country's workforce.

A country's fears do not show up as frightened faces. In the summer before the war, Parisians crowded into the city's cinemas to see Disney's *Snow White* and a comforting cartoon world in which the heroine's principal virtue was her meekness; Jean Renoir's *La Règle du jeu* drew angry catcalls for its attack on a life of lies and compromises and the film was banned as bad for French morale. Maurice Chevalier, meanwhile, drew whistles of approval for his cheerfully anodyne parody of Hitler in song at the Casino de Paris. Hitler himself could have sat in the audience and taken no offence.

Hélène's address book included contact numbers for the German firms of Mercedes and Auto-Union; her sympathy cards after the São Paulo accident included one from a young relation of the German First World War hero, Captain Manfred von Richthofen, resplendent in his air force uniform. She had no feelings of hostility. On the contrary, she was eager to be taken on by one of the German firms which were producing the most powerful cars in Europe. Early in the spring of 1938, she offered her services to Adler as a works driver. Conscious as always of her value as a marketing tool, she enclosed an attractive photograph with her career summary. Adler, however, expressed no interest; they would, the manager crushingly informed her, be relying on drivers who were more familiar with their cars for the challenging Liège–Rome–Liège Rally in which she had expressed a wish to drive.[15]

A possible reason for Hélène's choice of Adler, rather than a French firm, lay in a new friendship.

Post-war events in her life have caused much emphasis to be laid on the fact that Hellé Nice was, in the words of one journalist, 'tempted' back into rally driving in 1938 by 'that suave womanizer and SS member [Huschke] von Hanstein'.[16] In fact, she had already made several vigorous attempts to return to the racing circuit; no further temptation was required. The Hanstein connection does, however, merit consideration. He was, with the exception of Hans von Stuck*, the only German driver with whom she struck up a friendship shortly before the war.

Huschke von Hanstein was, at twenty-seven, a dashing young man whose zest for danger was matched by a flair for publicity which later served him remarkably well as the manager of Porsche. Later photographs show him looking like a cartoon character, with

---

* 'Hans von Stuck von Villiers and Paula' was how Hélène's address book listed the couple, together with their home addresses in Berlin and Potsdam.

a grin of tombstone teeth and outsize glasses; in 1938, however, he was wirily attractive with a string of conquests to his name. Eyebrows are sometimes raised today about the fact that his new BMW 328 Roadster had the number-plate SS-333;* in 1938 the plate would not have been regarded as particularly sinister by French drivers. Hélène's colleague Anne Itier had already driven professionally with Hanstein in 1937 and enjoyed a whirlwind romance after he helped to rescue the car she was driving with Marguerite Mareuse from a desert storm which had submerged their car in sand during the Rallye du Maroc. Shortly after this, Itier was invited to partner Hanstein at Le Mans, where he was driving an Adler.

By 1938, then, Hélène was aware that Adler were using French women drivers. A damaged shoulder had temporarily put Hanstein out of Grand Prix driving, but he was still participating in rallies. He asked Hélène to partner him in a German-made DKW in the Rallye de Chamonix, starting from Beaulieu. What Arnaldo Binelli thought about this is unknown, but Hélène's own record of the race leaves much to be guessed at and little explained. They were, she wrote, penalized after arriving late because they had become lost in the mist ('nous sommes trompés de route à cause du brouillard'). From a woman who had survived crossing Estonia in the depths of winter on roads covered in black ice, the explanation seems limp and unconvincing. Remembering the romance with Itier after her desert storm, one wonders whether Hanstein was playing a variation on a familiar theme.

No letters exist; no allusion is made to Hélène in the memoirs written by Hanstein's wife, although she had some acid comments

---

* The car was raced as part of the motorized section of the SS; Hanstein felt no shame about driving with the SS insignia on his uniform in the 1940 Mille Miglia; he did so, he later explained in his autobiography, in order to encourage his team.

to make about Itier. The only reference which has survived to connect Hanstein to Hélène Delangle is a single record, made in her own schedule notes, of the Chamonix Rally. Despite the puzzle of how they got lost on roads she knew so well, it does not add up to much; the address book which Hélène kept up to date until the war does not even mention Hanstein's name. Perhaps, in seeking explanations for the misfortunes which overtook Hellé Nice after the war, Hanstein's name has been given misleading prominence. No harm ever came to Anne Itier in France through her own well-known romantic connection with him, a year earlier.

Huschke von Hanstein

It was Itier, the following summer, who enabled her friend to prove that she had lost none of her racing skills. Itier had always been interested in promoting single-sex racing for women; pragmatically, she may have accepted that this was the only way in which women racers might hope to make their mark. In 1939, she began, through the Union Sportive Automobiliste (USA), which she helped to set up, to negotiate for a series of all-female races which would take place on the same day as a Grand Prix. Itier then approached Renault and argued that it was in their interest to sell their cars into the female market by running them in these races. The idea was not new; Hélène had competed in a similar competition for Peugeot 301s in 1933.

Renault, who had recently produced a cost-conscious but sporty car called the Juvaquatre – the first to have a single-shell body – were enthusiastic. On 11 June, on the same day as the Picardy Grand Prix, Hélène was one of ten entrants for the morning race of ten sturdy Juvaquatre Renault saloons. It was a family car, not intended to be driven at fierce speed in bad conditions; the circuit of Péronne, north of Paris, was awash with rain that day, while a driving wind kept the spectators huddled under the limited protection offered by a modest grandstand. Hélène must have been delighted; this was her first competitive event since the accident and she was only just beaten to first place by a younger driver, Yvonne Simon, over a 68-kilometre course. The near-win was a spur: two months later, she drove south-west to Saint-Gaudens and the familiar tricks and trials of the mountain-encircled course of Comminges. She had always loved a good audience; she had her wish here, perhaps because there was some hint in the air that trouble was ahead and that the convivial, raffish noisy days of the old-fashioned French race meeting were coming to a close. For whatever reason, it was as hard to find a standing-spot with a view of the Comminges track on 6 August as to find a reader that summer who had not borrowed or bought *Gone with the Wind*, the summer's international bestseller.

'Le Critérium Automobile Féminine', as it was grandly named, took place during the morning of the perfect summer day, bright, windless and warm. The spectators, ready to enjoy themselves, cheered as the best women drivers in France climbed into the neat row of unspectacular Juvaquatres and revved them in preparation for the starting signal. Simone des Forest, Madame Marinovitch and Itier herself were Hélène's most serious challengers for the prize; in the closed cars, they were identifiable only by the numbers.

It was her day; by the end of the first few laps, there was no doubt that she was going to be the winner. Charles Faroux, writing for *L'Auto*, remembered how he had admired her handling of this notoriously difficult course in earlier years. Now, he watched how boldly she handled the hardest sections, where the road twisted steeply downhill, gaining herself another five-second advantage on each lap. Her control was, he wrote, outstanding, as was her ability to keep up an average of 90 kph in a family saloon. In all, Faroux felt ready to honour Hellé Nice as the fastest and the most technically skilled woman driver of her times. Neither he nor she could have known it, but this was the glowing tribute which would crown and close her professional racing career.[17]

The day was hers, but she had always looked down on all-female events as less of a challenge. There must have been a moment of wistfulness as she watched her friend Jean-Pierre Wimille, remembered now as one of the great drivers of their time, take second place in the afternoon Grand Prix at Comminges. He, more loyal to the make than she, was driving a Bugatti. They spoke to each other after the race. Wimille had just been in England with Jean Bugatti, visiting the new premises of the Bugatti Owners' Club at Prescott, in Gloucestershire; he must have shared Jean's dismay at the news which reached them from Paris. The bank with which the Bugatti family had always dealt had decided, after a panicky year, to extend no further credit. Bankruptcy could only be staved off by taking part of the company out of the receiver's long grasp. With Jean's agreement, Ettore Bugatti went to Belgium to arrange with his friend King Leopold for the setting-up of a new factory at Antwerp.

Hearing the gossip at Comminges, Hélène hugged Wimille, bringing a smile to his austere features, as she wished him good luck for his next race, on the sand track of La Baule. It is unlikely that she or even Wimille himself knew how closely Jean Bugatti had involved himself in preparing the car the driver was to use.

Jean had always loved speed: late in the evening of 11 August, two days before the La Baule race, he decided to give the car, a 57C tank model, a final run on the long straight stretch between Molsheim and Strasbourg. Mechanics had been placed on guard at the side turnings to make sure that the route was kept clear. Still, at ten at night, Jean felt safe to assume that he would have the road to himself. He let the heavy supercharged machine out to its full speed, 235 kph.

Sometime shortly before midnight, Ettore Bugatti was called to the telephone at Laeken, the palace belonging to King Leopold. He was told that a cyclist had pedalled off a sideroad and into the path of the Bugatti. The bonnet, swerving, caught him at an angle and tossed him clear, although with broken wrists. The car, out of control, swung left, smashed into two trees, lurched right, hit another tree, and split in half. When they found Jean's body, his hands still gripped the wheel.[18]

For Ettore, roaring through the night towards Molsheim in his great Royale, the sense of bewilderment and loss was devastating. All his efforts to keep Jean from racing, to protect his life, had come to nothing. He had lost his oldest son and with him, the company's brightest hope for the future. Jean, since 1933, had been in charge of the factory and, although Ettore had sometimes been unwilling to acknowledge it in the past, producing designs as innovative and visually ravishing as his own.

On 26 August, King Leopold agreed to the immediate mobilization of Belgium's troops to protect his country from invasion; it was tactfully indicated to Ettore that he, as an Italian national, at a time when Italy was supporting Germany, could no longer expect to be provided with factory space at Antwerp. Dazed by Jean's death, Bugatti accepted his friend's decision.

Three weeks later Hitler's armed forces invaded Poland. Under instruction from the War Ministry, Ettore Bugatti began to arrange the transfer of all machinery from the threatened province of Alsace west to Bordeaux; here he was to undertake making crankshafts for Hispano-Suiza V-12 aircraft engines.

A million Frenchmen were mobilized and sent east to defend the Maginot Line; Arnaldo Binelli, as a Swiss national, was not at risk of being conscripted. Perhaps both he and Hélène were among the optimists who still believed that appeasement would save France from Hitler's attention. Perhaps, as apprehension sent the Riviera into a decline, with shops closing every week and the abrupt cancellation of the first Cannes Film Festival, the couple were simply bored, pining for the vitality of the city. Life was desolate on the hillside above Beaulieu sur Mer when many of their neighbours had closed up their houses for the winter and when the weather grew too severe for their daily bicycle rides and strolls on the deserted shore.

For whatever reason, in the icy January of 1940, Hélène and Arnaldo packed most of their possessions from the Villa des Agaves on to a trailer, hitched it to the back of Hélène's great Hispano-Suiza, and headed north for Paris. They were there, five months later, when Hitler's troops marched into the city.

13

AND WHAT DID YOU DO DURING THE WAR, MADEMOISELLE?

Ami, entends-tu le vol noir des corbeaux* dans la plaine?
Ami, entends-tu le bruit sourd d'un pays qu'on enchaîne?

MAURICE DRUON

Pusillanimous though Marshal Pétain's pursuit of an armistice seemed in the terrible June of 1940, there was no realistic alternative. The army, gallantly attempting to defend the heart of France after its retreat from Paris, could never have withstood the devastating efficiency of Germany's blitzkrieg attacks, a form of warfare for which the armed forces had been completely unprepared. Almost a hundred thousand lives, both military and civilian, had already been lost; occupation, so long as the rules were obeyed, offered no further immediate threats.

For the prudent northerners who had already packed their bags and moved southwards, the zone governed by Pétain and his subordinate Pierre Laval from Vichy offered a substantial if morally threadbare umbrella. For the remaining 25 million who now found

---

* *Corbeaux*, or ravens, was a term which came into use for German soldiers in France during the war.

themselves prisoners in a gigantic German state, which was being subsidized by France to the tune, by 1942, of a staggering 500 million francs a day, there might seem to have been only two options, to collaborate or to resist. Between these dramatic alternatives, however, lay a muddy and uncharted land of compromise; few were able to refrain from making some concessions in order to survive as food and fuel became scarce, and transport almost impossible.

In Paris, the swastika-emblazoned flag of the occupiers hung above eerily quiet streets. The most familiar sounds of the city by 1941 were those of Hélène's country childhood, the whirr of bicycle wheels and the clatter of wooden-soled shoes (leather had been requisitioned for German use). Each morning, with the precise steps of mechanical dolls, the troops of the occupiers marched along the Champs-Elysées towards L'Etoile. Every day, the press and the wireless projected the same triumphant message: the war had already been won here in France. For the rest of Europe, it was only a matter of time.

For Ettore Bugatti, a blossoming love affair with a beautiful young fashion model, Geneviève Delcuze, brought consolation, but he had lost his brilliant heir and was bitterly conscious that he himself had been the chief bar to his son's happiness. Among the papers opened after Jean's death was a love letter to the Mexican dancer Reva Reyes which he had written in 1938, after Ettore had successfully opposed their marriage plans. The letter disclosed Jean's arrangements to make Reva, together with his siblings, his principal heir.

Death on the eve of the German invasion spared Carlo Bugatti, the patriarch of this extraordinary family, from the humiliation which now faced his son. The newly established factory at Bordeaux was swiftly placed under German control and was, as such, bombed by the RAF in November 1940. At Molsheim, Ettore was obliged to accept a compulsory purchase of the Bugatti workshops by the German firm of Trippelwerke, a manufacturer of torpedoes for use by submarines. The splendid Molsheim chateau and the little Hostellerie du Pur Sang were abandoned, while the winter garden, which had housed some of Rembrandt Bugatti's finest bronzes, fell into ruins.

W. F. Bradley published the first biography of Ettore shortly after the war, in 1948. Having met the car designer at a time when he was a devoted husband, Bradley chose not to reveal that Bugatti, when he returned to Paris in the late autumn of 1940, had left his ailing wife and eighteen-year-old son, Roland, at a house near Bordeaux while he began a new life with Geneviève Delcuze. Neither did Bradley choose to say more about the Molsheim works than that Ettore had left them at the recommendation of the Air Ministry and had subsequently been forced to sell to the occupiers. In fact, Ettore, viewed as a natural ally by Germany because of his Italian birth, had been paid the considerable sum of 150 million francs, enough to recoup what he had lost in acquiring the gigantic Château d'Ermenonville north of Paris shortly before the war, and to finance the production of new designs being produced by his trimmed-down works team in Paris.[1] There had been a time when Ettore had contemplated turning his new chateau into a base for the factory; now, serving as a hostel for Russian refugees during the war years, Ermenonville also became a safe hiding-place for the vast collection of antique carriages formerly kept at Molsheim, and for Ettore's Bugatti Royale. However well-disposed the Germans might have been towards an Italian-born car-maker, it is unlikely that they would have allowed him to keep such a princely car for his personal use. Sacha Guitry, it is true, managed to hang on to his Hispano-Suiza, but Guitry was willing to do almost anything, short of treachery, to keep in with the Germans.

Ettore, while he was ready to make use of some valuable connections to protect Lébé, his older daughter, from being sent to work for the occupiers in Germany, was no collaborator. He was fully aware that, between 1943 and 1944, several members of his staff and three of his best drivers were working actively for the Resistance. Bradley, drawing on private information given to him by the Bugatti family and staff, stated that Ettore provided them with a meeting place at his first wartime home on Avenue Hoche, and that he provided forged passes and identity cards. These, in the years when a man could be shot for entering the unoccupied zone without an *Ausweis*, or official pass, were invaluable to the men who were ready to risk their lives in Resistance work.

Robert Benoist, the man who finally led the operations in which the Bugatti workforce were most closely involved, was forty-six when the Occupation began. 'He had the most striking face,' wrote another former Bugatti works driver, René Dreyfus, 'the profile of an eagle, with sharp features, piercing eyes. Through his face, you could see something beautiful, his honesty, his nobility, his class. He was a true chevalier.'[2]

Benoist was serving as an armaments officer when the Germans entered Paris, having been refused permission to fly – he had been an outstanding airman in the 1914–18 war – because of his age. He was at Le Bourget airfield, away from his unit, when news came through that Paris had fallen. Struggling to find a way through the fleeing and terrified crowds, Benoist was arrested by an armed convoy moving towards the south-west. Using his professional skills, the prisoner waited for an opportune moment to swerve away from his captors and into a minor road before putting his foot down on the throttle of his sports Bugatti and driving at full tilt through the abandoned country lanes. Reaching an isolated farm which belonged to a friend, Benoist hid his own car and borrowed an old machine in which to rejoin his unit. Subsequent events show that he was contacted by a fellow Bugatti driver, Charles Grover ('Williams'), who had rejoined the British Army at the outbreak of war to drive for the Signal Corps.

A bilingual upbringing and his knowledge of France made Grover a natural choice for the Special Operations Executive (SOE), who trained their men in many different skills, including industrial sabotage, before providing them with detailed missions and dropping them back into France. On 31 May 1942 Grover was parachuted into occupied territory near Le Mans – a familiar landscape to a racing driver – with orders to form a new Resistance network under the codename Operation Chestnut. Making his way to Paris, he linked up with his fellow Bugatti drivers Benoist and Jean-Pierre Wimille. Use was made of Ettore's offices as a cover while the three men began the sensitive task of recruitment; their own wives were among the first to join. A young radio operator reached them from England in March the following year; over the next three months Operation Chestnut built up an impressive supply of arms and equipment at Benoist's secluded family chateau in the forest of Rambouillet, just south-west of Paris.

The occupiers had, in 1940, seemed friendly and eager to be accepted. 'Ils sont corrects' was the grudging catchphrase of the first few months as the German soldiers offered their respects to the tomb of the unknown soldier, paid their bills and obeyed their own orders to be off Paris's darkened streets at the curfew hour. By 1941, however, the mood had hardened; the assassination in October of a German officer at Nantes, where Hélène had once played at leading her Roman troops in a Lenten fête, was swiftly countered by the execution of twenty-two hostages, followed by the killing of fifty more at Bordeaux. The first acts of armed subversion by the Resistance were followed by the arbitrary arrest that December of 700 Jewish Parisians and the execution of a further group of hostages at Mont-Valérien, not far from the city. The following year, 1942, mass deportation commenced; in June 13,000 Jewish Parisians, including a large number of women and 4,000 children, were rounded up and held like cattle before being deported. The transit camp where they were held was the indoor Vélodrome d'Hiver, the popular sports centre where Hemingway had cheered on six-day cyclists in the twenties. In Vichy, meanwhile, 40,000 more victims were handed over to the enemy. Later, it was discovered that René Bousquet, head of the Vichy police, had been in charge of arresting the families confined at the Vélodrome d'Hiver, where many died of exhaustion and dehydration before they could be put on the trains.

In 1943 growing fears of an Allied invasion led to an intensive German crackdown on the Resistance. In June, seven networks were infiltrated; among them was Operation Chestnut. At the end of July, their radio operator was captured and tortured until he revealed the least incriminating name, that of Robert Benoist's brother. Maurice Benoist, unfortunately, knew enough to disclose the site of the hidden arms cache to the Nazi Security Service: it is not clear whether it was the German police or the equally brutal French *Milice* who promptly made their way to the Benoist chateau at Auffargis, where they arrested Charles Grover. Imprisoned and then transported, he is thought to have been executed at Sachsenhausen in March 1945, although one writer suggested that he was able to buy his freedom and to continue working undercover for MI6.[3] (The fact that a parcel of his clothes was despatched to his brother in England in March 1945 from Sachsenhausen suggests that this was not the case.)

Robert Benoist, captured in Paris three days after Grover's arrest, made a hair-raising escape, first from a German car and then from a friend's house on Avenue Hoche – it may well have been the Bugatti residence – by climbing out and over a roof. Rescued by a British RAF plane and taken to England, he was back in France in the autumn of 1943 and at work with Jean-Pierre Wimille on a new sabotage mission called Operation Clergyman. The objectives this time were the destruction of two large electricity pylons at Ile Héron above the Loire, the destabilization of a railway line used by German troops and the preparation of an effective interference group ready for D-Day in the Nantes area.

The danger to a Resistance fighter of being caught cannot be overstated. A radio operator was the only means of communication by which coded plans could be made to receive arms and ammunition for the sabotage operations, but the Germans had become increasingly successful in capturing the radio operators and issuing misleading signals. If the message was successfully transmitted, there still remained the problem of the drop itself. The location was indicated by the flashing of an agreed morse letter with torches, but it was always possible that the torches would be seen by the enemy and the drops still had to be transported to a safe place and hidden before daylight. M. R. D. Foot, in his exemplary study of the SOE's work in France, has noted that Benoist was able, in a single night and with the help of only two men, to receive and conceal seventeen heavy containers. He was also, by virtue of his courage and his remarkable qualities as a leader, able to rally some two thousand Resistance fighters from his own area in the Rambouillet forest and to begin preparing them for action.[4] Sainte-Mesme was nearby; it would be pleasing to think that Hélène Delangle's brother Henri was one of Benoist's intrepid followers.

Benoist had made many remarkable escapes; in June 1944 his luck ran out. Arrested while visiting his dying mother, he was taken to the notorious prison at Fresnes on the outskirts of Paris. Ettore Bugatti's secretary, Stella Tayssedre, and her husband, were taken at the same time, but the police were convinced that many more were involved in the conspiracy. Tortured, Benoist refused to yield more than his own name (he was identified in his papers as 'Daniel Perdridge' with the field name 'Lionel'). 'Never confess', he scratched defiantly on the wall of his cell at Fresnes, and added his true initials for identification.[5] Stella Tayssedre was five months' pregnant when she was rescued on the verge of transportation by a group of Red Cross workers at Compiègne station north of Paris. Her husband, together with Benoist, was transported to Germany. On 6 September thirty-six officers, including Robert Benoist, were hanged with piano wire in an underground cell at Buchenwald. The type of wire used suggests a grim joke; radio operators working with the Resistance were always referred to as 'pianists' in SOE directives.

The quiet and deeply religious Jean-Pierre Wimille had been more fortunate. In the summer of 1944 he had been arrested with his wife, the former ski champion Cri-Cri de la Fressange, at one of Benoist's family homes, together with Denise Bloch, the 'pianist' for Operation Clergyman. While his wife and Bloch were being held, Wimille escaped by dodging between cars parked in the driveway and out to a stream where, by submerging himself and breathing through a straw, he held out until the search had been abandoned. Denise Bloch was eventually executed at Ravensbrück; Madame Wimille made a last-minute escape from deportation when a cousin, who was at the Gare de l'Est with a Red Cross van, lent her a white coat and smuggled her out as one of the medical charity's workforce. She was at the Bois de Boulogne, on 9 September 1945, to see her husband triumph in the race they had just named the Coupe des Prisonniers, and to watch Ettore Bugatti arrive in the great Bugatti Royale he had retrieved from its hiding-place at Ermenonville. This was a day for honouring heroes; the first race of the day was named the Coupe Robert Benoist.

Not all racing drivers behaved so courageously. Louis Chiron spent his war years in neutral Switzerland with his friend Rudi Caracciola and with Alice Hoffman, the clever and strongwilled woman they had once shared and whom Caracciola had married in 1937. Another Bugatti driver, René Dreyfus, was safely in America when Germany invaded France. Dreyfus was a courageous man who had signed up in the autumn of 1939 to help defend the Maginot Line;

Delahaye's generous American patron, Lucy Schell, may have been instrumental in saving his life. The name Dreyfus was evidently Jewish, and René had rashly neglected to toast his German hosts or their country on his last racing visit to the Nürburgring in 1939. It seems likely that Lucy Schell was concerned for his safety when she insisted that he should be chosen to represent Delahaye at Indianapolis in 1940; Dreyfus remained in America throughout the war and and went on to become, with his brother, the owner-manager of a successful New York restaurant.

Among the women, Anne Itier did voluntary work for the Ministry of War while the younger Simone des Forest drove lorries for the Red Cross in the Vichy-governed area where she had grown up, and where she still lives. Violette Morris was not so virtuous.

The Amazonian woman who had competed against Hellé Nice at Montlhéry in the early thirties had supported the Nazi Party since her invitation to the 1936 Olympic Games at Berlin. Shortly afterwards, she became a secret agent, supplying detailed plans of the Maginot Line defences, together with other pieces of valuable military information. Back in Paris during the occupation, Morris was given the job of infiltrating Resistance networks;* her success rate made her elimination a priority for the French section of the SOE. Despite the fact that her home, a barge docked on the Point du Jour quay, was well-known, Morris managed to evade capture until 1944. On 26 April she was driving a long-bodied black Citroën of the kind always used by gangsters and Germans in 1940s films, when five Resistance fighters stopped the vehicle and opened fire. She died at the wheel, shot to shreds by sub-machine-gun fire. Not surprisingly, Morris's name seldom features in French histories of the early women racing drivers.

* Morris also allegedly worked as a torturer at the Gestapo headquarters on Avenue Foch.

And what, meanwhile, of Hellé Nice? 'I have never been in any trouble, civil or military,' she said in her own defence after the war. Did she want to convey only that she had escaped accusation? It is not necessary to imagine that she betrayed some Jewish neighbours or that she became a spy; her collaboration, if she was guilty of it, might only have taken the pragmatic form of being on good terms with the occupiers. She liked enjoying herself; it is not necessary to suppose that she would have turned down an invitation because it came from a German.

She would not have been alone. 'Whatever their outlook, during these years, the French have all more or less been to bed with Germany, and whatever quarrels there were, the memory is sweet', was the brazen declaration made by Robert Brasillach, wartime editor of the repellently anti-Semitic and pro-German *Je Suis Partout*.[6] The journal was renamed *Je Chie Partout* (I shit everywhere) by patriots during the Occupation and, derisively, *Je Suis Parti* when it vanished from sight after the Liberation. Brasillach was executed as a collaborator in 1945. Yet there may have been a grain of truth in his assertion. In the early years of the war, many people believed that Hitler was going to win; in Paris, it seemed an appalling certainty.

The presence of the occupiers in Paris was impossible to miss. Over a thousand Germans were helping to supervise the occupied zone from their headquarters at the Hotel Majestic on Avenue Kléber. The police had moved into the Claridge on the Champs-Elysées, the Gestapo were carrying out nocturnal interrogations at 74 Avenue Foch and 11 rue de Saussaies, while the deeply unpleasant Sicherheitsdienst (SD) were established at the Crillon. Every day the soldiers' march along the Champs-Elysées became more of an affront. The commendation: 'Ils sont corrects' had changed to a bitter 'ils nous prennent tout' in 1941 when it became apparent that Hitler's plans for France reached no further than its exploitation. Everything of value was reserved for German use, while the French were left to manage as well as they could. 'Le système D', which became part of the language, translates as 'getting by'. Le système D, by 1941, was the only way to survive.

Photographs of the lengthy queues for increasingly meagre rations show scrawny women, bare-legged, their skirts cut short for cycling, their unkempt hair valiantly hidden under turbans, their faces haggard with anxiety. Civilians who did not fraternize with the Germans or have access to goods through the booming black market were starving. A walk in one of the city's gardens was often undertaken with the hope of braining an unwary pigeon; posters warned that it was unhealthy to eat stewed cat. The fortunate, with kind relations in the country, depended on the food parcels of which 300,000 reached Paris in 1941. The enterprising bred rabbits in their cellars to enliven a stomach-knotting diet of beans, swedes, tiny lumps of fatless cheese and, for a treat, grey, gelatinous sausages. In years when an egg was a magnificent luxury, food was increasingly associated with the idea of power. The Germans alone had regular access to good food in Paris; while their hosts starved, they ate like victors.

Freezing weather provided some of the harshest memories for those who lived in Paris during the Occupation. The winter of 1940 was bitter; the winter of 1941 was worse. Hélène Delangle, like her sister Solange, suffered from poor circulation: she could have been among the many who, threadbare coats padded with newspaper to keep out the cold, roamed the windy streets in a ceaseless hunt for treasures to lay in the grate: chestnuts, twigs, a sheet of cardboard, or, if they were lucky, a piece of broken furniture. She and Arnaldo might have joined the scavengers of suburban ditches, uprooting clumps of grass to use as tobacco for cigarettes. It is likely that they made slow, humiliating journeys to Sainte-Mesme each month to beg for anything that could be offered, a loaf of bread, a precious lump of butter wrapped in paper.

It was not the only way in which the Occupation could be survived. Life could seem almost normal in occupied Paris, if you were willing to put your conscience to sleep or to be – it was a much-used word – *realistic* about the situation. Officially, the Parisian evening ended soon after dusk. Street-lamps heavily veiled in navy cloth gave the city the haunted air of a Picasso painting from the blue period. The Métro signs gleamed dimly; in the back streets, where every window was tightly shuttered in obedience to the regulations, the darkness of the blackout hours was profound and eerie. Yet Colette wrote of her friend Georges Auric, a member of the group of composers known as *Les Six*, that he had been out drinking and dancing at two in the morning with a German officer friend and the Vicomtesse de Noailles when his leg was crushed: 'nightclub,' she noted cryptically, 'two in the morning, champagne, accident'.[7] Maxim's and Le Tour d'Argent were crowded every night of the week during the war and not all of the tables were occupied by men in grey uniforms, although officially non-Germans were always placed in a discreet side-passage. French audiences as well as Germans turned out to watch an ageless Mistinguett sing and dance at the Casino de Paris; a blind eye was turned to the fact that Django Reinhardt had gypsy blood and performed long after curfew hour at the Hot Club.

This was the brighter aspect of life; there were blacker tales. The sign on the door of the Casino de Paris instructed all Jews and dogs to keep out. Philippe de Rothschild's beautiful wife, Lili, prudently reverting to her maiden name of the Comtesse de Chambure, lived on good terms with the occupiers until, in the month of the Normandy landings, she refused to sit next to the German ambassador's wife, Frau Abetz, at a dinner-party. The order for her arrest went out that week. Philippine, her ten-year-old daughter, was smuggled away by a resourceful grandfather; the Countess was taken from the Gestapo headquarters to a Paris prison and then to Fresnes, before being deported to Ravensbrück. A female friend who had been a Resistance fighter was at Ravensbrück with her and survived to report that Countess Lili had been beaten, tortured and was still alive when she was thrown into the oven.[8] Philippe de Rothschild himself, after serving eight months' imprisonment in Morocco, and then at Clermont-Ferrand, had escaped to Spain before joining his brother James under de Gaulle's command in England. He arrived home in the Normandy landings. Later, after hearing of his wife's death, he volunteered to join the delegation investigating Belsen and the children's camp at Hamburg-Neuengamme. His own twelve-year-old cousin proved to be one of the children brought here for use in medical experiments and then hanged.[9]

Such dark stories did not come near Hélène Delangle. Or, if they did, she chose to obliterate them. We can try to imagine her sharing the discomfort of the majority of civilians in Paris; we can guess that an instinct for survival allowed her to make some useful compromises. A woman whose career had been an exotic mix of dancing and racing would not have escaped some flattering attention and invitations. She may not have turned them all down.

Guesses are all that can be made since every scrap of evidence concerning Hélène Delangle's life in occupied Paris has disappeared; no allusion to the war survives among her papers, perhaps for good reason. All that is known is that Arnaldo Binelli was able to continue the development of his ideas for making an improved form of bicycle mechanism and to employ a patent attorney's help to take out three separate patents, registered in Paris, between 1941 and July 1943. This would not have been cheap and Binelli, estranged from his Swiss parents, was dependent on Hélène to pay for his enterprises. Her passion for the handsome young man had not lessened; there was nothing she would not spend to keep him with her. His schemes might even have seemed a shrewd investment when bicycles and vélo-taxis had become the only mode of transport for non-Germans in Paris. Taxis only returned to the city, and at a rate which put them outside most citizens' reach, in 1946.

Hélène's identity card for 1941 provides a few more clues. The photograph, taken in semi-profile, shows that she had kept her good looks. The years of driving have left no mark on the pretty and for once, rather pensive face; her hair, still expensively bleached to the pale blonde she claimed to be her natural colour, is drawn back behind her ears. The *préfet de police* has, however, firmly revised her age; her claim to have been born in 1905 has been corrected to 1900. The address, 1 Avenue Jeanne d'Arc, Arcueil, shows a considerable drop in living standards from the elegant apartment above Rondpoint Mirabeau; here, Arnaldo and Hélène were living out in the suburbs, south of the city.* A collaborator might, without too much difficulty, have retained the handsome apartment above the Seine; in Arcueil, it would have been easier to maintain a low profile. They were nearer to Sainte-Mesme, a source of food in hungry times. A few small bistros had survived in the Arcueil area; keeping themselves and their customers on Le système D, they provided a threadbare illusion of life as it had been.

A more striking detail emerges in 1943. That autumn, Hélène and Arnaldo travelled south to Nice.† There, they settled into a newly built villa of some considerable splendour. The Villa des Pins, on avenue Jean de la Fontaine, is a film star-style home, hidden behind tall gates at the end of a secluded drive. The road up to it, exhilarating to a practised hill-climb driver, is an ascending spiral of fast corkscrew bends which allows for no pause. Beyond the gates, a terrace projects from the cliffside. The city spreads out below; at dusk, the line of the Riviera coast road uncoils a necklace of lights beside the sea.

* The only previous connection to Arcueil is that this was where Hélène had maintained her Hispano-Suiza, at the Heigel Garage.
† This was made possible for the first time as Germany occupied the Riviera and did away with the restrictions on travel between occupied and unoccupied zones.

*Hélène's wartime identity card, showing that she failed to get away
with taking five years off her age.*

The villa, with its large light rooms and glorious views, was magnificent, but Nice itself was not a pleasant place for a patriotic Frenchwoman to make a new home in the autumn of 1943, however great her hunger for warmth might have been after the bone-chilling winters of Paris during the Occupation. The fact that Hélène was able to acquire such a luxurious abode there, at this time, raises questions she might not have been eager to answer.

The Italian occupation of Nice, which began in November 1942, had been relatively benign; until September 1943 the city offered a friendly haven to Jewish refugees, despite the strenuous efforts of SS Hauptsturmführer Dannecker, the assiduous chief of the Gestapo's Jewish office in France. Thanks to Dannecker's visit to the town in July 1942, however, two streets with Jewish names had been renamed and a handful of Jewish businesses were closed down; in August 1942 some immigrant Jews were identified in Nice and sent to Drancy, the half-finished housing estate outside Paris which served as a holding station for Auschwitz victims. Ugly though these events were, they were rare and extremely unpopular with citizens; more typical of Nice under Italian control was the fact that a French attempt to attack a synagogue in the town was quelled by the carabinieri.

In September 1943 all of this changed as Germany took possession of Nice and began preparations for defending it against an anticipated attack by the Allies on the Riviera coast. In October cyclists were barred from the Promenade des Anglais; by January 1944 the Promenade had become a military zone, guarded by concrete barricades and defended by machine guns and anti-aircraft emplacements. The tranquil crescent of the Baie des Anges was drilled with trenches and fortified with barbed wire before mines were laid. The extravagant and absurd Jetée Promenade, Nice's favourite and most absurdly kitsch tourist attraction, was stripped of metal for ammunition until nothing remained to show its former splendour but a skeleton cupola and a row of sea-bound stumps. Nice's citizens were ordered to surrender their household metals or face a fine; candlesticks, fenders and copper pans were carried in baskets to the Atlantic Hotel on boulevard Victor Hugo, to be weighed and added to the stockpile. The people, here as in Paris, were starving.

Was this a pleasant place to be? To choose to be? Not unless you were prepared to compromise, to ignore what was unpleasant, to pay with your company, your smile, and perhaps a little more, for a life of ease and freedom.

In September 1943 SS Hauptsturmführer Alois Brunner established his headquarters at the splendidly ornate Hotel Excelsior. You can still stay at the Excelsior, in a room looking on to a courtyard of iron balustrades and cascading plants; you would have no idea, either from the surroundings or from the anodyne brochure which extols their placid atmosphere, of what this place had once become.

The Jews who had seen Nice as a haven fled from it as the German troops marched south in the early autumn of 1943, but not fast enough. Initially, a distinction had been made between *les juifs*, who were French-born and entitled to some protection, and *les Israélites*, immigrant Jews who had been forced out of Germany, Poland, Russia and Czechoslovakia. Now, all wore the yellow star over their heart from the age of six upwards, and all were under threat. Forty-five were arrested trying to cross the River Var; a hundred more were culled from a railway-station platform. From the moment Alois Brunner established himself at the Excelsior, the Jewish population were hunted out of Nice like rats, taken from their beds, from the pavements, from the station, from the beach, even, hurried away in shorts and sunsuits to be shunted north to Drancy, and out to the German camps. Three thousand were arrested in the space of a few weeks; many of the names had been supplied by local informers. The reward for such assistance was excellent, up to 5,000 francs a head.[10]

Was this the crime of which Hélène would stand accused after the war? The money she had been paid in compensation for her crash at São Paulo was running out, seven years on, and she had borne the considerable expense of her lover's enterprises, none of which reached completion. The city archives do not show the name of the previous occupant of the Villa des Pins. Favours may have been done. Was a Jewish family eased out to provide the home of her choice? It is possible that the occupiers were willing to adopt a laissez-faire policy towards a charming woman who could have formed a paradigm for German womanhood, an image of blonde strength and singlemindedness, a French Brünnhilde.

Far below the Villa des Pins lies Nice's Baie des Anges. Standing on her terrace, shaded by the one superb pine which has given the villa its name, Hélène could have watched over the destruction of the Jetée pier and the conversion of the beautiful bay into a minefield. The Hotel Excelsior was hidden from view. Out of sight, out of mind; perhaps she and her young lover passed the last phase of the war here in effortless isolation, unscathed by temptation, as untouched by the presence of the occupiers and their steely mission of extermination as by the coming of the Allies.

Perhaps, between 1943 and 1945, Hélène and Arnaldo did nothing but play with the dogs, make love, drive up and down the corkscrew road and close the gate against anybody who came asking awkward questions.

Perhaps.

DISGRACE

14

THE ACCUSATION

'Vôtre place n'est pas ici, vous.'

LOUIS CHIRON,
QUOTED BY HELLÉ NICE TO ANTONY NOGHES,
13 DECEMBER 1949

On 26 August 1944 Paris was stripped of its Nazi flags and proclaimed a free city. Six months later the last of Hitler's troops were forced out of their final stronghold in eastern France. They left behind them a poor and ravaged country. The Allies had bombed ports and factories; Resistance saboteurs had smashed electricity supplies and communication lines. A map of the French railway system for 1945 gives the measure of their success; it resembles a handful of scattered dressmaker's pins.

In 1945 Marshal Pétain returned to France to face his trial. The jurors, aware that he had given the order in 1942 to fire on Allied troops, recommended that the former war hero should be imprisoned for life. Pétain died at the age of ninety-five in an island fortress off the coast of Brittany. His former deputy, Pierre Laval, condemned to death for activities which included an energetic commitment to the deportation of Jewish women and children, was shot at Fresnes after making a botched suicide attempt two hours earlier. Fellow prisoners, while recognizing Laval's guilt, were nevertheless discomforted by the brutality of his execution.

Philippe Viannay, writing an article for the Resistance publication *Défense de la France* in March 1944, had called for the destruction of all those who had aided the enemy. 'Kill without passion, without hatred,' he wrote. 'Never stoop to torture; we are soldiers, not sadists.'[1] There were, despite this appeal, atrocities. One shocking photograph in the book which quotes Viannay's words shows a group of naked and shaved women, daubed with swastikas and encircled by a staring crowd. In the summer of 1944, a chateau-owner guilty only of being a suspected monarchist was given a series of punishments which included being stabbed in the back and throat and doused in petrol which was then set alight. (His torturers were subsequently tried and imprisoned.)[2]

Bitterness at such crimes as the burning alive, on the orders of German officers, of the women and children of the village of Oradour, in a locked church, during the vicious summer of 1944 – the men were taken to nearby barns and shot – strengthened a thirst for revenge which was fuelled by poverty. To have eaten and dressed well during the Occupation seemed now to have been a form of treachery: how had such a way of life been maintained if not by collaboration? In Paris, Louis Aragon's testimony saved Maurice Chevalier from being tried in October; his fellow entertainers Tino Rossi and Sacha Guitry were sent to Fresnes, where so many celebrities were imprisoned immediately after the liberation that one star-struck guard made a habit of taking an autograph book on his patrol. Coco Chanel had not been the only couturier to sell her wartime creations to the occupiers; her perceived crime, in times of hunger and privation, was to have lived comfortably at the Ritz with her German lover. The actress Arletty, who played the beautiful, elusive Garance in Marcel Carné's *Les Enfants du Paradis* (1945), briefly joined the all-star cast in Fresnes as a punishment for similarly unpatriotic behaviour.* Robert Brasillach, the disgraced former editor of *Je Suis Partout*, was arrested, tried and executed; the Duke and Duchess of Windsor, meanwhile, returned to Paris with 134 pieces of luggage after visiting Hitler and passing their wartime years in the Bahamas.

Photographs of the trembling, skeletal survivors who sang the *Marseillaise* to the crowds welcoming them back from the German camps were widely published in the newly uncensored French press. Inadmissible guilt – few had fully understood the true horror of the camps – was mixed with outrage as the stories of starvation, torture and mass incineration began to emerge. Strict rationing, a rash of strikes in 1946 and the painfully slow return of industrial confidence – only five thousand cars were manufactured in France in 1947, a number barely sufficient to provide post-war Paris with a working taxi fleet – added to the sense of bitterness. The identification and persecution of collaborators offered an outlet for such feelings. A cousin of Philippe de Rothschild's witnessed the occasion on which a Free French officer recognized a former collaborator while they were both attending an elegant party. Identified, the man was requested to leave while the icily silent guests lined themselves into two long rows between which he was forced to walk to the door.[3]

Some revenges were more subtle. It was now known that Ettore Bugatti had received handsome compensation from the Germans for the loss of his Molsheim factory. His first claim for its restitution was rejected, despite the fact that he had finally consented to become a French citizen in 1946, following his marriage to Geneviève Delcuze. (Barbara Bugatti died, after a long illness, in 1944.)

---

* It is sometimes suggested that the turban which Arletty wore as 'Truth' in the film's opening scenes concealed a shaven head. The film was made in 1944, the year of savage recriminations.

Officially, the opposition to Bugatti's claim was made by the communist-run trades unions which wanted the Molsheim factory to be run as a cooperative, liberated from the Bugatti family's authorative control; unofficially, resentment was fuelled by the belief that Bugatti had taken a fat bribe to support a comfortable life in Paris and had therefore forfeited his right to ownership. Such feelings would not have been surprising; Alsace had suffered considerable humiliation during the Occupation, when French had become a forbidden language and the franc was replaced by the Reichsmark, returning it, in all but name, to the status of a German province. In May 1947 Ettore was driven back to Alsace in his Bugatti Royale, to the war-battered town of Colmar; here, once more, he appealed for the restoration of his estate. A savage attack on his character was made by the lawyer representing the trades unions. The appeal seemed certain to be rejected. Driven away by his chauffeur Toussaint, a despondent Ettore asked to be taken to the factory, but the gates were barred against his entry. Paying his respects at the stretch of road where his son Jean had died, Ettore collapsed. The stroke and a subsequent coma robbed him of the news that the Colmar court had finally decided to grant his claim. Ettore Bugatti died on 21 August and was buried beside his son in the family vault at Dorlisheim.[4]

A photograph of Hélène dining out in Cannes with an unknown companion in 1946 reminds us how frequently the word 'agitated' was now being used to describe her.[5] She has lost her look of gleeful insouciance. The radiant smile has gone; in its place, there is a look of strain. She is dressed with smart severity. It is a photograph which makes the viewer want to know what it was that these two were talking about. She was still living at the Villa des Pins. Arnaldo Binelli, a poor businessman, had been allowed to take control of her financial affairs. It is possible that, as Hélène saw youth disappearing from her features, she tried to hold him

Hélène and an unknown companion in Cannes, 1946.

with bribes. 'Pour Naldo, tout ce que je possédais était à lui,' she told a woman friend, Janalla Jarnach, in the 1970s. The expression is ambivalent. I gave him all I had, or, so far as Naldo was concerned, everything I owned was his. Both may have been true of the circumstances.

In January 1946 the former racing driver Marchese Antonio Brivio Sforza sat down in Milan to write an answer to a letter he had received from a former girlfriend in the South of France. He had, while alarmed by its contents, prudently waited to talk to the managing director of Alfa Romeo before making a reply.

In 1938 Alfa Romeo had come up with a remarkable new model, the 158. It caused a sensation at its Livorno debut that year; between 1950 and 1951 it would establish itself as one of the most successful racing cars of all time, winning 47 times out of its 54 appearances. In 1946, however, the model was still safely under wraps in the Italian cheese factory where it had spent a restful war. Its glory lay ahead. The startling gist of the letter Hélène had posted off to Tony Brivio late in 1945 was that a 158 had been stolen. The theft could only be of value to another firm who were intending to examine and adapt it for their own use.

Brivio Sforza was closely connected to Alfa and he was President of Milan's Automobile Club. His hair must have stood on end when he read Hélène's news. But the story was without foundation. No model 158 had been stolen from the cheese factory; neither had any of the other Alfas which were still under guard. 'And so,' Brivio wrote back with a bluntness which only just kept on the right side of mockery:

> I really can't think what kind of car you might be talking about. Anyway, thank you so for such a charming reminder of times past and I do hope we get the chance to meet again at a race course in France, or in Italy, one of these days. Best wishes, Antonio Brivio.[6]

There had, it seems, been a mistake and Brivio's letter, so coldly casual in tone, was a blow to any hope that Hélène may have had of attracting his interest and re-establishing herself as an Alfa driver.

She had lost none of her eagerness to resume competitive driving although, in her mid-forties, it had become hard to convince the organizers of races that she was not past her best.

It was her red-haired rally-driving friend Anne Itier who reached out once again to bring her back to the wheel. In the autumn of 1948, remembering Hélène's magnificent performance in a Renault at Comminges in the summer of 1939, Itier wrote to suggest that they should partner each other for the Monte Carlo Rally of 1949. Hélène was overjoyed. On 17 January she went into

Nice and bought a new Renault for just under 320,000 francs from the local showroom. She had six days left in which to refresh her driving skills on the approach road which twisted up to the lonely Villa des Pins.

The first Rally to take place since the war was an ideal event at which to stage the return which Hélène was planning (she had already opened negotiations with the Automobile Club of Reims). Renault were eager for publicity and few people in the racing world had shown a more spectacular ability to attract it than the former dancer. For the car firm, as for her, Monte Carlo provided the perfect showcase.

Glamour had returned to the Riviera, once again a favourite winter playground of the fashionable world. Orson Welles had just acquired a villa at Mougins; Aly Khan was staying at his opulent Château d'Horizon with Rita Hayworth. The Bal d'Or, held at the Sports Club of Monte Carlo, was a dazzling occasion, the walls of the club's dining-room newly brightened by gold leaf to match the Maharanee of Baroda's splendid evening dress and the elegantly wrapped presents which were handed out by a gleaming bevy of gold-frocked ladies. At Cannes, the widow of the great aviation pioneer Louis Blériot put in an appearance to welcome John Derry, who set a new record when he flew down from Paris in 44 minutes. Crowds assembled to watch the British pilot give a sea-skimming demonstration of air stunts in his Vampire the following day.[7] And crowds gathered in the steep little town of Monte Carlo on the morning of 23 January to watch the drivers, masked by their goggles and well-muffled in the heavy protective clothes they would need, as they checked their cars and provisions for the gruelling journey out across a Europe which had, for the past ten years, been made inaccessible. This was not simply a rally; it was a symbol. The roads of Europe were open again, and freedom tasted sweet at the wheel of a speeding car.

One would like to know what conversations took place as the

Renault drove out of Monte Carlo that morning. The night before, in the shocked presence of Anne Itier, Hélène had undergone the most humiliating experience of her life. Dressed for a splendid night out, she attended the reception which was being given for the pick of the rally drivers, in their honour. She had been deep in conversation with Itier and their friends, Yvonne Simon and Germaine Rouault, when a tall figure detached himself from a male group on the far side of the room and made his way towards them. Jabbing a finger at Hélène and raising his voice so that nobody could fail to hear his words, he denounced her as a Gestapo agent. It was, he boomed, a disgrace to Monaco and to the rally that this woman had been allowed to participate. Why was she here?

Silence fell as the drivers turned to stare at Hélène, white-faced, mute with shock. Politely, they waited for her to defend herself. 'I was,' she said afterwards, 'so staggered to hear myself being called an agent that I simply didn't know what to say. I didn't even react.'[8]

It might have been better if she had; and yet what, in such circumstances, could she possibly say, and who would believe her, when the man who had accused her was Louis Chiron, the adored king of motorsport in Monte Carlo? Monegasque by birth, Chiron had put the principality firmly on the tourist map when he founded its own Grand Prix in 1929; he had been one of the most spectacular winners of the national Grand Prix in 1934; a superb driver, he had the charisma of a film star – and the vanity.

Immaculately dressed in his light blue overalls and with a polka-dot scarf knotted at his neck, Chiron was a man who enjoyed the company of beautiful women and relished the flattery of the press. Photographs of him show a man who loved the camera and responded to it like a showman. It is conceivable that he resented a woman who excelled at diverting press attention to herself; it seems incredible that he would have sought to defame her for such a petty reason. It may be that Hélène had rejected his advances, or that she had angered him by gossiping about his long relationship with Alice Hoffman, the wife of his first influential sponsor. Yet none of these reasons could justify such a vicious and calculated act of revenge.

Chiron had chosen the place and time at which to make the denunciation with cruel skill. Hélène was French; if she chose to challenge Chiron, she would have to make her claim in a Monaco court, outside French jurisdiction. Antony Noghes, with whom Chiron had founded the Monaco Grand Prix, was President of the Automobile Club of Monaco. He also headed the committee in charge of the Monte Carlo Rally. Noghes was the man to whom any complaint would have to be addressed. He was one of Chiron's closest friends.

Itier and Hellé Nice completed the Rally without distinguishing themselves.* Shortly after their return, Hélène wrote a long and dramatic appeal to Antony Noghes whose name, it is worth noticing, was so unfamiliar to her that she misspelt it as Nogues. The letter, of which she preserved a copy, described the nature of the accusation, the horror and shame Chiron had caused, and the damage to her reputation. 'I can promise you that what he said was bad enough to have influenced everybody who heard him – and they all did,' she told Noghes, naming her women friends as principal witnesses. She protested her innocence, pointing out that this was the first time such an accusation had been made. She asked Noghes to take note that gossip was already spreading. At Reims,

*Hélène identified a photograph of herself with Itier in the Rallye de Monte-Carlo in her scrapbook and noted that the rally had ended disastrously that year when the Renault skidded into a canal in Amsterdam. She dated the Rally, inaccurately, to 1950. The sports magazine *L'Equipe*, in ten days of reports on the 1949 rally, noted that car no. 156, driven by 'Hellé' and Itier, had crashed, but gave no further details. Renault, however, wrote to Hélène on 9 February 1949, congratulating her on a splendid drive and offering publicity shots of her triumphant return. This could have been a careless oversight on their part, or awkward diplomacy; certainly, the return was neither victorious nor triumphant.

a hasty decision had been taken to ban her from further contact with their course; she had learnt this on her return from the Rally.

From indignation, she turned to threats. In the first place, she told Noghes, she expected a full written apology from Chiron. If this was not produced, she would take the case to Monaco's tribunal, where her own name would be cleared and Louis Chiron's blackened as a teller of untruths. Unchivalrous untruths, she added for good measure.

On 25 February Noghes dictated a short and carefully non-committal response. Louis Chiron was unfortunately visiting England for an undetermined period. He would be shown the letter on his return. No assurances were offered; the nature of the accusation was not even mentioned.[9]

And then? Applications to the city archives of Nice and Monaco have yielded nothing concerning a trial. The Automobile Club of Monaco, which has a splendid bust of Louis Chiron on show to greet visitors, lacks any evidence of the dispute. The Court of Appeal in Monaco, a magnificently ecclesiastical building, has no files on a case brought against Louis Chiron in the period between 1949 and 1955. Hélène herself kept only the copy of her letter, together with Noghes's response. It is hard to believe that she would not have kept an apology from Chiron, or proof that she brought a case against him, with a successful outcome. But there is nothing.

Is it possible that Chiron had grounds for his terrible attack on a fellow racer? An article which was published about Hélène in 1997 has suggested that suspicions were aroused by her friendship with Huschke von Hanstein; why then, did he spare Itier, who knew the German driver, had a brief affair with him and was standing beside Hélène when he made his accusation?[10] Even if Hélène did have a brief fling in 1938 with the man later known as 'the racing baron', would he have encouraged her to become a Gestapo agent? The idea is frankly absurd: Hanstein was himself arrested by the Gestapo in 1943 and given six months in prison for the pitiful crime of going to a Brazilian embassy party in Budapest. Sent to the Russian front, Hanstein finally succeeded in making his way home and kept a low profile for the rest of the war. Nobody who ever met him regarded Huschke von Hanstein as anything other than an ebullient racing and rally driver who later became a brilliant public relations manager for Porsche.[11]

There is another possibility. One of Hélène's carefully preserved photographs shows a handsome airman in his plane, while another shows the same man in his German officer's uniform. This was General der Flieger Freiherr Friedrich Leopold von Richthofen, who wrote to wish her well after the São Paulo crash. It may be that these photographs hold a secret and that this was a friend who could have lured Hélène into working for the enemy. Even if this was the case, it seems unlikely that she would have been careless enough to keep a photograph of him in full uniform, when

The photo of Friedrich Leopold von Richthofen, which he sent to Hélène, and which she kept until her death.

friendship with a German officer was all that was required for a charge of collaboration to be launched.

The French records of the war years show nothing relating to Hélène Delangle and there are no extant details of a court case, although the author of the 1997 article was confident that she took steps to clear her name after Chiron's denunciation. Neither are there any details obtainable in France of native spies who were employed by the Gestapo; the question is, indeed, such a delicate one that a response is extremely hard to obtain.

The Germans are more forthcoming and, on this issue, more thorough. A detailed list has been created at the Bundesarchiv in Berlin; it gives what is thought to be a comprehensive account of all agents working with the Gestapo in France during the Occupation. Application was made to the Bundesarchiv during the course of researching this book; Hellé Nice is known to the archive keepers neither by her pseudonym nor by her true name. They concluded that she was not, as Chiron had alleged, a Gestapo agent.

But would she have been prepared to go to court in an unsympathetic principality to prove her innocence? It is possible that the writer who claimed in 1997 that she did so was misinterpreting the evidence. Several of the photographs in the American archive[12] to which he was given brief access show Hélène sitting in what appears to be a court-room; they were in fact taken at an official meeting before the Biella Grand Prix of 1935.

I am, despite that misleading photographic evidence, inclined to share his view. Had a woman as well-known as Hellé Nice proved to be a former Gestapo agent, only four years after the war, the newspapers would have been full of the news and she would have been severely and publicly punished for it. Her crime would be remembered. Since no reference appears anywhere to such a charge, other than in her own copy letter to Noghes, it seems safe to conclude that Chiron backed down. The fact that she never again referred to this humiliating experience need not cause surprise; all that mattered was the clearing of her name. Silence, even after a victory, would have been prudent.

Let us assume, then, that the case was due to come before the Tribunal of Monaco and that Chiron withdrew his allegation at the last moment. Hélène was vindicated, but her public career was over. She made a last gallant effort to return in 1951. Entered for the local Nice Grand Prix, she was replaced at the last minute by a fierily brilliant young driver, Jean Behra, whose reputation was made the following year when he won the Reims Grand Prix. The decision was not surprising; she was over fifty and she had not competed against men in a Grand Prix since her accident in Brazil. She still had her Renault and the will to drive it, but rallying partners fell away after Chiron's revelations. Nobody wanted to be seen keeping company with a woman who had been accused of working for Germany; however thorough the vindication had been, the taint of an unsavoury history lingered.

Arnaldo, while sympathetic and affectionate in the early stages of Hélène's indignation and unhappiness, grew tired of offering reassurance, especially when it seemed to produce so little effect. She was no longer the strong, attractive woman he had been enchanted by at their first meeting in 1935. Volatile in her moods ever since the São Paulo crash and impossible as a sleeping companion – she would wake after two or three hours, often drenched with sweat after a nightmare in which the moments leading up to the crash were replayed – her hatred of Louis Chiron, her destroyer, was beginning to mark itself on her face. Lines pulled down her laughing mouth and emerged like gullies in the anxious frown which had become her most recognizable expression.

Arnaldo began to look elsewhere for pleasure. The unoriginal cover story of playing cards with a few friends in the afternoons was soon blown. Caught and forgiven, on the first occasion, he was trapped between the desire to leave a woman to whom he was no longer attracted and the fact that he remained financially dependent on her. Awkwardly, he tried to change the nature of the relationship, making light of his infidelities, seeking her advice about how to escape the advances of some unusually predatory lady. It seemed to him that Hélène was content in this role; years later, she was still wondering that any man could have been so obtuse. She had, she remembered, once asked him why he chose to tell her so much more than she wanted to hear. She never forgot his answer: 'Why, who else could I tell?'[13]

15

SANS EVERYTHING

'Je crois que la chance a perdu mon adresse.'*

HELLÉ NICE TO JANALLA JARNACH,
18 APRIL 1967

Arnaldo Binelli, according to Hélène's own account, was responsible for her financial ruin. In 1950 he met a Parisian businessman who persuaded him to borrow her savings for investment in a Liechtenstein-based company. The compensation she received after her crash at São Paulo had been changed from Brazilian milreis into gold in the Canaries; its value in 1950 was, by her own calculation, approximately three million francs (approx £42,000 in modern currency). Arnaldo, as a Swiss citizen, was legally entitled to take the money abroad; his business partner was not. The two men were arrested by the customs and imprisoned. They were eventually released but the money disappeared – along with the Parisian financier.

This was the bizarre explanation which Hélène produced for her vertiginous plunge from riches to poverty; telling the story in

---

* Loosely, 'Luck seems to have lost my number.'

1974, she was even ready to suggest that Arnaldo had fabricated the businessman in order to gain possession of her money and lock it up in a Swiss bank account.[1] She may have been fantasizing; she certainly exaggerated the sum involved.* There is, however, no doubt about the fact that the money had disappeared.

So, by 1960, had Arnaldo.

In 1957 the impoverished couple left the Villa des Pins for a modest home at Magagnosc, near Grasse. Hélène sold the best of her furniture and paintings to pay the rent and to cover their debts; the rest was put into store. In 1958, she made another sale, which produced enough to support them for a further year. By 1959, they were penniless. Arnaldo, still hoping for success from one of his inventions, applied to Jean Behra, the young driver who replaced Hélène in the Grand Prix de Nice of 1951 and who had gone on to become one of Ferrari's top racers. Behra, who was killed while competing in Germany later that year, told Binelli that his brother José might be interested in his plans (he wasn't); learning of the couple's financial difficulties, he also mentioned a new charitable organization which might be able to offer them assistance.

La Roue Tourne had no connection to the world of motor sports; the link which Behra had suggested was through Hélène's earlier incarnation as a music-hall star. Formed in 1957 by the widow of a Resistance hero, Janalla Jarnach, and by Paul Azais, a film star whose public career ended when he was knocked down by a lorry, La Roue Tourne's kindly purpose was to provide discreet help for anybody in the theatrical world whose career had been affected by a similar misfortune. With the great comic actor Fernandel as its president, the charity established itself at the building in rue Legendre from which it still operates.

---

* In 1981, she was ready to say that Binelli had 'stolen' the sum of five or six million francs (£70,000 or £80,000 in modern currency: Hélène–Janalla Jarnach, 18 May 1981).

One of the first recipients of La Roue Tourne's help was Henri Garat, a hugely successful performer in the 1930s.* A pleasant voice and a charming manner were replaceable talents and Garat had been superseded by the younger, more talented Tino Rossi. Depression, ill-health and an inability to manage money had done the rest; by the late fifties, Henri Garat was a ruined man. When he, his Swiss wife, Annaliese, and their young son, Marcel, met Binelli, they were already being discreetly assisted by the charity.

Hélène, in the letters that she wrote years after the event, consistently remembered that her relationship with Arnaldo entered its final phase soon after he made his first visit to La Roue Tourne. Suspicious of a new rival, she searched his pockets and found letters written by Annaliese Garat, who was then working at the charity's headquarters. 'Our unforgettable nights of love' were the words which lodged themselves in Hélène's memory, along with pleas for Arnaldo to start a new life with her. (Garat had meanwhile been taken into hospital at Hyères, where he died in 1959.) Annaliese was good-looking and determined; she had an attractive child who adored Binelli. He, according to Hélène, dithered wretchedly, announcing one day that he was going to leave, and the next that he was going to stay. Sometimes, he beat her up. On three occasions, he took money from her to cover the cost of visiting Annaliese at her new home in Grenoble.[2] In April 1960 he left for good. He and Annaliese were married in Switzerland where Marcel Garat adopted his stepfather's name. Interestingly, Binelli's parents were more enraged by his defection to Annaliese than they had ever been by his relationship with Hélène Delangle. Arnaldo was disinherited in favour of his stepson.[†3]

* Garat is the most probable original of the charming young singer in *An American in Paris* (1951) from whom Gene Kelly finally wins Leslie Caron.
† The reactions of Arnaldo Binelli's brothers, Orazio and Secondo, are not known.

In retrospect, Hellé Nice wanted to believe that it was she who finally ordered her faithless lover to leave; the letters she wrote at the time show that this was not the case. Binelli's departure was a devastating blow to her confidence. At the age of sixty, and in poor health, she was left friendless and without means of support. Everything she had, she bleakly wrote to Madame Jarnach, had been used for Arnaldo's benefit; now, nothing was left. And the rent was beyond her means. In a month, she would be homeless.[4]

Paul Azais and Janalla Jarnach were shocked and conscience-stricken; unnecessarily, they felt responsible for the fact that Binelli had met Annaliese Garat on the premises of the charity. Never having met Hélène, they promised to look after her. All she had to do was come to Paris.

Madame Delangle, having already grudgingly parted with a thousand francs to cover her daughter's immediate living expenses, was less sympathetic. Reluctantly consenting to store some furniture, she indicated that this would be a great inconvenience, depriving her of a useful woodshed. She wanted to know when Mariette, as she continued to address her, intended to find some gainful employment.[5] Her letter expressed no love and little concern for her ageing daughter's welfare.

In the summer of 1960, Hélène climbed the narrow staircase to the charity's office at rue Legendre; with her, she had brought her typewriter, a suitcase full of news-cuttings, photographs and the stamp collection which she had been making since she first travelled to America.* After being greeted by Madame Jarnach, a large, blonde, softly pretty woman, Hélène gaily announced that she was ready to turn her hand to anything; all she asked was to be

---

* The stamp book, dismantled after her death, was one of her greatest treasures. The interest, for a postmaster's daughter, may always have been there. It is reasonable to suppose that she began to collect as she began to travel.

given plenty of work. A little attic above the reception room, accessible by a steep flight of stairs, had already been cleared and provided with a bed and table. On the wall, Hélène hung up her favourite photographs of herself as a dancer; the frames were made of cheap black tape.

Visitors to the charity remembered her for her liveliness; Janalla Jarnach and Paul Azais – he was nicknamed Popole by Hélène, who adored him – were shocked by the intensity of her passions. Arnaldo Binelli was never far from her thoughts. She could not forgive him; as time passed, his remembered crimes increased. Finding a loaded pistol in the attic, Jarnach was shocked to learn that Hélène carried it everywhere in the hope that she would one day cross Binelli's path. Her plan, she said, was to shoot him in the knees. Prudently, Jarnach removed the bullets.[6]

During the days, the reception room at La Roue Tourne was busy and crowded; in the evenings, there were galas to be attended for the purpose of raising money. Hélène was at her happiest on these occasions; visits to the Olympia and the Casino de Paris brought back memories of a time which, in her increasingly confused recollections, was now bathed in glory. She, not Mistinguett, was the star in her own retelling of the past, scant solace for the fact that her racing triumphs counted for nothing at La Roue Tourne. The only significance of a turning wheel here was in the wheel of fate from which the charity took its name. Boasts of her triumphs on the international circuits did, however, produce one result: she was appointed as the charity's chauffeur. Her driving, according to Madame Jarnach, was not of a kind to reassure passengers.

Their new friend had, in Madame Jarnach's view, the air of happiness but not the conviction. It was evidently humiliating for her, a woman of renown, to find herself placed among people whose fame had been of a less dazzling kind. She hated her loss of independence. Frail – she often had to use a stick to walk – and suffering from bad circulation, she suffered acutely from the damp Parisian winters. The bedroom at rue Legendre was, however hard they tried to make improvements, impossible to keep warm. She pined for Nice, for the sun, for the light on the sea, for the daily pleasure of a stroll along the promenade.

These were the obvious causes of her unhappiness. The difficulties with her family were slower to show themselves.

There is something almost Atrean about the tragedies which befell the Delangle family. Three children had died in infancy, another at Verdun, a father while still in his prime. Hélène's career had been destroyed twice over, once when she crashed at São Paulo, and again, when she was publicly accused of being a Gestapo agent. In 1960 La Roue Tourne took her in. In 1961 Solange Delangle was confined in a psychiatric hospital in Paris where she was held for almost a year, during which Hélène paid daily visits and took over the care of her apartment. One evening in 1963, gentle, simple-minded Henri Delangle was knocked down by a drunk driver while he was ambling around Sainte-Mesme; his injured body lay undiscovered until the following morning. Visiting him in the local hospital at Estampes that afternoon, Henri's mother and sisters found him strapped to the bed, ready for electric shock treatment. The treatment was prevented – Hélène credited herself with having taken the initiative – but Henri had suffered severe cranial damage. Incapable of sustained concentration, he was now almost unable to write. He became, as a result, entirely dependent on his mother and on Solange, who had bought a weekend cottage at Sainte-Mesme.[7] The two women employed Henri as a useful labourer and decorator.

Henri and Hélène had always been fond of each other. The accident removed any chance of fraternal support in fighting the battle for her inheritance, something about which she was becoming increasingly concerned. The value of Madame Delangle's property at Sainte-Mesme was, by Hélène's own calculation, at least one and a half million francs.★ French law entitled her to receive a third of the property as her legacy. Unfortunately, however, only Solange's name appeared on the title deeds which had been drawn up in 1926, and the relationship between the sisters was not friendly. Hélène's frantic appeals to her mother met with the cold response that all future arrangements would be dealt with by Solange in an appropriate fashion. This was not reassuring.[8]

Hélène became hysterical during the summer following Henri's accident. La Roue Tourne had closed for the summer holidays; Paul Azais and Janalla Jarnach were spending a fortnight on the coast; she was alone. Unreasonably, she insisted that her benefactors should return; when they refused, she became abusive, screaming down the telephone and writing long, anguished letters which rambled from tales of one vendetta against her to another. Reminded of all they had done for her, and of their readiness to protect her until the end – 'you will always be our dear Hellé, always safe and in our thoughts', Madame Jarnach reassured her – she seemed to calm down.[9]

Returning to Paris at the end of August, the charity's founders saw that the attic bedroom had been emptied out. A jubilant letter arrived from Nice where the runaway blithely announced that she had found a charming place to live, with a kind landlord who put flowers in her room and allowed her cat, Minette, the run of his garden. The rooms were pretty and a little expensive, but if they only knew how wonderful it was to be in sunshine again, to be near the sea. She had, she added proudly, done the last part of the drive to the coast in record time;[10] Madame Jarnach did not remind her that the car in which she had taken off was the property

---

★ Hélène was speaking in 1962 but the franc was revalued in 1960. If she was thinking of old francs this would be 150,000 new francs, but whether she meant old or new francs is not known.

of La Roue Tourne. Full of forebodings, she begged Hélène to remember that her lodging at rue Legendre was still empty; would she not come back and join them?[11]

Her fears were soon confirmed. Madame Delangle's health began to deteriorate rapidly in 1964 and fierce discussions took place between her daughters. Solange wanted her put in a home; Hélène, perhaps still hoping to influence her and regain a place on the title deeds of the property, proposed to bring her to Nice. Henri sided with Solange; Madame Delangle was taken to 'La Domaine' at Boissy Saint-Léger, where she died in June 1964. Solange immediately took possession of the house at Sainte-Mesme and informed Hélène that her stored furniture was being sent to Nice. As for any chance of the bill being altered: 'I went to the lawyer,' Solange wrote. 'Hopeless. Nothing can be done. Still, I'll try to do the best I can for you.'[12] Hélène's possessions arrived a week later. Her silver trophies, although tarnished, were intact; the furniture, stored for four years in a damp shed, was sold by a local dealer in Nice. It fetched a disappointingly small sum.

Destitute and fearful, Hélène now became entirely dependent on La Roue Tourne. She moved to a grim basement room in the Cimiez area of Nice and then to Beaulieu, where she had once lived in carefree splendour, high on the hill. The Renault belonging to the charity was traded in for a secondhand Simca. In this, she travelled to local cinemas where, during the matinée performances, she sold the charity's funding envelopes. 'I live like a bird on a branch,' she wrote. 'I seem always to be cold, and so tired.'[13] Madame Jarnach sent an appeal for help, at her suggestion, to Marcel Mongin – 'votre ex-époux'. He sent back 50 francs. Henri Thouvenet contributed 200. At least, Hélène answered, she'd be able to buy herself a pair of shoes for the first time in four years. She would, she added with a touch of her old spirit, give Mongin a kick up the backside if she ever saw him again.[14]

In 1974, the year in which Paul Azais died, Hélène also learned of the deaths of her brother Henri and of Arnaldo Binelli. The loss of her brother produced a burst of grief. 'Mon petit Didi,' she wrote. He had been her favourite, so gentle, so harmless and kind: 'I loved him so much.'[15] The news of Binelli's death – it was cancer – stirred no such tenderness. 'Why should I regret a man who robbed me of three million francs?' she demanded. All she remembered of him now was that he had left her when she was penniless, when she had done everything for him. Hadn't she paid for every one of his useless schemes, for an operation on his kidneys, for journeys which, she now believed, had been made only so that he could enjoy himself with other women? 'Et tant et tant de choses,' she concluded savagely: no, there was nothing to grieve her in the news of Arnaldo's death.[16]

Writing to Janalla Jarnach, her last remaining friend, was Hélène's continuing solace in the last and terrible years of her decline. Some letters, like one in which she spoke of her plans to race again and retire in glory, bear witness only to her unstable mental state; others, when she poured out her hatred of Solange for having robbed her of her inheritance, are shocking in their ferocity. For the most part, however, the sheaf of documents typed or written in a small sloping hand on squared paper torn from an exercise pad chronicle the wretchedness of a woman living in extreme poverty, without friends, and in deteriorating health. Psoriasis, the curse of Solange's life, now afflicted her. Her skin bled from suppurating sores; frightened that her landlords would throw her out if she dirtied their sheets, she slept in her clothes, wearing the old trousers of which La Roue Tourne sent her a steady supply. Sleep became impossible. Her teeth were taken out. She no longer had the courage to appear at cinemas gathering money for the charity; she was too ashamed of her appearance.

Some comfort came, in 1975, when a new landlord, Raymond Agostinucci, expressed a good-humoured interest in her former

Hélène's last home on rue Edouard Scoffier, Nice, 1975–1984.

history as a racer. She spent her last nine years in a small, cold attic apartment at one of his properties in Nice. Rue Edouard Scoffier is a dingy street in a run-down area at the back of the city; here, in a house filled with Italian tenants who assumed that she was living rent-free, Hélène lived in solitude, poring over the newspaper cuttings which told of more glorious days, smoking the thick yellow Mais cigarettes which were her one luxury. Each day, clutching a tattered leopardskin coat around her like an amulet, she went across the street to start up the Simca and sit in it for a little while before climbing the stairs back to her room. Sometimes, if she could persuade them to take an interest, she showed one of the tenants her cuttings and the precious trophies which, even now, she could not bring herself to sell.

In 1978 she enjoyed a moment of glory when the postman told her that he had seen the film of her Brazilian crash on television the night before; invited to speak about it on Radio Monte Carlo, she was obliged to refuse. 'How could I do it?' she asked Madame Jarnach. 'I can't afford the journey and speaking's almost impossible since I lost my teeth.' Sometimes, she admitted, she thought of shutting the door, turning on the gas, 'and goodbye to Hellé Nice and her miseries. I'm often tempted.' Still, she added with a touch of her old merriment, 'at least I still have my dear Janalla's trousers to keep me cosy and my fur coat which is old now, really old – like me!'[17]

In 1983, she told Madame Jarnach that she had made one final bid to recover her lost inheritance. Frail though she was, she had driven the Simca to Sainte-Mesme and knocked on the door of the little house where her sister lived, having sold the maternal property.* Solange refused to speak to her. A young cousin was called in to explain that she must leave. 'It's incredible that a

---

* The orchard, well, and stretch of riverbank had apparently netted two million in old francs for Solange (Hélène–JJ, 14.6.1976).

legitimate child can be robbed like this,' she wrote 'and yet it's legal. I'm sorry to be writing badly but my eyes are terrible.'[18]

In September 1984 Hélène was taken into hospital for an operation on her legs. A friend of Madame Jarnach's, asked to visit and to take her some fruit and biscuits, found her lying in a coma. 'Bon courage chère Hellé,' Madame Jarnach wrote, but her words were never read. Transferred to a second hospital a few days later, Hélène Delangle died while still unconscious. La Roue Tourne, faithful to the end, organized a commemorative service at the little church on rue Legendre, Sainte-Marie des Batignolles, on 29 October. A small announcement had been placed in *Le Figaro*, but the church was almost empty.

Madame Jarnach, anxious to find some way of honouring the memory of a woman she sincerely admired, made the journey to Nice in 1985 and visited the dreary house on rue Edouard Scoffier. She was told, to her dismay, that everything had already been

messes

La Roue Tourne.
L'Association d'Entr'aide
du spectacle
vous prie d'assister, ce
lundi 29 octobre 1984, a
18 h 45, a la messe qu'elle fait
célébrer, en l'église Sainte-
Marie des Batignolles, 77, rue
Legendre, Paris (17ᵉ), en souvenir d'

HELLÉ · NICE
championne du monde
automobile

décédée récemment à Nice
et inhumee à Dourdan.

Hélène's obituary in Le Figaro.

dismantled and given away, the cuttings books, the trophies, the book of stamps. The room at the top of the house was stripped bare, its faded green shutters tightly shut. She returned to Paris, knowing only that the funeral rites had been properly executed and that La Roue Tourne had also paid for Hélène's ashes to be sent to Sainte-Mesme for burial in the family grave. Payment was made for flowers to be laid on the tomb every Sainte-Hélène's day, 18 August, as was proper. Everything concerning her death, at least, was in order.

Or should have been. The details confirming the transaction and payments are preserved at the Nice Mairie, but the instructions given by Madame Jarnach were ignored. The slab of stone commemorating the Delangle family in the graveyard at Sainte-Mesme is engraved with only three names: Alexandrine, Solange and Henri. Solange, who died in 1986, was living at Sainte-Mesme at the time of her sister's death. As the purchaser of the plot, she had the right to do as she wished with it. She chose to obliterate her sister's presence. With the trophies sold, the cuttings books lost and the place of burial unmarked, it would be as if Mariette Hélène Delangle (1900–84) had never existed.

AFTERWORD

When I first knew Warner Dailey, he was selling antiquities from his house in London. Outside, the street by a greasy canal set the scene for a 1950s gangster movie; Warner, narrow-faced as a fox under a black fedora, matched his row of sleek Packards and black Citroëns to perfection. Inside, the house was crammed with oddities which had taken his fancy: Winston Churchill's telephone, an eighteenth-century bed shaped like a Russian troika, dress-shop dummies, box cameras, a cardinal's chair, photographs of pale girls framed in plaits of their own hair.

Articles were written about Warner and his house; the guests who braved evenings in the dark and strangely menacing kitchen smiled in disbelief when told that their dinner rolls came courtesy of the dustbins at the Savoy or Claridges. (Their provenance, although they had arrived via the back door, was always of the best.) Warner, one of the few true eccentrics I have known, saw nothing strange in his collection or his catering arrangements.

Fifteen years later, Warner and his wife moved to the South of France. He was still in business. Every Sunday morning, he visited a car-boot sale in an olive grove at Cogolin, a few kilometres inland from Saint-Tropez. And there, one morning in 1994, he spotted a thick, slightly battered album of yellowing sports cuttings, for which the dealer was asking 700 francs. One of the newspaper items showed a girl with short blonde hair and an earsplitting grin, sitting at the wheel of a racing car. The caption read: 'Hellé-Nice, Champion racer.' Somebody had written a date beside it: '1929'.

700 francs (£70) was a considerable outlay for a collection of cuttings about an unknown woman, but Warner bought the book. A dealer mentioned another, very similar, which had been sold a few weeks earlier at a Nice flea-market. There was a good chance it might turn up again. Four months later, he had the chance to buy the companion book for a thousand francs. Whoever the unknown lady might be, her value was rising.

Peter Hawkins, the man in charge of Christie's car auctions in Monaco, helped him take the next step. The car which appeared most consistently in the albums was a Bugatti; the deed of sale, also with the cuttings, provided a registration number. If the car survived, its owner would be listed with that number at the Bugatti Trust. Six months later, Warner had managed to track the Bugatti to Ben Rose, an American with a passion for vintage cars. Rose, happy to reunite the scrapbooks with the Hellé Nice Bugatti, bought them for $7,000. Two years later, the books and car were sold, for a considerably larger sum, to another collector.

In August 2000 I met up with Warner and his wife after a long gap in our friendship. Over dinner, Warner announced that he knew a wonderful story which needed to be written. He told me about the albums; a few days later, he sent me a three-year-old article from a car magazine. Titled 'One Hellé of a Girl', it sketched the extraordinary life of a Frenchwoman who went from working as a striptease dancer to become the most successful female racing driver of the thirties before a liaison with a German driver led to accusations of Nazi sympathies, forcing her to clear her name in court. 'If only Hellé Nice had written her autobiography,' the article concluded; beside it, Warner had scrawled: 'Yes! But fear not! Miranda is on the case!'

He was right. I had fallen for that bold laughing girl in the car the moment I saw her face. The problem was that the scrapbooks had disappeared, along with the car; Warner had no clue who had bought them or how to reach Ben Rose and I was worried about researching a life of which so little was known, and for which all research was likely to be in a foreign language. Bugatti fans soon introduced me to a good point from which to start. *Souvenirs d'un bugattiste*, published in 1997, showed a photograph of Hellé Nice on its jacket; a picture of her draped in a scarf and nothing else was credited to the collection of the author, Antoine Raffaelli. It was rumoured that Raffaelli had acquired a huge collection of her papers in the south of France at about the same time that Warner Dailey picked up the first scrapbook. Diligently tracked to Marseille, M. Raffaelli kept his head down and answered nothing. Eventually, he said that he was unwell.

The new owner of the Hellé Nice Bugatti rang me on Christmas Eve 2001, apologizing for his delay. A month later, Oscar Davis drove me to his New Jersey office to inspect the scrapbooks and, for the first time in my life, to sit in a racing car. Her car, no less, the very one in which she beat the world record at Montlhéry in 1929. I didn't expect the Bugatti to be so pretty; I hadn't, until I drove one, fast, understood the exquisite adrenalin-filled rush it would bring, a feeling of exhilaration, of excited, dangerous joy. Few experiences could match the intense happiness of racing in a car like this.

The cuttings in the albums loosely confirmed the article I had read. I still had no idea of her beginnings, her family, her love life – with the exception of a reference to von Hanstein – or her end. I didn't even know where she had died, and I needed that information most of all. In France, unlike Britain, beginnings are found in ends; the details of birth are recorded alongside the entry of death. Common sense suggested that if the scrapbooks surfaced near Saint-Tropez, she must have been living somewhere nearby. Somewhere with a racing history: that narrowed it down to Monte Carlo and Nice.

Nice it was, and my elation faded as I walked up rue Edouard

Scoffier. I knew from the interviews in the scrapbooks that this was a woman who loved light, mountains, sunshine: it seemed terrible that she should have spent her last years in the cold shadow of the cliffs behind Nice, in this grey and desolate house. A friendly basement squatter let me in and left me to wander at liberty through the neglected rooms. Knocking at the house next door, I spoke to a woman who looked baffled by my questions. Hellé Nice? No, the name meant nothing. Nevertheless, I scribbled down her own name: Madame Louis Lavagna.

Hélène had been born, as I now knew, at Aunay-sous-Auneau, near Chartres. Here, and at Sainte-Mesme, it became possible to shape her early years. I saw the tiny house which had once been inhabited by the postmaster, the school she had attended, the Delangle home at Sainte-Mesme and the drab little building at the far end of the village where, I was given to understand, Solange Delangle had kept to herself, never speaking of her private affairs. An old neighbour remembered that he had, as a child, seen Solange's sister arrive in a big smart car; the local historian, Roger Delayre, established that Alexandrine Delangle, the mother, had passed as the wife of a M. Bernard during her life in the village. The gravestone was perplexing; I could not understand why, if Hellé Nice was recorded as having been buried here, there was no mention of her name.

Back in England, I decided to send a photograph of Hellé Nice to Madame Lavagna and see if it might jog her memory. It did. She had forgotten the name, she wrote back apologetically. Yes, she remembered her now, a shabby, lively little woman with a blue Simca who had been taken in by M. Agostinucci as a charity case. If it was any help, she could give me the name and address of the landlord's daughter; she might have kept something.

She had. In April 2002, when I was in despair of ever finding the material I needed, Andrée Agostinucci let me into her house on avenue Mendeguren in Nice, high on one of the hill roads which twist up from the back of the town. Hellé Nice had, as I now knew, once been her neighbour, although they had never met. Andrée, a small, graceful girl, explained that she had found a trunk of papers, letters and photographs in a garage on one of her father's properties. He was dead; nobody was interested in the trunk; she decided that it was worth rescuing. And she, like Warner and myself, had fallen under the spell of the woman whose story it disclosed.

Later that day, Andrée introduced me to the contents of the trunk. Here, at last, was the stuff of which biographer's dreams are made, letters, pictures, cuttings, piles of them, none of which had ever been seen before. One of the letters was from a Madame Jarnach at an organization called La Roue Tourne; Andrée urged me to get in touch with her.

Before then, however, I had another stroke of good luck. Antoine Raffaelli, having failed to respond for two years, sent me the address of Wolfgang Stamm, to whom he had sold his collection. He enclosed a photograph of Hellé Nice which I had never seen before. A present, he said kindly, to make up for having kept me waiting. It was one of the best pictures of her I had yet seen.

A fortnight later, Wolfgang Stamm and I met up in the foyer of a Heathrow hotel. After dinner, he opened his briefcase and spread a second feast on the second table. Here, wonderfully, was a naked Hellé Nice, arms upstretched to capture a fluttering white dove, Hellé Nice driving a Miller on an American speedway in 1930, Hellé Nice and her raffish American manager, Ralph Hankinson, Hellé Nice's boyfriend Billy Winn, scribbling a message 'to the sweetest little girl in the world' on a handsome picture of himself – and, of course, the picture we had all seen in Raffaelli's book, Hellé Nice scantily draped in a gauze scarf for a studio shot. Wolfgang Stamm said that I could use whatever I liked from the collection for my book. Such generosity is, in my own experience, rare; in my search for Hellé Nice, it was what I had come to expect.

The last great find came almost by chance. I had no expectations of finding anything in Paris, but it seemed courteous to pay a call on Madame Jarnach, since La Roue Tourne had evidently played an important role in Hellé Nice's life. Visiting a gracious chair-bound lady with a magnificent coiffure in November 2002, I was told that she had arranged for me be taken to lunch on the premises of the charity. Seeing my long face – I had planned to enjoy an off-duty afternoon – she added that I might find it quite helpful for my researches.

Lunch at La Roue Tourne was a cheerful experience, well laced with wine in honour of a dancer whose father had been a film stuntman, and whose birthday it was. My neighbour at the long table was a tiny ninety-year-old tightrope walker who showed off some of his skills after the meal. Later, Jeannine Chaponnay, the charity's secretary and general organizer, took me up to Hélène's little bedroom, grey and cold enough to make it clear why she fled back to the warmth of the south. They had, Jeannine added tentatively, kept some of her photographs and letters, if I was interested. Also, her address book. Everything, of course, was at my disposal, if I cared to borrow or make copies.

The last part of the story came together that afternoon as Jeannine, the retired dancer, and I sorted through the piles of close-written letters from Hélène – always Hellé in this correspondence – to her last and most faithful friend. Here was the pathetic story of the final years after the defection of Arnaldo Binelli, years in which, without the support of La Roue Tourne, she could not have survived. 'You will always be our Hellé, and we will always look after you,' Madame Jarnach had promised in one of her letters. It was evident that she had kept her word.

Gaps remain. I have used imagination to recreate the story of Hellé

Nice's earliest years; it is still not clear when or why she left Sainte-Mesme for an independent life in Paris, or how she became such an accomplished dancer. (Novelists will sympathize with my longing to have made something of the summer school for missionaries which existed at Sainte-Mesme while Hélène was a teenager; unfortunately, not a scrap of evidence could be found on which to build a link.) Her relationship with Henri de Courcelles ('Couc' in all the personal annotations) is conjectured from photographs and from the many pages of cuttings which she preserved about him, together with his obituaries. Marcel Mongin remains something of a mystery figure, as does Henri Thouvenet. The nature of her friendship with Ettore and Jean Bugatti is open to speculation; so is the mysterious loss of her wealth in the period following Louis Chiron's claim that she worked for the Gestapo.

Caution is required when relying on the evidence of a woman whose memory is defective and it is clear that Hélène's memory became unreliable after her crash in 1936. In one undated interview, given in 1938, she joked that she could no longer recognize her own mother's face or even her own apartment block. Research shows that many of the dates and circumstances noted in her albums were inaccurate. She remembered, to take a single example, having participated with Anne Itier in the 1950 Monte Carlo Rally; Itier did enter it, but with another partner. Hellé Nice was not a 1950 entrant. I have restored the true events wherever it has been possible to verify them.

The story I have told will not, I am afraid, satisfy the experts who would like to know precisely which cars she owned and which were loaned to her, the degree to which they were customized for her needs, the links between her and Itier, the way that she was perceived by her mechanics, the reasons that she chose to continue driving an outdated Alfa Romeo when she could, as it seems, have easily afforded to buy a more competitive machine. My aim has been to tell her story rather than to provide a technical history of her career. My hope is that I may have established the ground from which more detailed researches can be undertaken.

My wish, above all, is that her extraordinary life should not be forgotten. A heroine who rose from obscurity, and who now lies in an unmarked grave, deserves to be honoured and recalled as she was once described, as a champion of the world.

ACKNOWLEDGEMENTS

Without Warner Dailey, ably backed by his wife, Fiona, this book would never have been written. Andrée Agostinucci and Patrick Trapani, Brian Brunkhorst, Oscar Davis, Janalla Jarnach, Simon Moore, Antoine Raffaelli and Wolfgang Stamm have been immensely generous in allowing me to make use of their collections, and their time. Jean-Pierre Potier has been steadily kind and helpful in providing introductions and information; Dick Ploeg and Patricia Lee Yongue have been the best of email friends to me, supplying answers to my interminable questions with a patience and good humour far beyond the call of duty.

My thanks are also due, with apologies to anybody whose help has been neglected here, to:

Pierre Abeillon, at *La Revue des automobiles*; Joan Acoccella, Jean-Louis Arbey at The Bugatti Club of France; the Bugatti Trust at Prescott, with particular thanks to Richard Day and Sue Ward; the Brooklands Museum, where I gratefully remember John Tarring and the late John Granger; the Motor Museum at Beaulieu, where Malcolm Thorne helped me to find some wonderful material. At Beaulieu sur Mer in France, I was kindly assisted by André Cané; at Aunay-sous-Auneau, Raymond Barenton and the mayor, Monsieur Picault, were patient, helpful and informative. Thanks also to Philippe Aubert, Antony Beevor and Artemis Cooper, for book loans and valuable advice; The Military Archives of Berlin, the staff of the Bibliothèque Nationale; Alan Black, William Boddy, Malcolm and Ian Brackenbury, the staff of the British Library, William Cash, the Casino de Paris, M. Cavalier, Giles Chapman, Jeannine Chaponnay at La Roue Tourne, Tom Clifford, Ian Connell, Gerard Crombach, Gordon Cruickshank, Charles Dean, Roger Delayre at Sainte-Mesme, Elsie Burch Donald, Trevor Dunmore at the RAC library, everybody at Ivan Dutton Ltd, Irene Testot Ferry, Gregor Fisken, M.R.D. Foot, Simone des Forest and her family, Lynn Garafola, Andrew Graham, Robert Greskovic, Malcolm Harris, Malcolm Jeal at the Veterans Car Club, Louis Klementowski, Danielle Lallart at the archives of Aunay-sous-Auneau, Madame Louis Lavagna, Mike Lawrence, Katherine Legge, the late Joan Littlewood, the staff of the London Library, David Long, Maurice Louch, Mike Lynch, Alastair Macaulay, Stanley Mann, John Marks, Mike Marshal, Lester Matthews, the Midlands Motor Museum, the automobile club of Monaco, Lord Montagu of Beaulieu, the appeal court of Monaco, the Archives Municipales of Nice, with especial thanks to Mireille Massot, Louis-Gilles Pairault, Agnes Rougier and Auguste Verola; Patrick O'Connor, the staff of the Archives de Paris; Jimmy Piget, Sam Posey, Don Radbruch, Peter Rickley, Lord Rothschild, Roland Saunier, Joe Saward, David Sewell, Alessandro Silva, Leif Snellman, Evelyn Stottard, Ken Summers at CHH Motorcars, Simon Taylor, David Thirlby, Antonia Till, Gillian Tindall, David Venables, Nick Walker at the Vintage Car Club, Mick Walsh, author of the first – and, at present, the only – British article on Hellé Nice to be published after her death.

Thanks are also due to two splendid agents, Anthony Goff and Henry Dunow, and to my wonderful editors, Andrew Gordon, Martin Bryant and Ileene Smith. Thanks also to Pen Campbell and Alan Hollinghurst.

Especial thanks to my son and daughter-in-law, Merlin and Shula Sinclair, for support and company when it was most needed; and to Thomas, Sallie, and the matchless trio.

APPENDIX 1

Translation of a letter sent from São Paulo by Arnaldo Binelli to Charles Faroux, editor of L'Auto, *Paris, July 1936 (Agostinucci Collection).*

Dear Sir

I have just received the article about Miss Hellé Nice's accident which was published on 15 July. *L'Auto* seems not to know what took place as much of the detail is inaccurate. I am enclosing, to let you judge for yourself, a photo which was taken at the precise moment of the accident. You will be able to see that there was no barrier, no form of organization and people standing all over the circuit. You can see that the race was still going on and you will appreciate that there were fifteen more cars coming up behind at high speed.

You seem not to have have understood that the accident took place just 25 metres before the end of the 60th – and final – lap. Look at the photograph and you will see that the car on the left is de Teffe's and that Miss Hellé Nice is on the right, in the process of passing him. You can see that de Teffe is not making room for her, but the main cause of the accident is the crowd of spectators who ran out on to the circuit to cheer on the Brazilian who seemed about to lose third place so near to the end. The cars were doing about 140 kph. The inquiry has reached the view that the spectators were to blame and that Miss Hellé Nice was their first victim.

I am Miss Hellé Nice's mechanic and I was standing by the finishing line, 25 metres from the accident, so I saw everything.

All the French people out here are unhappy about *L'Auto*'s account. Miss Hellé Nice is doing reasonably well now and she should be able to explain everything to you herself on her return. She will also be able to produce photographs and a film which offer clear evidence of the events.

Yours sincerely
Arnaldo Binelli

APPENDIX 2

Yacco 1937 International records Class C[10] at Montlhéry
3 days at 143.78 kph
4 days at 144.08 kph
15,000 km at 143.77 kph
10,000 miles at 141.59 kph
5 days at 141.74 kph
6 days at 141.16 kph
7 days at 141.48 kph
15,000 miles at 141.48 kph
20,000 km at 141.39 kph
8 days at 141.29 kph
30,000 km at 140.88 kph
9 days at 140.83 kph
20,000 miles at 140.18 kph
10 days at 139.99 kph

World records
20,000 km at 141.39 kph
6 days at 141.16 kph
7 days at 141.48 kph
15,000 miles at 141.48 kph
8 days at 141.29 kph
9 days at 140.83 kph
20,000 miles at 140.18 kph
10 days at 139.99 kph

APPENDIX 3: RACE HISTORY*

1928

June   (Sunday) 2me Journée Féminine de l'Automobile, Montlhéry; also the Concours d'Elégance in a 10CV Citroën closed car with a body by Taramo

1929

1–2 June   3me Journée Féminine de l'Automobile, Montlhéry: 1st (Omega-Six; race no. 9) Championnat Féminin 150 km, 30 laps; handicap race: 15th from the very last starting position (Omega-Six)
(1st) Grand Prix Féminin 50 km, 10 laps: 1st (Omega-Six)
Concours d'Elégance: 1st of 12 in closed touring-car class (Omega-Six)

June (date unknown)   Le Touquet, Automobile Meeting: 1st in gymkhana event (Rosengart)

14 June   6me Championnat Automobile des Artistes, Parc des Princes: wins in the women's

---

* I am indebted to Dick Ploeg for the details given in this appendix. Hellé Nice's own record is rather less accurate, but has been preserved in the Brunkhorst collection.

	category and makes the best time of the day (of both sexes)
18 December	Montlhéry speed record trials, 10 km at average of 198 kph with a 2-litre 35C Bugatti (possibly no. 4863) on loan from Ettore Bugatti before an accident occurred

1930

29 March	Molsheim delivers 35C–4863 to Hellé Nice on temporary road registration 1647–WW5[*]
21 April	Casablanca Rally, Grand Prix du Maroc, a 709.5 km handicap race: having appeared with a 2-litre Bugatti, withdrew after her friend Count Bruno d'Harcourt's fatal accident
23 May	Signs a contract to do 'speed exhibitions in racing automobiles' for Ralph Hankinson in the USA
1 June	Bugatti Grand Prix Le Mans: 3rd (2-litre Bugatti, T35, race no. 32, road registration 2066–RD9)
20 June	7me Championnat Automobile des Artistes, Parc des Princes, speed demonstration and gymkhana event/gymkhana: 1st in the women's category (Bugatti Type 43A, road registration 2066 RD) Concours d'Elégance: 3rd in the women's category

[*] An earlier delivery of this car was made on 2 July 1927 to a certain Marco Andriesse of Amsterdam, but this earlier delivery, albeit unlikely, has also been associated with Hellé Nice (Conway, *Grand Prix Bugatti*). More recent research by Pierre-Yves Laugier shows that the 1927 Andriesse sale seems correct, while prior to Hellé Nice's purchase of 4863 it first came into the ownership of van Hulzen on 29 March 1929 with road registration 2048 NV.

June	Buffalo vélodrome, organized by the Automobile Club des Artistes: dirt track demonstrations
29 July	Arrives in the USA for 18 dirt-track and speed-bowl demonstrations. Cars used on American track tour included Ralph De-Palma's 1500cc blown Miller, Bob Robinson's 4-litre unblown Miller and Bill Robinson's Duesenberg
2–8 August	Harrington, Delaware
10 August	Woodbridge (half-mile board track), New Jersey: 10 demonstration laps in 4 minutes, 29 seconds using Larry Beals's Duesenberg
16 August	Middletown, New Jersey: five-eighths mile on Orange County Fair Speedway
21 August	Lancaster: five-eighths mile on dirt track
30 August	Flemington (Fair), New Jersey: half-mile dirt track
5 September	Pottsville, Pennsylvania: half-mile dirt track
6 September	Trenton, New Jersey: half-mile dirt track
13 September	Brockton, Massachusetts, half-mile dirt track
19/20 September	Allentown (Fair), Pennsylvania: half-mile dirt track in DePalma Miller
27 September	Bloomsburg, Pennsylvania: half-mile dirt track in DePalma Miller
11 October	Winston-Salem, North Carolina: crashed, but unhurt
12 October	Concord, North Carolina: half-mile dirt track in Hoffman Special
18 October	Langhorne, Pennsylvania: 1-mile dirt track
24 October	Kinston, North Carolina: quarter-mile dirt track

25 October	Wilson, North Carolina: quarter-mile dirt track
1 November	Spartanburg, South Carolina: 3-lap trial against the clock (driving Jimmy Patterson's Miller)
12 November	Richmond, Virginia: half-mile dirt track

After returning to Europe she resumed racing with a Bugatti

1931

5 July	Grand Prix de la Marne, Reims: 14th overall; 4th in 2-litre class; 2nd in Coupe des Dames (Bugatti T35C, race no. 54)
26 July	Dieppe: 7th (Bugatti T35C)
2 August	Dauphine circuit, Grenoble 1500cc class: 7th in Bugatti
16 August	7th Comminges Grand Prix (Saint-Gaudens): 9th (Bugatti Type 35 unblown, race no. 30, road registration 2066–RD9)
6 September	Monza Grand Prix
13 September	La Baule: 8th (Bugatti T35C–4921, race no. 8, road registration 2678–RB6 from Philippe de Rothschild); held 6th position till last lap
27 September	Grand Prix de Brignolles (Alfa Romeo)

1932

22 February	Paris–Saint-Raphäel rally in a blown T35 Bugatti
	Pougues-les-Eaux hill climb (part of Paris–Saint-Raphäel rally) (Bugatti T35C–4921)
24 April	Oran Grand Prix (Algeria) (Bugatti 35C)

16 (?17) May	Nîmes, Trophée Automobile de Provence (Bugatti 35C)
22 May	Casablanca Grand Prix (Bugatti 35C)
26 June	Lorraine (Nancy)
17 July	(Sunday) 5th Journée Féminine de l'Automobile, Montlhéry Trials: 1st (Bugatti 'course 2 litres') Championnat Féminin, handicap race of 20 km over 6 laps: 5th (Bugatti 'course 2 litres')
24 July	Dieppe Grand Prix: 7th in 2-litre class (Bugatti 35C)
7 August	Klausen hill climb: 6th (Bugatti 2-litre)
3/4 September	Mont Ventoux: Ladies' hill-climb record at 18 minutes, 41.1 seconds and 2nd in 2-litre class (Bugatti 35C–4921, race no. 42, road registration 2678–RB6 of Philippe de Rothschild)
25 September	1st Grand Prix de Marseille (Miramas): retired with broken oil pipe (Bugatti 35C–4921, race no. 18, road registration 2678–RB6 of Philippe de Rothschild)

1933

[date?]	6th Journée Féminine de l'Automobile, Montlhéry Trials (25 km): 2nd and 4th classified for final with 5 points (Peugeot 301) Championnat Féminin (50 km): 3rd and fastest lap (Peugeot 301) 4th Grand Prix Féminin: 1st (Peugeot 301?) Concours d'Elégance: 1st (Delage, Letourneur et Marchand)

16 July	Dieppe Grand Prix
31 July/5 August	International Alpine Trial (Coupe Internationale des Alpes): 3rd with 3 points lost in 2–3 litre class (Bugatti T43; with Roger Bonnet)
13 August	(Sunday) Coppa Acerbo, Pescara: (Bugatti)
27 August	2nd Grand Prix de Marseille (Miramas): 9th (Bugatti 35C–4921, race no. 28, road registration 2678–RB6)
10 September	(Sunday afternoon) Monza Grand Prix: 9th overall, 3rd in 2nd heat (Alfa Romeo 8C Monza
24(?) September	San Sebastián

1934

February	Paris–Saint-Raphaël Rally, co-driving with Odette Siko in an Alfa Romeo 8C Monza
20 May	Moroccan Grand Prix, Casablanca circuit: retired with rear axle defect (Alfa Romeo 8C Monza)
27 May	Picardy Grand Prix, Péronne
3 June	Eiffelrennen, Nürburgring, starting from the front row: did not finish (Alfa Romeo 8C Monza 2.3-litre, race no. 5)
15 July	(Sunday) Vichy Grand Prix: 7th in heat, did not finish in final (Alfa Romeo 8C Monza)
22 July	Dieppe: 7th (Alfa Romeo 8C Monza)
12 August	Targa Abruzzo 24th sports car race, Pescara: did not finish (Alfa Romeo 8C Monza, race no. 5, co-driving with Marcel Mongin)
26 August	10th Comminges Grand Prix (Saint-Gaudens): 8th (Alfa Romeo 8C Monza, race no. 22)

| 15 September | Mont Ventoux hill climb: 2nd and new ladies' record, 16 minutes, 43.2 seconds |
| 28 October | Algiers Grand Prix: 10th and 7th in heats; 7th overall (Alfa Romeo Monza) |

1935

24 February	Pau: 8th (Alfa Romeo 8C Monza, race no. 6)
21 April	La Turbie hill climb: 2nd in class (Alfa Romeo 8C Monza)
26 May	Picardy Grand Prix (Péronne): 4th (Alfa Romeo Monza 2.3-litre)
9 June	Biella, Italy: 7th in heat, did not finish in final
30 June	Grand Prix de Penya Rhin, Barcelona (race no. 24, starting from last row): did not finish
4 August	Comminges Grand Prix (Saint-Gaudens): 7th in final, 5th in 2nd heat (Alfa Romeo 8C Monza)

1936

1 January	South African Grand Prix, East London
26/29 January	Monte Carlo rally starting from Tallinn, Estonia and co-driving with Mme Marinovitch: 1st for the Ladies' Cup and 18th overall (Matford)
1 March	Pau Grand Prix: retired after only 2 laps with conrod trouble (Alfa Romeo 8C Monza, race no. 22)
9 April	La Turbie hill climb: 1st in over 2-litre sports car class (Alfa Romeo 8C2300) Paris–Nice Rally
7 June	Rio de Janeiro Grand Prix (Gavea): 8th (Alfa Romeo 8C Monza)

12 July	São Paulo Grand Prix, Brazil (a street race in the Jardim America district): (Alfa Romeo Monza, race no. 34)

1937
19/28 May	Montlhéry: part of an all-female Yacco record-breaking team, establishing 10 world record and 15 International class C records at average speeds between 140 and 144 kph (co-driving with Simone des Forest, Odette Siko and Claire Descollas)

1938
	co-drove a DKW in the Rallye de Chamonix with Huschke von Hanstein: did not finish

1939
11 June	68 km race, Péronne: 2nd (Renault Juvaquatre)
6 August	Critérium Automobile Féminine, Comminges (Saint-Gaudens): 1st (Renault Juvaquatre)

1949
24/27 January	Monte Carlo rally: abandoned after accident involving a truck (Renault 4CV–1060, 760cc, rally no. 156, road registration 2544 BA9, co-driving with Anne Itier)

1951
	Grand Prix de Nice: her last race (Renault 4CV); replaced in the team by Jean Behra

NOTES

1. BEGINNINGS

Hellé Nice (hereafter referred to as HN) lived at 6 rue Edouard Escoffier from 1974 until her death ten years later. Most of the material used in the first part of this chapter is based on the letters she wrote to Madame Janalla Jarnach, whose charity, La Roue Tourne, paid her rent and provided her with a modest allowance, 50 francs a week. The letters, of which there are approximately 120, written over thirty years, are in Madame Jarnach's possession and are used here with her kind permission.

Information given in this section is also based on information provided by Madame Louis Lavagna, a resident of rue Edouard Escoffier, and by Andrée Agostinucci, the daughter of HN's last landlord and the owner of almost all of HN's family papers, photographs and records. I am also grateful to the *Mairie* and City Archives of Nice for material which they enabled me to find. The account of HN's room, and the house, is based on the author's own visit to the premises in 2001.

In the second part of this chapter, descriptions are based on the author's visits to Boissy-le-Sec and Aunay-sous-Auneau in 2001. (The full name of the latter village has been shorted to Aunay in the chapter, for the sake of convenience.) The postmaster's house there has now been replaced by the more modern building of 1907, but the old house still stands. The full record of HN's older siblings, and their deaths, is given only on her personal papers. I have not been able to find any record or evidence of their graves at either village, or at Lèvesville-le-Chenard, where Léon Aristide Delangle is buried.

I am especially grateful to the *Mairies* of Boissy and Aunay-sous-Auneau for the information they located and allowed me to use, to Jacques Chatot, for his genealogy of the Delangle family, and to Raymond Barenton, the historian of Aunay-sous-Auneau who introduced me to *La Petite Marquise*, by Marie-Josèphe Guers (Mercure de France, 1993), a novel set in Aunay-sous-Auneau at the beginning of the twentieth century and based on written and oral records taken from the village. The archives of the postal service, both in Paris and at Chartres, have failed to yield any helpful information concerning the Delangle family.

I have introduced two speculative points. It is clear that the two branches of the Delangle family did not get along, but the reasons for this have been impossible to establish. HN, in later years, visited her relation Henry Delangle in Canada. I have assumed that this must be her father's brother, who was registered at birth as Daniel Benoist Delangle, who did settle in Canada, although not until 1921. It has proved impossible to verify the causes of Léon Delangle's illness and early death.

Among books on the Beauce area of France, Emile Zola's *Earth* is the best-known and, although prejudiced, provides a vivid account of farming life and villages there in the late nineteenth century. An excellent historical leaflet on Aunay-sous-Auneau has also proved helpful. I am sorry not to have been able to make use of its account of other celebrated former inhabitants, including Auguste Blanqui and François André Isambert, whose relevance to HN did not seem significant. It is not certain that Dr Poupon had already become mayor by 1900, although he was in this office by 1902.

2. 1903: THE RACE TO DEATH

1. HN–Janalla Jarnach, 14 June 1976 (La Roue Tourne: hereafter LRT).

   It is reasonable to suppose that the Delangle family would have joined the rest of the village in going to watch the great race, since it came so close to their own home. The account is drawn from several sources, among which I would like to mention one of the most vivid and least-known, given by René Ville in *De Dion Bouton en témoignages et confidences* (privately published by the friends of De Dion Bouton, 2001), pp. 79–82. Charles Jarrott wrote a vivid account of the race, the only detailed first-hand account given by an English driver, which can be found on the internet at www.ddavid.com/formula1/race.htm.

The Delangles' friendship with Chopiteau, the Aunay schoolmaster, is suggested by his having acted as a witness to HN's birth-entry at Aunay's town hall.

3. LOSS AND LEARNING

1. This paragraph is speculative. We know only the name of HN's grandfather, the profession of her uncle and the fact that her father was buried in the family grave at Lèvesville-le-Chenard.
2. I have drawn on the accounts given by Philippe Aubert, *Les Bugatti: Splendeurs et passions d'une dynastie* (Jean-Claude Lattes, 1981), pp. 109–12, and David Venables, *Bugatti: A Racing History* (Haynes, 2002), p. 24.

4. PARIS

This is a period of HN's life about which almost nothing has previously been known. The main source for my reconstruction has been the remarkable archive of photographs and news cuttings which was rescued by Andrée Agostinucci from the garage of one of her father's properties, following the death of Hélène Delangle, his tenant. All the photographs were annotated by their owner.

1. Jean Rhys, *After Leaving Mr Mackenzie* (1931), chapter 1.
2. I am grateful for comments made by Joan Acoccella, Lynn Garafola, Robert Greskovic and Alastair Macaulay, based on a study of photographs of HN dancing.
3. The account of HN's day in Paris is imaginary, but the Mallet-Stevens garage was highly regarded. Garages offered an exciting opportunity for architects; in New York, plans were drawn up for a skyscraper car park. In Paris, the new Banville Garage had a sweeping spiral ascent which tested the skills of racing-drivers while offering a stylish image to pedestrians.

4. Solange's relationship with HN is hypothesized from a number of photographs in which she appears in what seems to be a holiday group; and from the letters she wrote to her sister during the 1930s. Earlier letters have not survived.

5. Courcelles and M. Melon (Mongin) are listed at Brooklands as entrants for the race. The photographs of Hélène and her friends at Brighton are dated as 1920 and 1921 by her. The visit to Brooklands is speculatively described. It is still possible to take an illegal walk along the banked walls of Europe's oldest speed circuit; the place remains wonderfully evocative and part of the track is still used for special events. William Boddy's book on Brooklands is the definitive history; enthusiasts should also visit the library.

6. It is likely, but not certain, that Mongin and HN were at Montlhéry on the day of Courcelles's fatal crash. The obituaries, carefully preserved by HN, suggest that he died on the way to hospital; the most detailed report, in *La Vie Automobile*, 10 July 1927, pp. 243–5, states that death was instantaneous. All the tributes allude to his courage, his charm and his modesty.

5. THE DANCER

1. This account is based on photos of the couple in the Agostinucci collection.

2. The music described here is identified in reviews of their performances in 1927 and 1928.

3. It is possible that it was these private performances which made HN's fortune; the salary she received for her music-hall appearances was relatively modest.

4. *Le Journal*, 21 January 1927.

5. Willy's words have come down to us only through the review by Pierre Varenne which quotes him, n.d. (Brunkhorst).

6. Varenne's review, quoting Willy, appears in HN's cuttings books, but without an attribution or date.

7. HN's representations of her career are taken from her conversations with Madame Janalla Jarnach from 1960 to 1962. Madame Jarnach also provided the description of her bedroom

(author in correspondence and interview with JJ, autumn 2002).

8. It is significant that HN preserved a copy of the *Ailes de Paris* programme; with it she preserved a dossier of photographs signed by members of the cast with affectionate inscriptions to herself. She does not appear to have kept photographs of either The Dollys or Maurice Chevalier, although it would be odd if she had not approached them for similar signed pictures.

   Tempting though it is to speculate on an affair with Maurice Chevalier, there is no evidence. It is just worth noticing that when Chevalier's former love, Mistinguett, returned to the stage of the Casino de Paris for *Paris Miss*, in 1928, HN was not in the cast. Publicity shots do, however, leave no doubt that HN was at pains to imitate the most successful French music-hall star of the time. Miss's smile, her way of crossing her legs, her pose on a car bonnet: all were copied, with great success.

9. The Gala programmes and reviews were all kept by HN, as were the letters which thanked her for participating. The fact that she did not take part in 1929 is striking and does suggest this as the most likely year for her disastrous ski accident.

10. HN's own account of the accident is preserved in the scrapbooks (Brunkhorst).

6. 'LA PRINCESSE DES ALTITUDES, REINE DE VITESSE'

1. Sylvia Beach, *Shakespeare & Company* (University of Nebraska Press, 1991), pp. 80–1.
2. Ernest Hemingway, *A Moveable Feast* (Scribner's, 1964), pp. 64–5.
3. Concours d'Elégance had taken place in the Parc des Princes every 17–19 June since 1921, as part of the Actors' Championships. They had become widespread by 1928.
4. HN in conversation with JJ and Madame Louis Lavagna, as described to author, October 2002.
5. The reports and interviews which were given to Pedron and Marjorie are preserved in the HN scrap books (Brunkhorst).

8. LAPPING THE GOLDFISH BOWL

1. Winifred M. Pink, *Woman Engineer* (1928), 2 (17), pp. 235–6.
2. Details of the Pathé Cinema team's response are based on the account by a journalist who accompanied them during the week of HN's speed trial. The man from *L'Auto* could have been Charles Faroux, the editor, who frequently paid tribute to the outstanding quality of Hélène's driving (Brunkhorst).
3. HN's sensations are collated from several interviews which she gave after the speed trial, and from a journalist who was able to accompany her on a later record-breaking circuit (Brunkhorst).
4. The invoice is in the Brunkhorst collection and suggests that she collected the car from Molsheim. It is generally accepted that the car is one of two which were made available to her for the speed trial, and that it is the one which is now in the Brunkhorst collection.
5. *L'Intransigeant*, 7 February 1930 (Brunkhorst).
6. This is one of many undated cuttings in the Brunkhorst scrapbooks. I have based my account on the assumption that the details of HN's forthcoming trip to America, given out at Buffalo, mean that this second Actors' Championship must also have taken place in the summer of 1930. HN only went once to the US to compete on dirt tracks, and this clearly shows that all her cuttings about the Parc des Princes' events which mention America must relate to this summer. The Parc des Princes site was dismantled in 1930; from 1931, all Actors' Championships were held elsewhere in Paris at the Buffalo velodrome at Montrouge.

9. RALPH'S HONEY

I am especially indebted for material in this chapter to information provided by Professor Patricia Lee Yongue, and to a fine article she wrote on Hellé Nice's American adventure for *The Alternate* (2002). Also to an account given of the Woodbridge Broad Track by John Kozub in *The Alternate* (15 May 1992).

1. Henri Lartigue to HN, 18 August 1930, answering her letter of

3 August 1930. These, together with the Savoy Plaza accounts are in the scrapbooks (Brunkhorst).

2. Scrapbooks, n.d. (Brunkhorst).
3. Derek Nelson, *The American State Fair* (MBI Publishing Company, Osceola, Wisconsin, 1999), p. 78.
4. Albert R. Bockrock, *American Auto Racing: A History* (Cambridge, Patrick Stephens, 1974), p. 998.
5. Scrapbooks (Brunkhorst). Misprints crept in to newspaper articles, as did the name Helen Rice by which she was often known.
6. The car she used belonged to or was being driven that day by Larry Beals, but it is not certain whether it was a Miller or a Duesenberg.
7. Scrapbooks (Brunkhorst).
8. *Record*, 14 February 1931.
9. Account based on the letters of Teddie Caldwell to HN during the 1930s (Agostinucci).
10. *Record*, op. cit.
11. *France Soir*, 7 March 1961.
12. Previous owners of the car were Whitney Straight, whom HN knew well and Count Trossi, whom she did not. R. L. Duller was the last owner and is believed to have known her well.
13. *Record*, op. cit.

10. SEX AND CARS

1. HN–Janalla Jarnach, 3 March 1977 (LRT).
2. Erwin Tragatsch, *Das Grosse Rennfahrerbuch* (Agostinucci) (Bern: Hallwag AA, 1970), p. 238.
3. Teddie Caldwell–HN, 12 November 1931 (Agostinucci).
4. Teddie Caldwell–HN, 22 November 1933 (Agostinucci).
5. HN–JJ, 3 March 1977 (LRT).
6. Conjectural description.
7. HN–JJ, 14 June 1976 (LRT).
8. Teddie Caldwell–HN, 22 November 1933 (Agostinucci).
9. The second unsupercharged Bugatti, reg. 2066-RD9 went to an English driver, Charles Brackenbury, who drove it with considerable success during the mid-1930s.

10. Dame Joan Littlewood, *Milady Vine: The Autobiography of Philippe de Rothschild* (London: Jonathan Cape, 1984); interview and telephone conversations with author, June 2002.
11. Clive Coates, *Grands Vins: The Finest Châteaux of Bordeaux and their Wines* (Los Angeles: University of California Press, 1995), p. 64.
12. Henri Lartigue–HN, 30 March 1935; 5 April 1935 (Brunkhorst).

11. 'L'ANNÉE MALHEUREUSE'

1. Marcel Mongin–HN, 5 June 1936 (Agostinucci).
2. Henri Thouvenet–HN, 3 June 1936 (Agostinucci).
3. Ibid.
4. Marcel Mongin–HN, n.d. June 1936 (Agostinucci).
5. Accounts of the accident vary, but the film taken by Arnaldo Binelli (it is now in the Agostinucci Collection) was accepted as the most authentic record of the event in the subsequent application for compensation. Chico Landi, who took part in the same race, has given his own version on the www.atlasforum site (20 November 2001). Another account appeared in *Allgemeine Automobil Zeitung*, Berlin 1936 (no. 33), p. 16.

> The driverless car threw the nearest spectators to the ground, then ran them over, ripping arms and legs from them as if it was a monster, possessed. It finally came to a stop just over the finishing line. Five [*sic*] died on the spot; a further 35 [*sic*] were taken to the hospital. At the time, it was believed that the courageous woman driver was another victim; the first news bulletins announced that she was dead. She was taken to hospital in a coma and with severe injuries.

12. THE ROAD BACK

1. Solange Delangle–HN, 17 July 1936 (Agostinucci).
2. Marcel Mongin–HN, 24 July 1936 (Agostinucci).
3. Henri Thouvenet–HN, 18 July 1936 (Agostinucci).
4. Race records show that she was initially placed 4th, but that her

position was amended and she was given 3rd place (Brunkhorst).

5. Henri Thouvenet–HN, 21 August 1936 (Agostinucci).
6. HN–Janalla Jarnach, 3 March 1977 (LRT).
7. Léon Mouraret–HN, 29 December 1936 and 14 January 1937 (Brunkhurst). The reference to Bidon may help explain the nickname 'Bidon' which HN gave to the Alfa which she bought from Lehoux and which was looked after by his mechanic, also known as 'Bidon', meaning petrol can.
8. *La Gazzetta del Popolo della Sera*, dated by content. The Mille Miglia took place on 4 April that year (Brunkhorst).
9. Simone des Forest in an interview with author, 2001.
10. César Marchand, in *La Fanatique de L'Automobile*, August 1979.
11. The fullest account available of the Yacco trials is given by Anthony Blight in *The French Sports Car Revolution* (G. T. Foulis, 1996), p. 283.
12. Simone des Forest in interview with author, 2001.
13. Madame Janalla Jarnach, October 2002.
14. Julien Green, *Journal, 1926–1934*, in *Oeuvres complètes* (1975), IV, p. 338.
15. Heinrich Kleyer, Adlerwerke–HN, 21 February 1938 (Brunkhorst).
16. Mick Walsh, *Classic and Sports Car*, June 1997.
17. Charles Faroux, *L'Auto*, 7 August 1939, also quoted in Blight, op.cit., p. 522.
18. I have drawn on the account given by David Venables, op.cit., p 229.

13. AND WHAT DID YOU DO DURING THE WAR, MADEMOISELLE?

I am indebted to Antony Beevor and to Artemis Cooper for discussions and for the loan of some illuminating books on which I have drawn for this and the following chapter.

1. Details are taken from the accounts given by Venables, op.cit. pp. 230–1, and W. F. Bradley, *Bugatti, A Biography* (London, 1948), p. 144.

2. René Dreyfus, *My Two Lives: Racing Driver to Restauranteur* (Aztex Corp, 1983), p. 39.

3. Robert Ryan, *Early one Morning* (Headline, 2002); 'The Hero who Died to Live', *Sunday Times Magazine*, 16 December 2001. M. R. D. Foot is sceptical about this approach, as are MI6 (conversations with author, 16 December 2001).

4. M. R. D. Foot, *The SOE in France*, Appendix F (HMSO, 1966).

5. Bradley, op.cit. p. 140.

6. Quoted by David Pryce-Jones, *Paris in the Third Reich: A History of the German Occupation 1940–1944* (London: Collins, 1981), p. 62.

7. Colette, *Lettres aux petites fermières*, 15 December 1941, edited and annotated by Marie-Thérèse Colveaux-Chaurang (Paris: Le Castor Astral, 1992), p. 75.

8 Littlewood/Rothschild, *Milady Vine*, op. cit., p. 188.

9. Ibid., p. 187.

10. Robert Kanigel, *High Season in Nice* (London: Little, Brown, 2002), pp. 198–200.

14. THE ACCUSATION

1. Philippe Viannay, cited by Henri Amoroux, *Joies et douleurs de peuple libre* (Paris: Laffont, 1998), p. 472.

2. Ibid. p. 463.

3. Antony Beevor and Artemis Cooper, *Paris after the Liberation* (Penguin, 1994), p. 217.

4. For the best account of Ettore Bugatti's last months, see Venables, op. cit., p. 233.

5. Janalla Jarnach, in interview with the author, autumn 2002.

6. Marchese Antonio Brivio Sforza to Hellé Nice, 14 January 1946 (Brunkhorst).

7. These details are taken from the *Riviera News*, 1 March 1949.

8. HN to Antony Noghes, 13 February 1949, a handwritten copy (Brunkhorst).

9. Ibid.

10. Mick Walsh, 'One Hellé of a Girl', *Classic and Sports Car* (June 1997).

11. Tobias Achele, *Huschke von Hanstein, The Racing Baron* (Koneman, 1999).
12. The Brunkhorst collection, namely, HN's two incomplete scrapbooks, which were in the Christie's pre-Tarrytown sale collection or newly owned by Oscar Davis at the time when Mick Walsh had access to them.
13. HN to Janalla Jarnach, 'Réponse à Naldo', 1974 (LRT).

15. SANS EVERYTHING

La Roue Tourne, to which I am indebted for the loan of letters, photographs and many of Hellé Nice's personal items, continues its generous work with the help of private benefactors. It is still based at 56 rue Legendre, Paris 17me, and Madame Jarnach remains its president.

1. HN–Madame Janalla Jarnach, 1974 (LRT).
2. HN–JJ, 11 May 1981 and 'réponse à Naldo', 1974 (LRT).
3. Author interview with Madame Jarnach, November 2002.
4. HN–JJ, 18 May 1981 (LRT).
5. Alexandrine Delangle–HN, 1960 (Agostinucci collection).
6. Author interview with Madame Jarnach and correspondence. (August–November, 2002).
7. HN–JJ, 14 June 1976 (LRT).
8. Alexandrine Delangle–HN, 1960 (Agostinucci).
9. HN–JJ, JJ–HN, July–September 1962 (Agostinucci).
10. HN–JJ, 17 June 1963 (LRT).
11. JJ–HN, 21 June 1963 (Agostinucci).
12. Solange Delangle–HN, 1964 (Agostinucci).
13. HN–JJ, 26 June 1964 (LRT).
14. HN–JJ, 22 December 1965 (LRT). President Giscard d'Estaing also contributed the sum of 1,000 francs in 1977, following an appeal to him by La Roue Tourne.
15. HN–JJ, 19 June 1974 (LRT).
16. HN–JJ, 'Réponse à Naldo', 1974. Binelli's death was announced by his widow on 5 October 1974 (LRT).
17. HN–JJ, 11 January 1978 and another, n.d. (LRT).
18. HN–JJ, 28 June 1983 (LRT).

PICTURE CREDITS

The author and publishers wish to acknowledge with gratitude the following picture suppliers. Every effort has been made to contact all persons having any rights regarding the pictures reproduced in this work. Where this has not been possible the publishers will be happy to hear from anyone who recognizes their material.

Text pictures (page numbers)
Andrée Agostinucci: 22, 37, 46, 47, 50, 115, 143, 145, 155, 180, 184, 192, 231
Brian Brunkhorst: 85, 108
Bugatti Trust: 27, 30, 89, 103, 148
Janalla Jarnach/ La Roue Tourne: 56
Jean-Pierre Potier Archives: 149
Oscar Davis Collection: 163, 164
Private collection: 38
Wolfgang Stamm: 130, 198

Plate pictures
Andrée Agostinucci: 1, 2, 3, 5, 8, 29, 30
Brian Brunkhorst: 14, 15, 16, 17, 18, 21, 22, 24, 25, 26, 28
Bugatti Trust: 12, 13, 19, 20
Janalla Jarnach: 7
Jean-Pierre Potier: 10, 11, 27, 31, 32
Wolfgang Stamm: 4, 9
Michael Woolley: 6

INDEX

HD = Hélène Delangle
Numbers in *italics* indicate illustrations
Numbers followed by 'n' indicate notes

Bugatti cars
  production 27–8,177, 205–6,
    208–9, 229–30
  HD's love of, 48, 81–2, 93–4,
    151, 157, 158
  HD's own, *95*, *103*, 105–6,
    256, 257
  'the Thoroughbred Car', 82,
    92
  Philippe de Rothschild's, *152*
  models
    35/35C: xii, 82, 86, 93–4,
      148, 151, 157
    59: 157
    Royale: 82, *89*, 90
    T43A: 82, 86, 111
    T57: 166

Caldwell, Teddie, 133, 141,
    151, 194
Campari, Giuseppe, 143, 160
Camus, Albert, 149
Caracciola, Rudi, 96, 214
Carné, Marcel: *Les Enfants du
    Paradis*, 228–9
Carpentier, Georges, 120
Carrère, René (artist), 23+n,
    37–8, *38*, 43, 49, 55, 156
Carrière, René (driver), 156
cars/manufacturers:
  Adler, 200, 201
  Alfa Monza, 147, 157–8,
    160, 161–2, *163*, 166,
    169, 171, 190
  Alfa Romeo, 156, 157+n,
    182, 193n, 231–2, 261
  Amilcar, 78–9, 120n

Auto-Union, 156, 162, 165,
    200
Bugatti *see* Bugatti cars
Buick, 193
Citroën, 41, 54, 153, 215
De Dietrich, 15, 189n
Delage, 110, 148
Delahaye, 177, 215
Donnet, 78
Duesenberg, 132, 136, 159–60
Ferrari, 156, 182, 193n
Ford, 182, 195
Guyot, 51–4
Hispano-Suiza, 82n, 84, 97,
    140, 206
Hoosier Pete/Clemons
    Special, 128
Lorraine, 189n
Lorraine-Dietrich, 49
Matford, 168–9, 195–7
Mathis, 110, *112*, 195
Mercedes, 14, 96, 156, 162,
    170, 200
Miller, 113, 114, 116, 122,
    129–30, 132, 134, 135
Daubecq Omega Six, 75,
    76–9, *81*, 82n
Panhard, 14
Peugeot, 71
Renault, 203, 235n
Riley, 188
Rosengart, 83–4
Simca, 248
Sunbeam, 52
Talbot, 52
Voisin, 45, 71
Carstairs, Betty, 126

Caruana, Georges 'Lolo', 155n
Casino de Paris, 60, 61
Cecci, Joseph, xiii, 98, 100,
103, *103*, 109
Chambret, Dr Pierre, *155*
Chanel, Coco, 228
Chaplin, Sidney, 110, 114
Chaponnay, Jeannine, 260
Charles (mechanic, fictitious),
77–8
Chartres, 8, 13
Chevalier, Maurice, 62–3, *63*,
64, 114, 199, 228
Chiron, Louis, 52, 53, 139,
146, 159, 161, 164, 214
meets HD, 96–7
accuses HD of collaboration,
234–6, 238–9
Chopiteau (schoolmaster), 10,
15, 17
Citroën, André, 153
Clifford, Freddie, 157n
Cocteau, Jean, 61
Colette, 23, 24, 59–60, 61n, 67,
218
Comminges circuit, 147,
203–4
Constantini, Bartolomeo
('Meo'), 94–5
Coogan, Jackie, 124n
Coppoli, Vittorio, 182, 183
Coty, Frédéric, 42
Courcelles, Henri de, 42–3,
45–51, *46*, *47*, 76, 261
fatal crash, 51–4
Czaikowski, Count Stanislas,
146, 147, 160

Czaikowski, Madame, 160

Dailey, Warner, 255–6
Dalbaicin, Maria, *73*
Dallimore, Angus, 113
Dannecker, SS
Hauptsturmführer, 222
Daubecq, Jules, 75, 82
Davis, Dolly, 66
Davis, Oscar, 257
Défense de la France (journal),
228
Delage, Louis, 148
Delangle, Alexandrine Estelle
(*née* Bouillie; mother),
6–7, 8, 11, 12, 21, 25–6,
43, *143*
relations with adult HD,
142–5, 244, 246–7
death, 248
Delangle, Frédéric (grandfather), 20–1
Delangle, Gabriel (brother died
in infancy), 6
Delangle, Hélène (Hellé Nice):
appearance and dress
as a child, 15, 16, 21, *22*, 26
as young woman, xv, 36–7,
46, *47*, *50*
as dancer, xii, 59, 60
face used in advertising,
84–5, *85*, *130*
character
ambition, 139
attention to detail, 23
charming and cheerful, 83,
100